# When Good Enough Is Never Enough

ALSO BY STEVEN J. HENDLIN

*The Discriminating Mind: A Guide to Deepening Insight
and Clarifying Outlook*

# When Good Enough Is Never Enough

*Escaping the Perfection Trap*

Steven J. Hendlin, Ph.D.

A JEREMY P. TARCHER/PUTNAM BOOK
published by
G. P. Putnam's Sons
*New York*

A Jeremy P. Tarcher/Putnam Book
Published by G. P. Putnam's Sons
*Publishers Since 1838*
200 Madison Avenue
New York, NY 10016

Requests for such permissions should be addressed to:
Jeremy P. Tarcher, Inc.
5858 Wilshire Blvd., Suite 200
Los Angeles, CA 90036

Published simultaneously in Canada.

Library of Congress Cataloging-in-Publication Data

Hendlin, Steven J.
When good enough is never enough : escaping the perfection trap /
Steven J. Hendlin.
p.     cm.
"A Jeremy P. Tarcher/Putnam book."
Includes bibliographical references and index.
ISBN 0-87477-717-8 (hard : alk. paper)
1. Perfectionism (Personality trait)    I. Title.
BF698.35.P47H46    1992                     92-20476 CIP
155.2 ' 32—dc20

Printed in the United States of America
1    2    3    4    5    6    7    8    9    10

This book is printed on acid-free paper.
∞

*To Deborah,*
*and to the thirty-year memory*
*of my father,*
*Hale H. Hendlin*

# CONTENTS

# PREFACE

My vision for *When Good Enough Is Never Enough* is quite broad. It is written with a general audience in mind and aimed toward all those who are interested in growth, and are striving for excellence and confronting the problems of perfectionism. While the topic of perfectionism is one that is timely and relevant for everyone who grows up in our perfection-oriented world, in writing this book I have kept especially in mind those who know the self-inflicted pain of never-enough thinking.

Many of you who will read this book are high achievers and self-described perfectionists—and proud of it! When you pick up this book and consider whether it is right for you, you might wonder, "Is this the *perfect* book on perfectionism?" You may expect it to be perfectly written and have all the answers, and you may find yourself looking for signs that it isn't and doesn't. You'll be judging this book (and, indirectly, its author) by the same high standards you have set for yourself. Be attentive to how your high standards influence your reading of this book, because this may reveal valuable information about your own perfectionism.

My intent is to lighten the burden of your perfectionistic tendencies and convince you that energy aimed toward perfection can be spent more productively and meaningfully in striving for excellence—and to make sure you know the difference between the two. I hope to convince you that perfection-seeking is a losing proposition, not something you should aim for or claim as a virtue.

Many of you who pick up this book are concerned less with

perfectionism in yourself; you are looking for ways to understand and live with someone who is a perfectionist. The ideas and tools presented here will help you, if you take them seriously and work with them thoughtfully.

After reading through the chapters, carefully considering the ideas, and doing the exercises along the way, some of you may want to explore the subject of perfectionism more thoroughly. The sources listed in the endnotes and bibliography will enable you to trace more thoroughly the history of the concept of perfection in psychology, philosophy, and religion, and to recognize the more subtle nuances of its relationship to the plague of perfectionism. You will discover, in more depth than a self-help book can possibly cover, how some of the brightest minds of our time and previous times have wrestled with the concept.

May your journey take you toward excellence and beyond the never-never land of performance perfection. And may you find the perfection of essence that your heart and soul desire.

Steven Hendlin
Laguna Beach, California
Summer 1992

# Acknowledgments

I would like to thank the following people for their supporting role in the creation of this book. Each in his or her own way has helped ensure that *When Good Enough Is Never Enough* would be a good-enough book:

My literary agent, Daniel Strone, at the William Morris Agency in New York, for his sense of good timing and his polished interpersonal skills.

Jeremy Tarcher, publisher, for suggestions regarding content.

Connie Zweig, for her immediate positive response to my proposal and for editorial suggestions that added to the popular appeal of the book.

Dan Joy, who critiqued the first draft of the manuscript and worked closely and cooperatively with me in mindfully editing the second and final drafts. His suggestions regarding developmental sequence, content, and style enhanced the quality and flow of this book.

I thank the many patients who have contributed to my understanding of perfectionism. Their names have been changed to insure confidentiality when their stories have been used as examples in this book.

My family has been emotionally supportive from start to finish, always knowing that someday my perfectionistic tendencies would pay off. Thanks to Susan Hendlin Phillips, Martin Phillips, brother Ricky, and sister-in-law Terry for love and encouragement. Thanks to my brother Timmy for the years of growing up together on and off the golf course that taught me the benefits and limitations of sibling rivalry.

And finally, I acknowledge Deborah, my wife and colleague, who tuned me in to the vital interest in the topic of perfectionism and encouraged me to write about it. Her helpful comments in early discussions of content were appreciated. Her equal measure of loving tolerance and boundary-setting confrontation of my perfectionistic tendencies during our 15 years of mostly blissful marriage makes her an expert at living with a perfectionist. It is to her that I dedicate this, my second book.

# INTRODUCTION

IF, AS THEY SAY, it takes one to know one, my personal history certainly qualifies me to write this book. A competitive junior golfer from the age of 11, I was obsessed with golf—until I was 19, it was the single most important activity in my life. My ambition was to play golf as perfectly as possible. I practiced and played every spare hour—after school, on weekends, and all summer from early morning until late at night, often hitting practice balls at the driving range under the floodlights until my hands were sore, sometimes bleeding. I loved practicing even more than playing. I felt deep satisfaction when I could hit dozens of consecutive shots perfectly. I nagged my parents relentlessly to take me to the golf course and became sullen when my demand was not satisfied.

When I wasn't playing, practicing, or talking about golf, I was reading golf magazines, memorizing more statistics than any kid had a right to know. I knew the names and annual earnings of all major professional golf champions for the previous five years. I could recite the personal preferences and idiosyncrasies of the top 50 touring pros as if they were my relatives. What I didn't know about the details of golf equipment wasn't worth knowing. By age 12, I had given up all other sports and interests to focus my attention exclusively on golf.

My dream was to play on the pro tour someday. Every summer from age 11 through 17 I played on the junior tour. One or both of my parents drove my brother Timmy and me from one tournament to another, where we competed against the best in our age group in Southern California. It was very serious business for me and my fellow competitors, who included many of the best junior players in the country. A few of them would go on to succeed on the pro tour. The majority, however, became very good amateurs, settled for club pro jobs, teaching golf, or making names for themselves in local professional competition. Their dream to succeed on the pro tour, like mine, never became a reality. While I won my share of trophies and was respected by my young peers, I never stood out as the best as I had hoped to do. I certainly wasn't perfect.

To add insult to injury, Timmy, from age 10 to 13, was winning everything in sight. I told myself that he was in a younger age group where the competition wasn't so stiff. And while that was true it was also true that when he was hot, he could occasionally beat me in head-to-head matches. I envied all the trophies he won and was jealous of the adulation he received from our father.

My father had started me at this seductive game at age 8. He was my first and only significant teacher, a demanding, perfectionistic instructor who expected the highest achievement from me. He believed that the way to excel was to choose one sport at a young age and concentrate on it, even if this meant a lack of exposure to a spectrum of activities and choices. He was very critical when he believed I wasn't practicing hard enough or committed enough to the game. Despite his perfectionism, he was able to express his underlying unconditional love for me and impart a sense of good sportsmanship and the thrill of competition.

We would spend countless hours in front of a super-eight movie editor dissecting, frame by frame, every movement and nuance of my golf swing. We would then critically examine the swings of the top pros and compare my form to theirs.

Often I watched my father peruse the two scrapbooks full of newspaper clippings attesting to his achievements in tennis, boxing, fencing, and other sports. He wanted me to be as dedicated to golf as he had been to tennis when he was young. Consciously or unconsciously, he wanted to create me in his own image. While he praised me when I won, much of the time I felt I wasn't quite measuring up to his standards.

The stress resulting from my father's own driven perfectionism, especially in the arena of sports competition, had contributed to three heart attacks, even though he was otherwise in superb physical condition. On an early fall evening, when I was 14, my father and I were alone in the living room—discussing golf, as usual. He settled into the·sofa, puffing on his after-dinner pipe. Suddenly he choked, dropped his pipe, and died in front of my eyes of his fourth heart attack. He was only 52.

When I moved on to high school, I tried to keep alive the dream of playing professional golf. I scheduled my classes to begin in early morning so I could be out at the golf course by noon. I wrote a weekly column on golf for the school newspaper during the spring competitive season. While my heart and mind were still dedicated to my dream, the spark of fire in my young soul had been extinguished. I had lost my teacher and was on my own.

I was good enough but not perfect. I was good enough at age 16 to win my country club's overall junior championship, beating a 15-year-old. (Last year that golfer, now 42, won the prestigious United States Amateur Golf Championship. His victory made me wonder once again, as I had so often before, what my future in golf might have been had my father lived.) The same year, I was one shot above qualifying for the country's most important event, the National Junior. From hitting hundreds of thousands of practice balls, I had developed a beautiful swing. I had a smooth and deadly putting stroke and was willing to take on anyone for money in a putting contest, regardless of age or expertise.

I could shoot in the mid and low 70s by age 16 but not consistently. I got nervous too easily when the pressure was on. I was good enough to earn a varsity letter as a freshman in high school, but I wasn't steady enough to win the league finals, even though I was leading with only a few holes remaining. I was often close but rarely at the top. My temper was too hot—I would curse, yell, throw clubs, and get very angry with myself. I expected to hit every shot perfectly and could not tolerate being beaten by players whom I knew to be less talented than I but who had better control of their tempers. Because of the pressure I put on myself, combined with all my ranting and raving when things didn't go perfectly, I periodically suffered migraine headaches.

During these years, I frequently lost touch with reality. I would forget that I was playing a gentleman's game on beautiful green courses with gorgeous trees, peaceful ponds, and cavities filled with glistening white sand. When I was playing poorly, it all looked like a man-made hell. The sparkling dew on the early morning grass became an obstacle to slow down the roll of my ball on the fairway. The graceful branches of the towering trees became arms that would reach out and grab my ball, prematurely terminating its flight when I didn't hit it straight enough. Shimmering ponds became evil hazards that could swallow my ball and cost me a two-stroke penalty. Gently sloping, immaculately manicured putting greens became slick and speedy carpets of grass that could humiliate me with a three-putt.

The golf course became a maze to be negotiated, a dragon to be slayed, instead of an enjoyable walk in the park. I didn't realize how lucky I was to grow up playing on beautiful courses, where I didn't have to worry about poverty, hunger, disease, taxes, earning a living, or being able to afford to join these exclusive country clubs. Because I was so competitive and driven to win, I had created my own torture chamber out of luscious pieces of manicured real estate—all for a trophy and a smile of approval from my father, whom I now imagined was watching my efforts from some spiritual plane.

About halfway through college, the dream began to fade; my interests changed. My perfection-seeking shifted into the academic arena. Although I took it for granted at the time, it was important to me to perform at the highest scholastic level and to do it as quickly as possible. After two years at San Diego State University, I transferred to the University of California at Berkeley. I graduated Phi Beta Kappa from Berkeley in a year and a half, for a total of three and a half years of undergraduate work. This rapid pace did not deter me from immersing myself in the counterculture and radical political activities of those vibrant times in the late '60s. I wanted to be a part of everything.

After rewarding myself for my good work with six months of travel around Europe, I began graduate school in psychology. Attending school full-time, including summers, I received both a master's and a Ph.D. in psychology in three years. This included a one-year clinical internship and completion of my doctoral dissertation. I was 26 and thought I was one smart cookie. No one at the graduate school had ever completed two degrees that speedily, and I don't think anyone has since. I passed the state licensing exam for practice as a marriage, family, and child counselor. While it was patently obvious to me that I was not old enough to think of a mature, committed relationship myself, here I was, licensed by the state of California to professionally assist others as a marriage counselor!

My Ph.D. was followed by a year's postdoctoral clinical internship working with heroin addicts. By 27, I was teaching graduate-level psychology classes and had begun a private practice. When I was licensed as a psychologist at 28, I was told that I was one of the youngest in the state. By then, I had already been writing articles for professional journals, presenting workshops, and delivering papers at conferences for a couple of years. While all this did not exactly put me in the genius category, it did make me think I was special. Although I did not know it, at a young age I had become ensnared in the perfection trap, where I was unable to let myself be satisfied with a good-enough performance.

Our expectations for our lives today have increased. For one thing, many of us believe that we ought to find and enjoy the perfect job or career. This was not true even 25 years ago, when a job was primarily seen as a means to earn a living. Whereas the common conception in the '60s and earlier was that one should learn a trade, skill, or profession and practice it for one's entire work life, today it is common for people to change careers one or more times. One important reason for changing careers is to find work that will satisfy needs that go far beyond survival. These needs include peer recognition, self-respect, status, social contacts, the satisfaction of accomplishment, and the need for creative self-expression through work. We seek the perfect job that will act as a vehicle through which we may satisfy all of these criteria.

In the same way that we have come to expect to find the perfect job, we also hope to find the perfect lover and marital partner. Unlike those in previous generations most of us do not allow ourselves to be forced into prearranged marriages of power and convenience at the will of our parents. Ideally, we marry for love, and we believe it is our right to seek the most perfect partner we can find. We search for a mate who will complement us and help us find the marital bliss and satisfaction promised by the perfect "love connection," a match that feels like it is made in heaven. With this hope for ideal love comes the high expectations that can lead us into the perfection trap, where good enough is never enough. It is not surprising that more marriages than ever before—at least 50 percent—end in divorce, or that more people are choosing to marry later in life.

Perfectionism is a timely issue in today's lightning-fast technological world. In a society geared toward efficiency, productivity, and speed we are constantly under pressure to perform at higher and higher levels. Whether we know it or not, we become victims of *technostress*, expecting that we ought to perform as fast and as perfectly as the computers and other high-tech gadgetry that pervade our lives. We frequently become irritated and critical of ourselves and others when human performance pales in comparison to these machines.

We may get so caught in this techno-perfection trap that we prefer to spend our time with technological tools that can make us feel that perfection is possible. We become dependent on car phones so we can work while we drive, and on personal computers with processors whose speeds are measured in billionths of a second. VCRs allow us to capture events to be viewed later so that we need not interrupt our busy schedules. We can't live without fax machines that move our messages across the world in seconds. We become media junkies, unable to tear ourselves away from instantaneous news and live pictures of a high-tech war that is being waged in real time halfway around the world and beamed to us through the miracle of satellite signals from space. Consciously or unconsciously, we think, if these high-tech tools can be perfect, why can't we?

We have been influenced both positively and negatively by the '60s human potential movement in psychology, which spawned the pop-psychology and pop-spirituality movements of today. We are promised heaven on earth and taught to want more than we ever thought possible from our bodies, minds, and relationships. We are hungry for growth, self-understanding, and enlightenment. We relish the satisfaction of pushing past our limits, stretching ourselves to test the boundaries of human possibility. And yet not only do our increased expectations not necessarily lead to more fulfilling careers, marriages, or personal and spiritual growth, they can often leave us feeling greater frustration, regret, suffering, and disappointment.

We devour self-help books, TV shows, cassettes, and videotapes that promise us self-actualizati on, peace, and serenity. We throw ourselves headlong into various New Age psychologies, fad diets, religions, self-help groups, workshops, therapies, and philosophies, and bow at the feet of "perfect masters"—all with the hope of becoming the best that we could be. *Many of us have come to expect nothing less than perfection.*

For these reasons and others that we will examine in this book, the issue of perfectionism is vital to our lives today.

Part I, comprising the first three chapters, focuses on clarifying the nature of the perfection trap. The first chapter defines the term *perfectionist* and distinguishes between striving for excellence and pursuing perfection. Common characteristics of perfectionistic thinking are identified and contrasted to those of excellence thinking. An extended inventory is offered to help you determine whether you are a perfectionist. Chapter 2 explains the meaning of the phrase *good enough is never enough.* Examples illustrate various forms of never-enough thinking and behavior and demonstrate the futility of perfection-seeking. We examine why people often refuse to acknowledge that perfection-seeking is a problem and not a virtue. Chapter 3 details the suffering that can accompany perfectionism, the physical, mental, and emotional disorders related to the perfectionistic mentality.

Part II focuses on how we have become ensnared in the perfection trap. The cultural roots of perfectionism and the ways in which our society influences, sustains, and rewards the pursuit of perfection are examined in chapter 4. Chapter 5 takes us inside the mind of the perfectionist, examining the psychological roots of perfectionism from a variety of perspectives. The Western religious and Eastern spiritual roots of perfectionism are covered in chapter 6. We see how the psychological roots of perfectionism are reinforced when religious heritages emphasize the conscious, deliberate, and willful pursuit of the perfect.

Part III takes us into the belly of the monster, identifying basic aspects of daily life that are affected by perfection-seeking. Included are examples and exercises that aim at lessening perfectionistic behavior in each of these areas. Chapter 7 traces the early shaping of the "perfect child," identifying family patterns and parent-child dynamics that produce perfectionism in children and adolescents. Problems experienced by adult children of perfectionistic parents and how they can be addressed are examined in chapter 8. This chapter also discusses issues related to having perfectionistic siblings and suggests a method for transcending the need for parental approval.

Chapter 9 focuses on the problems encountered by the perfectionist at work, including how to cope with a perfectionistic boss and perfectionistic company. Chapter 10 addresses the perfectionist at play and leisure, areas of life also subject to the drive to be the best. In chapter 11, we look at our search to find the perfect partner and achieve the perfect relationship. Common unrealistic expectations are analyzed, and relationship excellence is contrasted to the fantasy of perfection. Various tools toward relationship excellence are offered.

Part IV offers practical guidance to help you escape from the perfection trap and transform perfectionism into the more healthy and moderate pursuit of excellence. Chapter 12 is for those who are living with a perfectionist. It points out the positive aspects of living with a perfectionist and offers coping strategies for the more difficult aspects. Chapter 13 concentrates on personal tools for redirecting perfectionism into a pursuit for excellence. A tool for defining good-enough performance is offered, and the various elements of excellence are identified. We see how these elements may be applied to transform the perfectionist's life. Chapter 14 briefly addresses some philosophical issues about our individual uniqueness. It suggests how we can, indeed, find forms of perfection in an imperfect world.

As you read this book and consider the various ways the perfection trap affects your life, you will begin to think more clearly and consciously about how to transform the pursuit of perfection into a striving toward excellence. Many exercises and tools will be presented to challenge your preconceptions about perfectionism, and to help you make this shift in perspective. You will begin to understand some of the unconscious reasons why the pursuit of perfection became such an overwhelming force in your life.

You will encounter many examples, both serious and humorous, of the important concepts presented. You will no doubt identify with some of them. If you have struggled with trying to be perfect, you can learn to relax and back off from this burden. The methods for escaping the perfection trap will help you learn to value yourself and create meaningful and satisfying goals and projects without having to perform perfectly.

While this book will take you partway down the path, please remember that perfectionism is not a characteristic that will easily be thwarted just by reading a self-help book, no matter how good it may be. Don't expect the book to solve all your problems. This book will not take the place of psychotherapy with a qualified professional, if that is what you need. Nor will it magically change a lifetime's worth of learning and patterns.

It can be difficult to overcome perfectionism, and any self-help book has limitations. However, working with the ideas and tools provided here will help you gain a *sense of understanding and control* over your perfectionistic thoughts and behaviors, which you initially might not have believed possible. You may begin to experience how good it feels to learn to value and trust your inner, intuitive self and your individual uniqueness, and how satisfying it feels to slow down and reorient the driven need to gain power and status over others into a more moderate striving for excellence. In making this orientation, you will open yourself to more gratifying love, work, and family relationships.

Learning to live in the present and appreciate the ongoing flow of life, rather than being caught in the goal-oriented future, brings a powerful realization of the immediacy and joy that are possible in our lives. The relief that accompanies this reorientation can make you feel lighter, happier, and able to view yourself and the world with more humor. You will find renewed energy to express yourself creatively and spontaneously, with motivation that comes from within yourself, rather than from the nod of outside approval.

# PART ONE

# The
# Nature
## of the
# Trap

# ONE

# Perfection or Excellence?
## *Dancing on the Razor's Edge*

*Friend, don't be a perfectionist.*
*Perfectionism is a curse and a strain.*
*For you tremble lest you miss the bull's-eye.*
*You are perfect if you let be.*
Frederick S. Perls

"What's the problem with being a perfectionist? Isn't being a perfectionist a virtue, a label to wear proudly? Why a book on overcoming something I view as a badge of honor?" If you're a perfectionist, these might be the first questions you asked as you picked up this book. Despite our conditioning to view perfectionism as a virtue, there are many negative and often unacknowledged consequences of the pursuit of perfection that create much pain and suffering in our lives as we strive to measure up to what is ultimately an impossible ideal. Some of these consequences are:

- feelings of anxiety and fear about performance failure, often leading to a paralyzing procrastination
- nagging self-doubt and regret over lost opportunities and perceived failures

- crippled self-esteem, security, and self-respect
- fearful inhibition of learning new skills, tasks, sports, and hobbies
- stifled creativity in work and personal projects
- frustration and self-disgust resulting from stubborn refusal to allow good-enough performance to be fulfilling
- desperate attempts to establish self-worth by seeking love, acceptance, approval, recognition, and admiration from parents, authority figures, relatives, friends, and peers
- inability to form and sustain intimate friendships and love relationships
- unrealistic performance expectations and critical judgments of others that hinder the formation of satisfying work relationships and often create anger, resentment, and bitterness

Perfectionism plays a role in creating or aggravating a wide variety of common psychological, physical, and emotional problems and illnesses. These include the following, which we'll look at in later chapters.

- eating disorders such as anorexia, bulimia, and obesity (chapter 3)
- manic-depressive mood disorder (chapter 3)
- obsessive-compulsive disorder and the need to control others (chapters 5 and 6)
- feelings of specialness, entitlement, and self-absorption (chapters 5, 7, 9, and 11)
- feelings of emptiness; lack of personal and spiritual meaning in life (chapters 5 and 6)
- cosmetic surgical procedures that can cause pain, disfigurement, even serious injury to the body (chapters 3, 4, and 7)

- guilt, envy, and jealousy (chapters 5, 8, 9, 10, and 11)
- inordinate desire for power, fame, and status (chapters 4 and 5)
- substance abuse (chapters 3 and 5)
- physical problems such as high blood pressure, heart attacks, poor digestion, skin disorders, sleep disorders, and various stress-related illnesses (chapter 3)
- loneliness, withdrawal, and depression (chapters 3 and 5)

## THE ESSENTIAL MOTIVATOR

As I intend to make "perfectly" clear in this book, perfectionism is not limited to those who proudly identify themselves as perfectionists. It affects not only those overachievers who, unaware of their limits, aim for perfection. *Perfectionism is consciously and unconsciously built into the very cultural, psychological, and religious foundations of our achievement-oriented upbringing.* Because of this, it is an issue that affects everyone, to some degree (see chapters 4–6).

One of the most common concerns that arises when we think about giving up perfectionistic standards is that, without perfectionism, we will have nothing to motivate or guide our behavior. We fear that individually and as a society, we might fall apart—that people would stop doing anything productive. Without the standard of perfection to motivate society to work, we might wonder, what standard will we replace it with to motivate us to succeed?

In this book, I do not suggest that we stop trying to perform at a high level or give up our motivation to achieve. I do suggest that we need to have appropriate personal standards rather than pie-in-the-sky ideals that are impossible to meet. In place of perfection, our standard for performance will be excellence. By the time you finish this book, you will understand the crucial differences between these two standards and realize that advocating excellence in place of perfection is not just a matter of semantics.

## More Books Than Anyone Alive

Arnold was 43 when he came to see me about his broken relationship and his nagging sense of failure despite his many impressive accomplishments. From our interviews, he had me convinced that he had done enough already to fill two lifetimes.

Always a little jittery, Arnold was unable to sit still very long. He would either tap his foot nervously while he spoke or move around in his chair. He couldn't quite get comfortable in the present and just settle into being with me.

He had earned a Ph.D. in his early 20s and gone on to write a number of widely adopted textbooks. He boasted to me that he had written more books in his specialty than "anyone else alive." I discovered that Arnold was telling me the truth about his publishing success, although I was skeptical about the "more books than anyone alive" part. Curious about his writing, I asked him to bring in some examples of his books. These were scholarly, informed, and moderately demanding textbooks that he had become adept at churning out on a variety of subjects. He claimed to have written more than 70 books, though many of these were revisions of his earlier works.

I was impressed by his productivity and by how he had been able to extract himself from the teach-and-research academic world. His books had sold so well in high schools and colleges that he could live off the royalties, even if he never wrote another word.

Arnold maintained that he couldn't find any friends who came close to having his range of interests. His friends might share one or two interests with him, but much of the time he pursued his activities alone. As he put it, "I work hard and I play hard—nobody can keep up with me."

His fascination with his intellectual prowess made it difficult for Arnold to see others as more than satellites of himself. He tended to relegate everyone else in life—his parents, ex-wife, girlfriend, children, secretary, colleagues, and employees—into secondary roles. Arnold's concern with what others could do for him left little room for him to consider that others might need from him.

It wasn't difficult to see why Arnold had developed a distorted sense of self-importance. On the surface, he seemed confident. He had done an impressive amount of scholarly work and was talented in a number of sports and hobbies.

Arnold was a good example of what is called the classic Type A driven personality (see chapter 3). He had great difficulty totally relaxing and doing absolutely nothing. He felt a chronic sense of urgency in his life and did everything fast. Nothing seemed right to him unless it was done intensely. For Arnold there was only one setting on the performance dial: Full Throttle, High Intensity.

Unfortunately, his urgency made it impossible for him to slow down and catch his breath. Rarely could he allow himself to stop producing or showing off without feeling anxious and unworthy. Arnold's accomplishments did not give him a sense of true inner security.

Arnold wasn't satisfied with being at the top of the heap in the textbook field; he wanted to be the best in every activity he took on. He wanted to be a man for all seasons, and so he became a skilled surfer in the summer and an expert skier in the winter. He could not stand to see someone do anything better than he. Thus he practiced skiing until he could handle the downhill as quickly and adeptly as his teacher. He considered becoming a professional photographer but decided that pursuit wasn't demanding enough. He had run in a number of marathons and completed at least one "Strong-Man" triathlon contest.

This obsession to prove his manhood also affected his sex life. Arnold seriously believed he deserved to have sex at least once per day. Without daily sex, Arnold believed an opportunity for The Perfect Day had been ruined. He felt something was wrong with his relationship if this daily sex bout did not take place. He could not appreciate that his girlfriend might be tired of this compulsive ritual or might not feel like making love. And, even when his girlfriend tried to meet his demands, he was unable to simply enjoy it. He had to be a long-distance performer in bed as well.

What brought him to my consulting room was the anxiety that

ensued when his girlfriend finally left him, driven away by his excessive demands and rituals. She had found a less demanding and more accepting man. He simply could not accept that she could leave him and his comfortable lifestyle for another man.

Arnold had the intelligence to understand that he could not continue to be oblivious to the needs of others if he wished his own needs to be fulfilled. With the help of psychotherapy he began to be less demanding and critical of his children, to slow down his hectic pace, and to seriously seek to understand the psychological dynamics behind his perfectionism. He began to accept the limitations of others instead of ridiculing them, and he slowly began to ease up on himself and accept that things did not have to be perfect.

By looking at the unconscious motivations for some of his high expectations of himself and his need to do everything to the extreme, Arnold began to slowly modify some of his obsessive all-or-nothing thinking as well as alter his daily patterns. He began to question his motivations and started to see how self-centered and self-obsessed he had become. He wondered whether he was capable of really loving a woman. He wondered whether he was able to really care for anyone. He began to realize that underneath the accomplishments and the boastfulness was a part of him that felt very insecure and empty; and that, as smart as he was, he nonetheless didn't know much about his own mind. He began to understand that he was caught in the perfection trap, where good enough is never enough.

## FROM EXCELLENCE TO PERFECTION

Arnold represents both the positive (striving for excellence) and negative (the trap of perfectionism) poles of our desire to be and do our best. He illustrates what happens when we fall over the razor's edge from one to the other.

One of the basic values of the Western world is the pursuit of excellence. Our competitive culture teaches us that we should strive to be the best. It is this pursuit of excellence that accounts for our highest individual and collective accomplishments in science, the creative arts, technology, sports, business, and human relationships. It is this same pursuit of excellence that pushes us to surpass ourselves, to always want more from ourselves in our quest for individual happiness and personal satisfaction. We all want to actualize our highest potential.

Pressured by our society's emphasis on achievement and excellence, something curious happens—as we grow up we get confused along the way. What began as the pursuit of excellence becomes the pursuit of perfection. Most of the time, we don't even know that we have taken a wrong turn. The path we follow in pursuing perfection is a perilous and unending one, fraught with the persistent danger of losing our fragile sense of self-worth.

The quest for perfection is guaranteed to lead to frustration, false pride, self-disgust, anger, regret, resentment, envy, and jealousy, any of which could become all-consuming. What we ultimately discover as we pursue this path is that *it is impossible to come out ahead.* For the perfectionist, what should be seen as good enough is viewed as *never enough.* The belief that we can become perfect in our behavior is a common falsehood. It simply can't be accomplished.

## WHO IS A PERFECTIONIST?

*A perfectionist is someone who thinks that anything short of perfection in performance is unacceptable.* A perfectionist is unable to feel a sense of satisfaction from his efforts because he never seems to do things well enough. Unable to determine appropriate limits, he sets his goals beyond reach and reason.

Here are some of the basic characteristics of perfectionistic thinking long identified by many of those writing on the topic of perfectionism.[1] All of these traits will be discussed in greater depth later in this book.

*The perfectionist is motivated not by the desire for improvement but by fear of failure.* As we saw in Arnold's case, the perfectionist's desire to excel can only be self-defeating. Achievement brings no sense of joy or satisfaction. The perfectionist runs *away* from the negative rather than *toward* the positive.

*The perfectionist tends to view the world in absolute, all-or-nothing terms.* Everything is either black or white, wonderful or horrible. The perfectionist's underlying assumptions about the world are framed in absolute terms, such as *always* or *never.* For example: "I'll never be able to complete that project." "I'm always the last one to be given any attention from the boss." "My wife never buys me what I want." "I must always get the respect and admiration from others that I deserve." With this thinking, the perfectionist illogically generalizes on the basis of a single incident. For example, the perfectionist believes that if she doesn't measure up in one area of work, she will not be able to measure up in *any* area of work; or that if she can't master her first attempt to learn a new song on the guitar, she will *never* get it right.

*The perfectionist has a large number of severe self-commands.* No one can live up to what the perfectionist demands of herself. For example: "I should be the best wife, mother, friend, lover." "I should never get angry." "I should always achieve my goals without any difficulty." "If Jane Fonda can be a superwoman, then I must be, too." "I must be the best dressed at the party or I won't enjoy it."

Albert Ellis, a well-known psychologist and developer of Rational-Emotive therapy, calls this *mustabatory* thinking. "I *must* have it my way or else I can't stand it." "She has *got* to go out with me or I'll never be desirable to anyone." Ellis also says that "shouldhood leads to shithood." He means that when we continually put these "shoulds" on ourselves and then can't measure up, the result can only be feelings of inadequacy, self-disgust, guilt, shame, and misery.[2]

*Perfectionists measure their self-worth in terms of unachievable goals of accomplishment and productivity.* Any deviation from the perfectionistic goal is likely to be accompanied by moralistic self-criticism (guilt) and a lowered sense of self-worth. In this manner, the perfectionist can drive himself crazy, continually falling short of the mark and continually feeling like an absolute "nothing" for not making the impossible grade.

This feeling of being a "nothing" is the feeling of shame. We will talk more about guilt and shame and the differences between them in chapters 3 and 5. For now, the main idea is that the inability to measure up to one's unrealistically high goals leads to severe self-criticism and feelings of worthlessness, both hallmarks of the perfectionist.

*The perfectionist tends to focus on the negative in a situation and exclude the positive.* He quickly zeros in on what is lacking and overlooks what is present. He tends to see the glass as half empty rather than half full. Example: The perfectionist notes the few remaining smudges on the floor that has been waxed twice, and then redoes the whole floor rather than just the small area that was overlooked. In this way, the perfectionist is able to justify his self-critical judgments.

*The perfectionist is quick to jump to conclusions based on inadequate information.* The perfectionist tends to interpret situations in a negative way without taking the time to gather sufficient information to warrant the judgment. One way she does this is by "mind-reading," believing she knows what another person is thinking based on unwarranted assumptions that often turn out not to be true. As a consequence she may become defensive and fear disclosing her thoughts and feelings to others because she assumes she will be judged negatively. In another example of jumping to conclusions, the perfectionist tends to give up quickly on a new project, assuming that he will never learn the skill simply because he got off to a slow start.

*Perfectionists, although often as critical of others as they are of themselves, tend to blame themselves for what is not their doing.* They may hold themselves responsible for events that are out of their control. Example: A father feels responsible when his son is unable to make the varsity basketball team. Believing he has failed as a coach to the boy, the father blames himself and then gets upset with his son, since his son is not making him look good. Both father and son end up feeling miserable.

*Hard-core perfectionists have obsessive-compulsive tendencies.* An obsession is an idea, emotion, or impulse that repeatedly forces itself into awareness even though it is unwanted. Obsessions lead to compulsions, which are uncontrollable, impulsive actions, driven by anxiety. For example, someone who is obsessed with having everything on her desk in perfect order may develop the compulsion to spend so much time tidying the desk that she is unable to concentrate on productive work.

## Dancing on the Razor's Edge

The balancing act required to keep us from falling into the perfection trap may make us feel at times like we are dancing on the razor's edge. It is not always clear to us what differentiates the unhealthy pursuit of perfection from the healthy striving for excellence. Too often, we think they are the same. In our pursuit of excellence, some of us have accomplished at high levels and yet have suffered quietly, feeling driven to push ourselves to still higher levels. We do not derive as much satisfaction from our work and relationships as we think we should or as we see others enjoying. We may have sensed that something was wrong, but because of our need to feel in control and deny that our striving could be a problem, we seduce ourselves into thinking that we are pursuing excellence when, upon closer examination, we are showing signs of unhealthy perfectionism.

Our predicament is further complicated by the fact that even if we are legitimately striving for excellence, we may pay a price. We may experience problems related to our need for high levels of accomplishment, even if we have managed to avoid pathological perfectionism.

On the other side of the razor's edge are those whose lives are affected by perfectionism in a devastating way, sometimes to the point of severe mental illness and even suicide. Unable to control the direction in which their strivings lead them, these people end up severely emotionally disturbed despite their accomplishments. Psychologists have studied many such people in an attempt to understand the relationship between creativity, genius, and mental illness.

This thin line is partly a result of our competitive and individualistic society, which tends to reward the push toward excellence and hard work, and to ignore the casualties that result when one crosses over the line into perfectionism. In fact, as chapter 4 will show, our culture in many ways encourages outright perfectionism. Once one has fallen off the edge into the perfectionism trap, it is not easy to come back.

## STRIVING FOR EXCELLENCE

We can help clarify the distinction between succumbing to perfectionism and seeking excellence by describing the healthy characteristics of someone who strives for excellence. Keep in mind that, in our balancing act, which category we belong in is sometimes only a matter of degree. Those striving for excellence are:

- able to accept a less-than-perfect performance without feeling inadequate
- able to derive personal satisfaction and pride from a good-enough performance
- motivated by the joy of achievement and the challenge of reaching a goal rather than driven by the fear of failure and disapproval from others
- able to appreciate and enjoy the successive steps achieved toward a goal as significant rather than focusing only on the end goal

- able to utilize previous accomplishments to build a reservoir of self-confidence and self-esteem as support when taking on new challenges
- able to feel sympathetic joy for the accomplishments of others without feeling envious or diminished by their success
- able to transcend the tendency to make their identity, self-esteem, and self-worth dependent exclusively on personal performance and accomplishments
- able to take on tasks, and play sports, games, and amusements for pure entertainment, doing their best but not turning the activities into competition
- able to lose gracefully and be good sports, to walk away without feeling that their self-worth has been diminished
- able to overcome depression and feelings of anxiety, hostility, anger, and resentment when they don't come out ahead
- able to enjoy their accomplishments without having to boast or put others down
- able to demonstrate a sense of modesty and humility, a realistic perspective on their accomplishments

## THE HENDLIN PERFECTIONISM INVENTORY (HPI)

If you are not sure whether you are a perfectionist, or you would like to determine how perfectionistic you are compared to others, take the inventory below. For each statement, fill in the blank with the number from the scale below that best describes how you feel. Try not to ponder each answer for more than 20 seconds, and don't go back to change any answers.

0 = disagree strongly     3 = agree somewhat

1 = disagree somewhat     4 = agree very much

2 = feel neutral about this

1. I think of myself as a perfectionist. _____

2. I take pride in telling others that I'm a perfectionist. _____

3. I am easily annoyed when others don't measure up to my expectations. _____

4. If I can't do something well, there is no reason to try it at all. _____

5. I am hard on myself when I lose a game, contest, or competition. _____

6. I set very high goals for myself no matter what I'm doing. _____

7. I like my material possessions to be in order and get upset when they are disturbed. _____

8. I like my workplace very neat and clean and find it hard to work if it is disturbed. _____

9. I have trouble accepting the fact that others don't expect as much from themselves as I expect from myself. _____

10. I get angry when people I care about don't perform up to my expectations. _____

11. I get impatient and annoyed when I have to waste time because of others' incompetence. _____

12. I find it hard to accept that people can do sloppy work and get away with it. _____

13. I can't imagine ever thinking I am too thin. _____

14. I don't like to have to be a beginner at learning something new. _____

15. I like to teach others the best way to do something. _____

16. Striving for perfection keeps me performing my best. _____

17. It is hard for me not to zero in on the inadequacies of other people. _____

18. It disturbs me that the world isn't a more fair place than it is. _____

19. If I couldn't excel at and be acknowledged for at least one thing I do, I don't think I could live with myself. _____

20. I often think to myself how other people are idiots when they make mistakes or don't perform as I think they should. _____

21. I get paralyzed by procrastination when it comes to tackling new tasks. _____

22. I hate to admit feeling envy when I find out that someone with whom I feel competitive has achieved something I haven't. _____

23. Once I make a mistake, I should never make it again. _____

24. When someone does something better than I, I tend to silently berate them and minimize their accomplishment. _____

25. When someone criticizes something about my character, I feel attacked and tend to get defensive. _____

26. I feel shame when I don't measure up to the goals I have set for myself. _____

27. When my work is criticized I feel injured and humiliated. _____

28. When others get awards and recognition I feel left out. _____

29. I feel very frustrated when I can't express my good ideas perfectly. _____

30. I get a perverse feeling of satisfaction in watching those with whom I feel competitive lose or fail, especially if they are losing to me. _____

31. I prefer the perfect world of my inner thoughts and fantasies to the outer world of human error and folly. _____

32. Those who are close to me tell me I expect too much of myself. _____

33. An average performance is not good enough for me. _____

34. People in my life don't seem to appreciate my special skills and talents. _____

35. Compliments on my physical appearance are important to me. _____

36. When my life is not in perfect order, I get anxious and do whatever is necessary to get things back in place. _____

37. If I don't wear exactly the right clothes for an occasion, I feel embarrassed. _____

38. Making jokes about others' foibles makes me feel superior to them. _____

39. It is hard for me not to boast to others when I have done something well. _____

40. Most of the time I don't feel satisfied with how my body looks. _____

41. I sometimes imagine that when I die and go to heaven, everyone there will be perfect and all my needs will be perfectly satisfied. _____

42. My feelings of emptiness go away for a while when I stuff myself with food or take mood-altering substances. _____

43. Getting attention in my family meant having to accomplish a lot. _____

44. I felt I had to earn my parents' love rather than be loved just for who I was. _____

45. Being hard on myself when I don't measure up will make me do better the next time. _____

46. Sometimes I wonder if someone like me belongs in this less-than-perfect world. _____

47. Sometimes I do something over and over until I get it just right. _____

48. At all times, I try as hard as I can to be morally and ethically correct. _____

49. I tend to judge my sexual performance and technique and wonder how I compare to other men or women my partner has been with. _____

50. Sometimes I wonder whether my spouse/boyfriend/girlfriend is the right partner for me and fantasize being with somebody more perfect. _____

51. I wonder what others think about me and what private things they say about me behind my back. _____

52. I am proud of my overall body strength and muscle tone. _____

53. I can't stand doing anything partway—it's either all or nothing for me. _____

54. I like to fantasize how my life would be if I finally got the recognition and status from others that I deserve. _____

55. I don't like to be around people socially who are not at the same level of accomplishment and social status as I am. _____

56. Sometimes I have dreams about others giving me recognition and treating me special. _____

57. I try to improve my partner to make myself look better. _____

58. It really matters what others think about me. _____

59. The thought of giving up the standard of perfection that I have set for myself fills me with anxiety because I wouldn't know what else to use to guide my behavior. _____

60. I feel driven to accomplish more and more in my life. _____

## Scoring

Add up your score on all 60 items. Your score will fall somewhere between 0 (if you disagreed strongly with all 60 items) and 240 (if you agreed strongly with all 60 items). In an inventory of this type, your score will be affected by various subjective factors (for example, your truthfulness in answering the statements) and statistical factors. Therefore your "universe" score is probably in the range of 15 points above or below what you have calculated, which you may want to consider when interpreting the results. Calculate the following:

_____ actual score                    _____ low universe score
                                         (subtract 15 points)

_____ high universe score
     (add 15 points)

## Interpretation of Scores

In using the interpretive guidelines presented below, please remember that not all general statements will be accurate in your particular case. One inventory instrument is not enough in itself to draw absolutely valid conclusions as to where you stand in relation to perfectionism. The HPI has not been rigorously tested or validated with significantly large samples; it is for experimental use only. Interpretations should be used only in a general way, to find out where you fit along the perfectionism scale.

Also remember that one of the main themes of this book is that no one who has been taught to value individualism, competitiveness, the desire to excel, and to gain personal recognition escapes the perfection trap completely. The question is how deeply we have become ensnared. With all of that in mind, if your total universe score for all 60 statements falls in the range of:

*80 or less.* Assuming you have answered the statements truthfully, you do not have a problem with perfectionism. But while you appear to have escaped the push of our society to strive for excellence, you could actually be on the other end of the scale—neither expecting much of yourself nor feeling much motivation. This may or it may not pose a problem depending on your chosen lifestyle and values.

*81–120.* You have a healthy degree of perfectionism. You do not overly pressure yourself to perform and have learned to value yourself independently from your accomplishments.

*121–160.* Your degree of perfectionism is mild to moderate. A score in the mid-range of this category (140) means you had an average score for all items of 2.3, or only slightly stronger than neutral. This category indicates perfectionistic strivings that are under control for the most part. You may have areas of perfectionism in your life that get the best of you.

*161–180.* You have a moderate to high degree of perfectionism. A mid-range score in this category (170) would mean an average of 2.8 for all items, clearly an indication that perfectionism is part of your thinking and behavior. You might be a high achiever who expects a lot from yourself. A moderate amount of your self-worth is determined by your accomplishments. You need to learn how to manage your desire for high performance to begin to untangle yourself from the perfection trap.

*181–200.* You have a high degree of perfectionism. You have gone beyond striving for excellence and definitely are ensnared in the trap of perfection. Good enough is never enough for you. You may have a driven need to succeed, and strong feelings about how you and others ought to be in this world. You are in touch with yourself enough to know that you are perfectionistic, and very likely you view perfection as your standard of excellence. You may be anxious about giving up this guideline because you would not know what else to use to determine your self-worth.

*201 and above.* You have achieved the category of "perfect" perfectionism! Believe me, you don't want to hear any more of the interpretation for this category. Penance: Say three Hail Marys, read this book four times from cover to cover (or until you have committed it to memory), and then proceed immediately to consult a qualified psychologist.

### Not for Compulsives Only: Taking It a Step Further

*Item and cluster analysis.* The HPI can be broken down into seven clusters of statements, based on different aspects of perfectionism. They are listed below, with their corresponding statement numbers.

- perfectionistic self-identification: 1, 2, 16, 55, 59 (5 items)
- narcissistic traits (superiority, grandiosity, envy, need for attention, etc.) 14, 15, 17, 20, 22, 24, 25, 27, 28, 30, 34, 38, 39, 42, 51, 54, 56 (17 items)
- body image: 13, 35, 40, 52 (4 items)
- severe judgments of self and others: 5, 11, 32, 45, 49, 50, 57, 60 (8 items)
- unrealistically high expectations of self and others: 3, 6, 9, 10, 12, 18, 26, 33, 43, 44 (10 items)

- all-or-nothing thinking: 4, 19, 23, 29, 37, 53 (6 items)
- obsessive-compulsive traits: 7, 8, 21, 31, 36, 41, 46, 47, 48, 60 (10 items)

By examining your answers to specific items within these clusters, you can get a more exact idea of the aspects of perfectionism with which you tend to identify. Look especially at items you scored 4 in each cluster.

# TWO

# When Good Enough Is Never Enough:
## *Caught Between Image and Reality*

*When we are ruled by our desires,*
*more is never enough.*
Ram Dass

*He who knows when enough is enough*
*will always have enough.*
Lao Tze

When it comes to human beings and their actions in the real world there is no such thing as absolute perfection. *Our behavior cannot be perfect.* Our lack of awareness of this simple fact creates much frustration and suffering in our lives. This is one of the reasons the pursuit of perfection is a trap. As the psychologist Rabbi Reuven Bulka has said, "Perfection is not for human beings, perfection is for angels."[1] What is the fundamental misunderstanding that leads us to believe that perfection in our performance is possible?

## Conceiving Versus Achieving

Philosophers from the time of Plato have conceived of and written about mental perfection, the perfection of thought forms and ideas.

Some psychologists believe the concept of perfection is one of the archetypes (unconscious collective mental templates) with which we are born (see chapter 5).

The fact that we can conceive of the perfect thought form or image does not mean these images can be actualized. *Our ability to conceive of a perfect image, combined with our failure to understand the impossibility of actualizing this image in our behavior, is the basic confusion that sets the trap of never measuring up for the perfectionist.*

It is as if our mind plays a cruel trick on us, taunting us to actualize the perfect images it produces. Our task is to learn to recognize and appreciate the images without believing they can be made real. This is not easy to do. We are told, "You'll see it when you believe it," and "You create your own reality," and other slogans that tantalize us with the notion that we should be able to turn all of our images and fantasies into real-world behavior.

When we fail to make this crucial distinction between the perfect mental image and real-world behavior we have taken the bait and stepped into the perfection trap. Once we begin to separate our images from our behavior, we are free to enjoy these images without the burden of needing to make them real.

This is why we say that perfection is a fantasy, a mental image or idea of what we consider to be the ultimate standard as we wish it could be realized in the world. In our striving for excellence, we can only *approach* what we consider to be the perfect athletic performance, perfect body, perfect relationship, perfect health, perfect vacation, perfect lifestyle, or perfect religious experience. Such an experience may feel whole, complete, and satisfying, but no matter how close the perfectionist comes to the image of perfection, the knowledge that he has fallen short results in feelings of inadequacy. For the perfectionist, *good enough is never enough*. If we can learn to sever the false but powerful unconscious connection between *conceiving* of perfection versus *achieving* it, we can spare ourselves much of the suffering that accompanies this impossible pursuit.

There is an alternative way to think of perfectionism. We can view it as "the practice of demanding of ourselves and others a higher quality of performance than is required by the situation," as one psychological dictionary defines it.[2]

## NEVER-ENOUGH THINKING

Our list of perfectionistic traits in chapter 1 dealt primarily with the way perfectionists think about themselves, the world, and others in general. The following list focuses on how the never-enough mentality influences the way perfectionists think and behave around a specific issue of overwhelming importance to them: their own performance.

*Perfectionists set unrealistically or even impossibly high goals for their performance.* For example, JoAnn tells me that she considers herself a failure because not all of the articles she has submitted to a magazine have been accepted for publication. Even though a number have been accepted, she is unable to handle the sense of worthlessness that lasts for days whenever she gets a rejection notice. Her all-or-nothing thinking casts a shadow on her accomplishments and diminishes her work. She says she just can't stand to have her acceptance record be less than perfect.

*Perfectionists cannot tolerate simply coming close to the goal.* They cannot tolerate anything less than hitting it on the nose. They leave little room for acknowledging gradual steps of successive approximation, or getting closer and closer to the goal with repeated practice. To the perfectionist, coming close is the same as failing. This all-or-nothing thinking can lead to feelings of self-disgust, anger, regret, and make the perfectionist try to blame others for the "failure."

*Perfectionists are not willing to be beginners.* They have little tolerance for the feeling of frustration that is natural to learning a new skill.

They expect they ought to be able to perform perfectly from the start. While they may realize this is irrational, they believe it nevertheless. If they can't learn a new skill immediately, they find some excuse for giving it up, because they cannot tolerate feeling foolish and dependent. In learning something new, we are often forced to get help from someone else, to depend on them to teach us and to surrender to their greater knowledge and skill. Perfectionists tend to avoid depending on others because they don't want to acknowledge their limits.

Unwilling to be beginners, they shy away from anything they have not already mastered. They especially don't like to be seen trying something new in public, where the potential for feeling embarrassment and humiliation is even stronger. If they do let themselves try something new, they prefer to do so privately, where no one can witness their trial-and-error efforts.

Sometimes perfectionists rationalize their avoidance of trying anything new as a lack of interest. They would rather tell themselves and others they are simply "not interested" than admit their inability to risk the vulnerable feelings of being a beginner. They need to believe that if they only had the interest, they could do anything well. And as long as they don't try new things, this belief is never put to the test.

*Never-enough thinking often leads to procrastination.* When the perfectionist is willing to try something new, it may be only after long procrastination. Whatever initial excitement may have been aroused at the thought of trying something new, is overcome by paralyzing fear of failure, possible humiliation, and feelings of shame. Procrastination protects the perfectionist from the dread of the less-than-perfect result, which she views as failure. Fear of failure may also lead the perfectionist to procrastinate with more familiar tasks and projects, stifling creativity and holding the perfectionist back from what she most desires—achievement.

Procrastinators often rationalize their inability to face their fears of rejection and humiliation with all kinds of "good" excuses for not beginning a task. Thus, they not only avoid taking on projects that may expose them to shame and humiliation, they also avoid acknowledging the real reasons for their behavior. Because of this, it is necessary first to help procrastinators admit that they are, indeed, fearful of a catastrophic outcome. Once they acknowledge this fear, they can work more directly with their catastrophic expectations and negative thinking.

*No matter how well perfectionists perform, they struggle to feel satisfied with the outcome. They feel an inner emptiness instead of the joy of accomplishment.* John, who is accustomed to doing outstanding work at graduate school, has just received word that his mathematics paper has been accepted by a prestigious journal. He says, "Yeah, I guess it's a feather in my cap. But it feels like I just measured up to what I expected of myself, so why should I make a big deal out of it?" He is unable to let this accomplishment sink in so that it can nourish him. Since he expects only the best of himself, he has simply measured up, so what is there to feel good about?

*Perfectionists are unable to savor the moment of accomplishment and unwilling to celebrate the event.* When they should feel excitement, joy, and satisfaction, they feel only an emptiness or deadness. Sometimes, the perfectionist is aware of this emptiness and says something like, "I know I ought to feel good about this but instead I just feel numb." Or he may ask, "Is that all there is to it? It didn't seem like the goal was hard enough to achieve," implying that there is no reason to feel good about an achievement unless the task was especially arduous. Sometimes he even uses the moment of accomplishment to put himself down: "Oh, it isn't all that important. I could have done even better."

This is the paradox of perfectionism: perfectionists want things to be magically easy to accomplish, but at the same time they are mistrusting of themselves if they accomplish something too easily. Since they basically don't trust whatever talent they have, they are suspicious of anything they don't have to work very hard to attain. This makes for a frustrating no-win situation—"If things come too easily, I won't value myself, yet I expect to be able to do everything expertly without much effort."

*The perfectionist fears being found out as an impostor.* When he does temporarily measure up, the perfectionist only succeeds in pushing away the fear of failure for a while longer. This is part of the reason why the perfectionist feels so little true satisfaction and joy. Failure is always lurking around the corner, with the next performance, promotion, or evaluation.

## FEAR OF BEING "FOUND OUT"

This fear of failure is related to the perfectionist's often-stated feeling of being a phony or impostor. He feels he is deceiving others; that he is not as competent or worthy as he appears to be. The impostor knows he will sooner or later be found out—it is only a matter of time. He almost wishes it would happen sooner so he could give up the anxiety-ridden charade.

Anne, a 38-year-old who teaches literature at a junior college, says, "I finally got the promotion I've been working so hard for. But I keep looking over my shoulder, waiting for the faculty to find out. Even though I know the material, I still feel like I'm faking it. Sometimes I dream of my students laughing at me as I stand in front of the class."

The impostor phenomenon was popularized in a best-selling pop-psychology book a few years ago. You can bet that many bought the book thinking to themselves, "Yes, that's me. I feel like an impostor, too," were those with perfectionistic tendencies.[3]

The fear of failure and of being found out is strong because the perfectionist lacks the inner self-worth to sustain any type of criticism. To be less than perfect is to be fallible, to make mistakes. And when the perfectionist makes a mistake, she believes others will make the same harsh, rejecting judgments of her that she makes toward herself.

When the part of the perfectionist's self-concept that strongly identifies with this role of being perfect is confronted by evidence to the contrary, she realizes that she is fallible like everyone else. Then, following all-or-nothing thinking, her inner critic tells her that admitting mistakes means that she is not only less than perfect but also incompetent and a phony. The reasoning goes like this: "If I think I am a perfectionist, but really I am fallible, then I am a phony, and my fallibility will be discovered and used to humiliate me. I'm really inadequate."

Perfectionists may also feel like impostors because they are able to create a surface picture of competence and control that covers their inner sense of confusion and turmoil. But as they achieve higher levels of responsibility, the fear of having their incompetence found out begins to crack the outer pretense of self-assurance.

*Contributing to the driven nature of the perfectionist is the "So what have you done for me lately?" mentality.* This type of thinking is generated both from within himself, as well as from outside, by our performance-oriented society. Movie and TV stars, no matter how many successful films or shows they have made, are "only as good as their last performance"; professional athletes are quickly forgotten by the public if they don't stay on top; the author who had a best-seller two years ago feels compelled to repeat his performance for his readers; the boss makes it clear that our last big sale was great, but, "Hey, that was two weeks ago. What can you do for me today?"

The message is clear: "You are only as good as your last victory or sale or performance. Don't stop—keep pushing for more." But this is heard and experienced by the perfectionist as, "You are only a good (lovable, worthwhile) person if you keep on performing. Don't stop now or you'll turn to dust." To stop performing is to diminish one's sense of self-worth, to feel empty, to have one's identity challenged to the core. The competitive nature of our society sanctions this "what have you done for me lately?" mentality (see chapter 4). It is never enough to set a record once or to have one outstanding performance; we must do it again and again. If we can't, sooner or later we are sure to be viewed as nothing more than a vapor trail.

## EXAMPLES OF NEVER-ENOUGH THINKING

A college high jumper easily wins his event in the conference finals by jumping seven feet. However, he's disgusted with himself for brushing the crossbar off with his foot on his last attempt at seven feet, two inches. He pounds his fist into the foam while he is lying in the jumping pit, then gets up and kicks the ground. When congratulated by the TV commentator on his victory, he smirks and says, "I was OK, but I should have been able to make that last jump."

Fourteen-year-old Melody gives a piano recital in front of her parents and a large number of guests and other students. She has been practicing for this event for three months. When the big day arrives, she plays almost flawlessly for her level of experience. Her piano teacher is elated with her performance, as are her mother, her friends, and the other students. Everyone is congratulating her. Her father walks up and Melody says, "Daddy, did you like it?" (Translation: "Daddy, do you love me? Was I a good girl?")

Her father looks at Melody with more than a hint of disapproval and says, "It was pretty good, honey, but your timing wasn't quite right." She feels crushed, forgetting all the praise she just received, as well as her own good feeling about her performance. What was good enough for others was not good enough for her father. And because of her strong desire to gain her father's approval, Melody feels that her effort was for nothing, and redefines her own evaluation of a good-enough performance.

Ray, 41, is an aerospace engineer who designs airplane parts. Although he is employed by a large corporation, he shies away from the normal social camaraderie with fellow employees, preferring to work and spend lunch time alone. He is afraid of disapproval and rejection by his boss, and avoids for as long as possible attending required performance reviews of his work. He is also afraid of looking foolish if he doesn't have all the answers, so he refuses to reach out for help or feedback from his colleagues when he gets stuck. His perfectionism comes through in his deep fear of being ridiculed should he need any help from anyone and his obsessive drawing and redrawing of his projects until they are error-proof.

Sandra, 30, is a sharp attorney who tells me how hard it is for her to take criticism from her boss in her work with a contract law firm. She proudly identifies herself as a perfectionist. Sandra wants her research briefs and contracts to be absolutely perfect and can hardly contain her rage when her boss comes to her with corrections or suggestions. While she rationally knows that she can't expect herself to know everything in her field after only a few years out of school, she nonetheless feels humiliated whenever her boss or any of the partners come to her with constructive criticisms of her work. Her humiliation is experienced only after an initial flash of rage. It is this rage that she wants me to help her learn to understand and control.

Gary, 48, works for a company that provides employee safety programs to small companies so they will comply with the law. His written work requires him to adapt various forms to fit specific companies. He complains that he cannot stay focused on one project at a time and is often unable to determine the priorities of his daily tasks. While working on one project, he will suddenly shift his attention, remembering that a call needs to be made or that a different contract needs to be sent that he had forgotten about. He confuses himself easily, unable to distinguish important tasks from small details that don't require immediate attention. He takes pride in some of the projects he completes but works weekends trying to make up for the time that has been lost during the week due to procrastination.

When I suggest to Gary that each morning he visualize a list of the tasks he wishes to complete that day in order of importance, he procrastinates working with the visualization, finding many excuses as to why he can't find the time to practice the exercise. He strongly resists my attempts to help him face his fear of failure, as his defenses require that he deny this fear. He prefers to blame his boss for over-working him. Not surprisingly, Gary also has trouble attending our sessions on time, as his procrastination problem greatly affects his skill at time management.

Mary, 26, works very hard to perfect her talent as a dancer. No matter how many times she is complimented for her graceful move-ments, she finds some reason to diminish all the compliments she re-ceives. Her dance teacher tells her that she doesn't seem to enjoy herself while she is dancing. Mary responds that dance is work for her, not something to enjoy. As a perfectionist, she believes that she doesn't have the luxury to enjoy her work.

## WORKING WITH THE CONCEPTS

Think about and then list the areas of your life (besides your body) where you know that you have judged yourself as not making the grade. What do you think your life would be like if you achieved a good-enough performance? Can you identify anything you gain by seeing yourself as inadequate? For a minute, imagine that all the areas in which you feel you haven't measured up no longer matter in your evaluation of yourself. How does this feel? Notice any resistance you experience to even briefly feeling good enough in every area of your life. What would you be giving up?

In what areas do you expect others to perform up to your high standards? How do you react when they fall short? For a few days, notice each time you either say or hear your inner voice (self-talk) make a negative judgment about the behavior of others. Try to notice how automatically these judgments come up. As you do this, make no judgment about your own judging of others. Just be aware of how often this judging goes on.

Many people feel strong anxiety at the thought of giving up their standard of perfection as the guide for their behavior. They fear not having anything else to push them to achieve. Imagine putting the standard of excellence in place of perfection. Think about how you could make this substitution without experiencing any loss of motivation. Can you imagine it? Would you lose anything? Might you gain something?

# THREE

# THE PERILS OF PERFECTION:
## Excess Leading to Illness

*Emptiness. The attempt to overcome it by intoxication by music, by cruelty, by blind worship. . . . The attempt to submerge oneself in any kind of working routine, any silly little fanaticism; a confusion of all means, illness as a result of a general lack of moderation.*
FRIEDRICH NIETZSCHE

WHAT KINDS OF PHYSICAL, mental, and emotional problems are related to perfectionism? In this chapter we will look at numerous examples of the role perfectionism plays in creating or exacerbating certain types of psychological difficulties, personality problems, addictions, and other forms of illness. Many of these problems can be alleviated when the pursuit of perfection is transformed into a more moderate, balanced, and self-forgiving pursuit of excellence.

## EATING DISORDERS

Research indicates that women with eating disorders show greater defeatism, regret, and body dissatisfaction than those who have had bouts of periodic binge eating but are now symptom free. Their perfectionism is indicated by an "excessive expectation of excellence regarding weight and diet control."[1] Further support for the relationship between eating disorders and perfectionism can be found in studies showing that adolescents who develop anorexia tend to be talented, have high expectations of themselves and a high need for self-control, and have a distorted view of perfection.[2-4] They strive to attain an unrealistic image of the perfect body and are severely critical of themselves when their body does not measure up to their unrealistic standards.

## Jeanne: Eating for "Full-fillment"

Jeanne, 35, is a high-powered attorney. Her nails are perfectly manicured, her accessories always match and she carries a stylish leather briefcase. She wears expensive silk blouses and attractive business suits that belie her inner insecurity. Jeanne is bulimic, and has struggled with the binge-and-purge cycle for three years. In psychotherapy, she is learning how her eating disorder relates to her perfectionistic standards.

Jeanne, like many bulimics and overeaters, is obsessed with food and feels seduced by it. She experiences eating as a euphoric high, like the mood-altering effect of a drug. Even though she feels guilty during a binge, food helps pull her through difficult times of stressful work. She says, "When I'm preparing for a trial, eating always makes me feel stronger—like I'm nourishing myself and will be able to stand up to the task. I experience a warm glow that makes me feel insulated and able to handle my fears."

The first bite of food that is inconsistent with her diet becomes Jeanne's downfall. Perfectionistic all-or-nothing thinking undermines her efforts at self-discipline. She gives herself no room to stray—even a little. She rationalizes that if one bite has destroyed her efforts to control herself, why not give up and indulge? "I know that once I blow my diet and begin eating crap, I give myself permission to eat everything in sight," she confesses. "Once I have been soiled by the first bite, it's like an internal switch is flicked and I no longer care about control. I have blown it; the first screw-up of my diet makes me feel like a total failure, and the only way to undo my feelings of failure is to purge, to make myself clean again. But first I indulge and let myself wallow in the food-mire like a pig."

Jeanne feels insecure about her skills in the courtroom, even though she receives nothing but praise from her superiors. For her, adequate performances in the courtroom are never enough, and so *she* is never enough. Food fills her with psychological and spiritual strength in the face of her doubts and fears about her competence.

Her task in psychotherapy is to learn how to trust her own strength, skills, and knowledge and how to "full-fill" herself without food. She needs to give up her all-or-nothing thinking and allow herself minor dietary slips without letting them lead to total loss of control. She has given up purging, realizing the danger to which she has subjected her body by using this extreme form of weight control.

## Myra: Eating Her Heart Out

Myra, 31, is a perfectionistic secretary, the mother of a 7-year-old child, and 40 pounds overweight. She wears attractive but loose-fitting clothes to hide her fat and giggles nervously when she talks about herself. As the secretary of a high-powered corporate executive, she needs to be on top of everything, and is very much in control of both the office and his schedule. Her excess weight is the only mismanaged aspect of her life.

Her mother is also quite obese. Myra recalls that she shared with her mother repeated halfhearted and ultimately failed attempts to diet. In her words:

> We would try to diet. We'd talk about diets and prepare diet food together. Our closest connection came when we were around food. But my mother never had what it took to lose weight. She loves eating too much to really make more than a surface effort. She didn't really care that she was 70 pounds

overweight. I think she liked throwing her weight around with my father. But I could see what a burden it was for her physically to carry all that extra weight. And I could see that she didn't really like herself.

Because she was overweight, Myra's own burden was a fear of being doomed never to marry. Despite her pessimism, after graduating from college she met a man at her first job, fell in love, and eventually married. He, too, is overweight and thinks Myra is just right for him physically. He puts no pressure on her to lose weight. But, being a perfectionist, she continued to put pressure on herself.

When Brad came into my life and liked me large, I couldn't believe I could be so lucky. We used to make jokes about sex being better for fat people. But I know I'm endangering my health like this and I know it means I've got psychological issues that get covered by all this fat. I want my body to be as perfect as my marriage and my job.

In psychotherapy, Myra began the painful process of examining her past relationship to her mother. She started to realize that the primary way she had felt loved by her mother was in the sharing of food. She began to confront some painful disappointments in her life. She saw that her weight was the one thing she allowed herself not to keep compulsively under control. Her perfectionism and her overweight both related to her unsatisfied desire for her mother's love.

## Adele: An Obsession with Being Thin

Adele, 41, has a Ph.D. in philosophy, teaches at a respected university, and is divorced. She is a high achiever who has published numerous papers on political and moral philosophy. She is very attractive and is fashionably thin without looking emaciated. She is a charming woman who carries herself with style and confidence.

But, like all perfectionists, good enough is never enough for her. She wants to lose another five pounds, even though she looks great just as she is. She exercises every morning. Four days a week she gets up at 7 A.M. and jogs at least two miles, following her run with 10 laps in her pool. On alternate days she goes to an aerobics class for an hour, then comes home and swims her 10 laps. She completes this routine with 20 minutes of meditation.

Adele is compulsively careful about her diet, counting calories and timing her meals to prevent any slip into indulgence. She eats small portions on a small plate using a small spoon, just as she learned from a behavior modification self-help book.

"I never look just the way I want to," she says. "No matter how many eyes are turned my way or how many compliments I get from men, I don't feel thin enough. My own image of how I should look is all I care about. I want to be the most perfect combination of brains and beauty any man could want. I'm satisfied with my mind—now all I have to do is shape my body into 41-year-old-perfection."

What is the motivation for all this compulsive activity? After six years of marriage, Adele's husband left her for a younger woman. Adele was determined to do everything possible to ensure that this kind of rejection could never happen to her again. Over months of psychotherapy, she began to confront her suppressed anger and rage toward her ex-husband. In doing so, she slowly began to ease up on herself and realized that she had turned inward (in the form of striving for physical perfection) the rage and resentment she felt toward him. This insight freed her to exercise in a more moderate fashion and to become more accepting and loving of her body.

## MANIC-DEPRESSIVE DISORDER

The manic phase of manic-depressive disorder is compatible with the perfectionist mentality of feeling driven to accomplish at very high levels. This, of course, does not mean that perfectionism causes this disorder (the cause is thought to be a chemical imbalance), but only that a segment of those who suffer from manic-depressive disorder exhibit perfectionistic tendencies.

Manic-depressive perfectionists love the energy and the creative flow of ideas and intuitions they experience during a high. They may get lost in their work for long stretches of time, sensing little or no need to stop for food or sleep. They feel on top of the world and have an inflated sense of their own worth based on their high productivity. While their flight of ideas may lead to a flurry of activity, they often find themselves unable to complete the many projects they have begun. When they inevitably fall into the depressive phase of the cycle, they lose all sense of self-worth. They are unable to keep up the driven, manic productivity that has sustained their good feelings about themselves.

Dennis, a perfectionistic manic-depressive who now takes lithium to control his mood swings, put it like this:

> Before I took medication, I'd have periods where I felt like I had the answers to everything. I would stay up for days at a time coming up with schemes for my business. And I would run around trying to do everything at once. I thought fast and talked fast. Half the time, no one could understand what I was trying to say. I felt like a whirlwind that couldn't be stopped. It was like being on speed.

For Dennis, these periods of driven activity reinforced his belief that he was capable of anything. He could, for a while, measure up to his standard of perfection, at least with regard to productivity. And he could silence the inner voice that labeled him a failure during phases of depression. He would bolster himself with the excess energy that carried him in a bubble of confidence and euphoria.

Dennis gave up the highs and lows for the more normally modulated mood swings that come with properly regulated body chemistry. With ongoing medication and psychotherapy, he learned to feel good about himself without relying on his manic periods of elation.

He now understands that the wild highs are not worth the price of the excruciating lows and that his perfection-seeking must give way to an acceptance of his physical and mental limitations. He has accepted the fact that his manic-depressive disorder results from a chemical imbalance that can be controlled with medication.

## SUBSTANCE ABUSE

It has been common knowledge for two decades that the old stereotype of the reckless, disorderly, and unashamed drunk is not an accurate picture of middle and upper-middle class alcoholics when they are not inebriated. Sober alcoholics are generally cautious, careful, overcontrolled, inhibited, and guilt-ridden. Many substance abusers are obsessive and perfectionistic, placing high performance demands upon themselves.[5] Their alcohol or drug habit may be their only relief from this internal pressure. The perfectionistic addict may have trouble learning how to relax and may use alcohol or drugs as a way to temporarily give up stringent control.

The term *codependent* is applied to the spouse or other person close to the alcoholic who attempts to control the alcoholic, many times covering up his or her drinking to family, friends, and employers. The codependent's own perfectionism does not allow him or her to admit there is a problem, for this would mean admitting to not having a perfect marriage and family. The codependent deals with shame by compliantly hiding the alcoholic's problem, thus enabling the substance abuser to keep living in denial.

### Perfectionism and Loss of Self-Control

Surface recognition of the perfectionistic strain in substance abusers and their codependents is evident in the popular alcohol and drug recovery movement literature and 12-step programs. Recovery groups focus some attention on learning how to be content with good-enough performance without having to be perfect. In addition, 12-step programs help the addict confront the various manipulative and controlling behaviors that are part of the psychological dynamics between substance abusers and codependents. But why is the addict often so reluctant to join a self-help recovery program?

One recovering alcoholic, in a booklet written for other addicts, draws the relationship between perfectionism, self-reliance, and the unwillingness to get help.

> As perfectionistic people, we simply expect too much of ourselves and others. Our attitudes keep us from using recovery methods, including the 12 Steps of Alcoholics Anonymous, which could lead us to a contented sobriety. People with perfectionistic values are true children of our individualistic society. They feel they must solve their problem of being chemically dependent by fighting it and trying to defeat it. But this problem will not be resolved through willpower or attempts to control ourselves or other people.[6]

The perfectionistic alcoholic's exaggerated self-sufficiency has led 12-step programs to emphasize the need for the addict to give up his struggle to control his addiction and passively put himself in the hands of God, or a Higher Power, "as he understands it." (The pronoun *he* is used here and below only for convenience.) Twelve-step doctrine teaches that it is only through giving up the attempt to control one's addictive behavior that one may find in a Higher Power the guidance and inspiration to overcome addiction. This has been a central aspect of recovery thinking that directly attempts to redress the spiritual emptiness that many authors claim is prevalent in substance abusers. It also emphasizes what is believed to be the futility of the addict's desire to overcome his problem through willpower.

Some perfectionists who come to psychotherapy and are also working a 12-step program confess to this being one of the more problematic aspects of 12-step doctrine, even though they may be benefiting significantly from the social and supportive aspects of the program. They feel resistance to the notion of turning decision-making over to a Higher Power, especially if this Higher Power is viewed as outside of themselves. The prevailing 12-step doctrine of passive surrender to a Higher Power tends to reinforce the perfectionistic addict's unconscious fear of losing *inner* control of his own mind.

In addition, passive surrender does not empower the perfectionistic addict to believe that it is *his own initial decision, and continual affirmation of this decision through choice and self-control,* that determine the outcome of his efforts. Passive surrender encourages a feeling of loss of personal control and responsibility, a feeling that one is at the mercy of an outside power. It also may foster dependence on the recovery group as a lifelong crutch in staying sober, so that one never "graduates" from the recovery program. Without group support and faith in God, the addict is taught to believe, he is always "just one drink away" from total loss of self-control and the dreaded fall from sobriety.[7]

In place of passive surrender, the recovery movement could adopt the concept of *actively* surrendering control. Active surrender acknowledges the addict's need to claim responsibility for his decision to begin and sustain treatment. It acknowledges his need to feel the fruits of his own positive choices, just as he has had to accept the painful results of his self-destructive ones. The active surrender to the influence of a Higher Power allows him to question his beliefs; it allows for the possibility that healing forces beyond his own willpower *but not necessarily outside of himself* may work to promote his physical and mental well-being.

## Shame and the Fear of Going Crazy

In much of the recovery literature, an important concept is that of shame, which is viewed as responsible for just about every kind of addiction and emotional disorder.[8] While guilt is the feeling that results when we transgress society's moral prohibitions, shame results from our own judgment of failure in reaching goals or living up to personal expectations.

Shame is the basic sense of being less than adequate (never-enough) that colors our world. It is rooted in a lack of early love, and a lack of *mirroring* (reflecting back through eye contact the infant's gazes so as to affirm his existence), and nurturing experiences with parents, especially the mother. (We will examine the differences between guilt and shame in more depth, and how they may engender different types of perfectionism, in chapter 5.) Because shame is a feeling with which almost everyone can identify, it has been an accessible and valuable cornerstone concept in explaining the roots of addiction.

Along with personal responsibility, other basic themes that have not been fully examined in 12-step recovery literature are the close connection between perfectionism, and the addict's unconscious sense of being out of control of his own mind and emotions, and how this relates to shame and the tailspin into addiction. Even though 12-step literature mentions the need to restore the addict's sanity, there is no real discussion about the deeper fear of losing sanity and how this may relate to addiction.

*Substance abuse not only facilitates letting go of outer control of behavior, it also acts as a defense against the more subtle and unconscious fear of losing inner control of one's mind.* It protects us and distracts us from the deeper fear of going crazy. With substance abuse one is able to give up control "safely" and even enjoy an altered mood, and thus avoid confronting the deeper fear of losing control of one's thoughts. While there is clear recognition that indulgence in alcohol or drugs allows temporary respite from the need to be in control of one's behavior and outer world, this deeper fear has not been sufficiently analyzed.

It is not surprising that this deeper dynamic is neglected in addiction and recovery literature. The addict already feels out of control, overwhelmed by his impulses and outer behavior, and so it is his behavior that receives much of his attention. He experiences ongoing guilt for his actions. He does not have the resources to face a still deeper, unconscious fear of losing control of his inner, mental world, even though *loss of outer control implies loss of inner control.* In labeling this fear unconscious, I am suggesting that it acts as a powerful underlying force to create certain defensive coping reactions, such as substance addiction and perfectionism. While it could be shortsighted to use this (or any) single dynamic as the only explanation for addiction, I believe it is nonetheless a significant one that has yet to be clearly acknowledged or analyzed.

### Links in the Toxic Chain

What I call the *toxic chain* is a cycle of misery created by the close relationship between our need for inner and outer control, perfectionism, addiction, guilt, and shame. The toxic chain begins with the idea that perfection in behavior is desirable and attainable. Like all perfectionists, the alcoholic perfectionist unconsciously becomes ensnared in the delusional trap that because he can *conceive* of perfection, he ought to be able to *achieve* it. Why should he want to achieve it? One motivation, as I have suggested, is that he is unconsciously defending against the fear of losing control of his thoughts and emotions. If he can prove to himself that he can perform perfectly, with no mistakes, he can reinforce his belief that he is in total control of his mind, emotions, and behavior.

While this deeper fear may be part of the picture for everyone who becomes perfectionistic, the substance abuser channels his awareness of being out of control of his outer world through his addiction. In the comfort of an alcohol- or drug-induced altered mood or state of consciousness, the abuser can forget, for a while, about the need to rigidly control all aspects of his life.

The toxic chain is intensified as the alcoholic, upon becoming sober, again becomes overwhelmed by feelings of guilt and shame resulting from having once again indulged in alcohol. As a perfectionist, he believes he should be able to control his actions and yet, repeatedly, he is forced to see that his habitual return to addiction means he is out of control.

He both wants to be out of control and fears it; he likes the relief but hates the destructive implications of relying on a substance. This realization of failure at self-control creates further feelings of shame, compounded by guilt in reaction to comments and actions from those close to the alcoholic. As pressure to control his drinking and perform perfectly continues to mount, the alcoholic is drawn again to the attractive escape of indulgence.

As long as the alcoholic continues down the path of perfectionism, the same negative feelings are bound to recur. *The toxic chain is fortified by the inability of the alcoholic to give up the pursuit of the impossible dream of perfection.* To break the chain, the alcoholic must realize that he is continually comparing himself to a standard of perfection that is impossible to achieve. Until he does, he is bound to continue in the self-destructiveness that creates so much misery for himself and others.

## A Relationship of Abusive Control

Jerry was a short, fast-talking, insecure, driven businessman who was accustomed to taking financial risks. He liked to remember the days when he had been a small-town college football hero. He was loud, demanding, and easily insulted at the least perceived slight. When Jerry came to see me, he was still in denial of his alcoholism.

His wife was in her late 20s while Jerry was in his mid-40s. She was terrified of him—and with good reason. He had broken her ribs during one drunken rampage. He had destroyed the dining-room furniture. Another time he had broken her arm. She always wore long-sleeved blouses to cover the bruises. The abuse had taken place over a period of five years before she sought therapy. He came for treatment reluctantly—the result of his wife's ultimatum. She had sought therapy elsewhere for herself, and she finally had the strength to demand that he seek therapy or she would leave him.

Jerry was neither serious about therapy nor ready to be honest with himself or me. He lied about the number of incidents of abuse as well as their severity. He could not face the truth about how he used alcohol to lose control and beat his wife. In fact, his denial and deeper humiliation made him avoid the real issue of wife abuse. Instead, during our first three sessions, he talked about his business failures.

Because he did not really want help, Jerry did not last long in treatment. He stomped out of my office in righteous indignation after about eight sessions, asserting he did not need help and did not "believe" in psychologists. Before he left, we did have time to talk about what would set him off to attack his wife. He explained that, "I just wanted things to be the way I like them to be."

When I asked him what that meant, he said, "No matter how many times I tell her how to prepare my salad at dinner, she always screws it up. I make it clear how I want the dressing put on the salad, but she won't do it. She just doesn't know how to do things right. I can't stand to have to tell her over and over again, and she still doesn't get it right."

Jerry expected his wife to wear only the clothes he thought she looked good in. He insisted she not leave the house after 8 p.m. He was self-conscious and insecure about being short but liked to feel like a big shot, which he was able to do by pushing his wife around. And he found it easier to feel outraged and righteous when he was drinking. "She provokes me to hit her when I'm drinking; I get so angry I just can't let her get away with the things she says to me."

"What does she say to you?" I asked.

"She tells me I'm a bully and an alcoholic. She calls me a wife beater. She tells me I want things to be perfect and that I expect her to be perfect."

"So, is she saying anything that isn't true?"

"No, it's all true. But when I'm drinking I just can't tolerate hearing it come from her mouth, that's all. I know what my problems are and I can handle them on my own."

In the substance recovery movement, the exaggerated self-reliance of the alcoholic and drug abuser receives considerable attention. As shown in the example of Jerry, the alcoholic feels a strong need to be in control and to believe that he can handle his own problems, whatever they may be. This leads to the common behaviors of lying, deception, and denial. Drinking and drug abuse provide a way to let go for a while and give up the strong desire to control that dictates the lives of addicts. This is why it has been said that "The god of the addict is the god of control."[9]

## Perfectionism and Cocaine

The widespread use of cocaine among upper-middle class professionals during the '80s was caused by more than it being the "in" thing to do for a recreational distraction from the stress of work. Cocaine gives a euphoric high that is much like the manic phase of manic-depression. When high on coke, these professionals felt like they could conquer the world. They could experience a temporary respite from the negative feelings that come with having to perform at higher and higher levels.

Many of those who became addicted initially only desired the boost that would help them through a stressful period of work. They were young, driven 30- and 40-something achievers who were trying to distinguish themselves in their professions. The boost from cocaine helped deliver the self-confidence and extra energy that allowed them to push even longer.

Tom had been using coke periodically for over two years. He was 36, blond, good-looking, had an MBA from Stanford, and was a manager in a large corporation. He wore Armani suits and drove a Turbo Porsche. Tom felt driven to move up the corporate ladder. His goal was to earn over $150,000 a year before he was 40. He had started using coke with friends on weekends and had considered himself a "recreational" user. However, he liked the effects so much that he began using the drug during the week. By the time he made it through my consulting room door, he was strung out. In his words:

"I feel like I can accomplish anything I want when I'm high. All of my dreams seem possible. All my doubts go away. For a while, it's like I've finally arrived in Perfection City. Everything looks great to me, especially when I'm out putting the Porsche through its paces. But I know it never lasts, that each time I'll come down and have to deal with depression."

In working with people like Tom, I have found that it is not until they are willing to get off the perfection-driven never-enough merry-go-round that they are able to seriously consider giving up their addiction. They view their drug use as simply a means toward an end rather than as a serious problem in itself. They need to learn to set their sights more realistically at excellence rather than perfection. They need to learn how to value themselves even when they are not at the top of the ladder and how to perform successfully without having to feel one up on the competition. They also need to learn how to relax.

## TYPE A BEHAVIOR AND DISTRESS

Now well-known in the popular-psychology world, the concept of Type A behavior was actually defined by two cardiologists while cataloging the behavior patterns of those prone to coronaries. Persons exhibiting these types of behaviors have been described as aggressive and extremely competitive, with strong needs to be in control and have power. They are impatient and show a high degree of perfectionism.

Research has shown that although Type A personalities are valued by their employers and are rewarded for their high productivity, this behavior pattern may not be healthy for the individual or the organization.[10]

The Type A personality needs to perform at full speed. To be around a Type A feels like being caught in a whirlwind of nonstop activity. They speak fast, walk fast, eat fast, make love fast, and don't know how to relax. They can be loud, pushy, and intimidating. There is an urgency to everything they do. Like perfectionists, these people need to win. They are very critical of others' performance as well as of their own. Not all perfectionists are Type A people, but many Type A people have strong perfectionistic characteristics. Let's look at a graphic representation of how the Type A perfectionist sets himself up for stress-related physical problems.

The first figure shows the distress model for the driven perfectionist. Stress overload wears this person down until vulnerable systems of the body collapse, leading to various psychosomatic symptoms and illnesses. The body spends too much time in a fight-or-flight response mode, with the various parts of the sympathetic nervous system in a hyperalert state, wearing down the body's immune response.

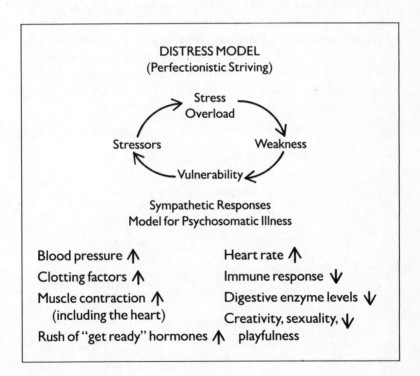

Figure 3-1

The second figure, in contrast, shows the healthy model of the person striving for excellence. In this model outside stressors, instead of leading to overload, are viewed as opportunities or challenges, which lead to reactions that enhance psychological and emotional growth. This genuine striving to meet challenges does not have to set off the "fight-or-flight" response cycle and can actually help the body build up resistance so that it can handle stress with less vulnerability.

Without the compulsiveness and fear of the perfectionist, the person striving for excellence can respond to stressors in ways that lead to creative solutions. This process further strengthens the mind, emotions, and body and leads to increased immune reactions that fight off possible disease and psychosomatic illness. This model of optimum response assumes that the right amount of striving, combined with the nourishment that comes from the satisfaction and joy of accomplishment can help us perform at high levels without pushing ourselves too far. Optimum response contributes to the peak performances of athletes, rather than to the stress overload that leads to burnout and illness in the perfectionist and Type A personalities.

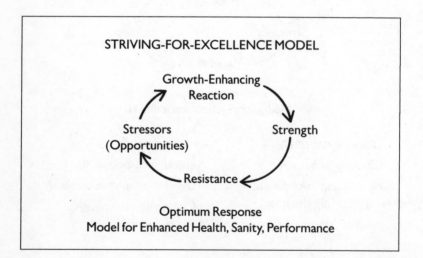

Figure 3-2

## TECHNOSTRESS: THE STRESS FOR PERFECTION

*Technostress* is a term used to describe the disease caused by the pressures of living in a high-tech world. According to psychotherapist Craig Brod, who coined the term, technostress manifests itself in two distinct but related ways: in the struggle to accept computer technology, and in the more specialized form of overidentification with computer technology, a condition described as *technocentered*. The symptoms of technostress include tension, paranoia, overstimulation, psychosomatic headaches, fatigue, lack of sexual desire, *psychic numbing* (i.e., "spacing out"), high anxiety, and low self-esteem. Brod believes that one result of technostress is that while we become tuned in to machines, we become starved for personal contact.

Our lives, both at home and at work, are bombarded with technology. VCRs, call-waiting buttons, modems, laser printers, satellite dishes, fax machines, cellular and portable phones are now commonplace. The psychological effects of being immersed in this technology include an impatience with anything that takes more than a few seconds and the inability to make decisions. Many people suffer a minor form of technostress when they are frustrated in their efforts to learn to set their VCRs, to operate a new computer program, or to master a new technological gadget such as a portable phone or video camera.

Among people involved with computers, from clerical workers to CEOs to computer programmers, Brod's research revealed "the striking effects computers were having on their lives." Besides experiencing the common stress reaction symptoms of headaches and fatigue, "they were beginning to internalize the standards by which the computer works: accelerated time, a desire for perfection, and yes-no patterns of thinking. These internalized standards combined to reduce the ability of the person to perform creatively or to relate to others in a loving way."[11]

According to Brod, high-tech environments create their own kind of stress—the stress for perfection. When life falls short of this computer ideal, technostress victims react with anger and hostility. For example, the acceleration of time is a common ingredient of technostress, especially for those technocentered individuals who spend large amounts of time working at a computer terminal. As the worker internalizes the rapid, instant-access mode of computer operations, his own inner sense of time distorts to accommodate the machine. Ultimately, experienced computer users become impatient with the computer's "slowness," and they seek more powerful machines with more memory and faster processors. One study showed that any computer-response time longer than 1.5 seconds resulted in impatience on the part of users.[12]

As the technocentered person strives to measure up to the perfection of the computer, human relationships become less important and are viewed as intrusive. He simply wants to be left to bathe in the warm glow of electronic stimulation, to be caught in what one fanatic calls the "undertow of the digital zone." The process of computer operation itself becomes highly pleasurable. The heightened stimulation of solving problems or making several choices a minute is a motivating force of its own and can be as exciting as sexual arousal.

For example, Michael Green, while producing a book that focused on the use of a popular graphics program with the Apple Macintosh, explains his feelings of fascination and seduction in his love affair with his computer. As he began learning to do extremely detailed graphic work, his obsession grew.

> I wanted to do *everything* on the computer. Even simple tasks that a pencil could handle just as easily. I was reluctant to turn it off after a day's work. . . . There was an intensity to this attraction far beyond the natural delight one gets from a superbly crafted tool. Know how when you first fall in love you want to share everything? Same thing! Only in this love story one's beloved didn't have a heart of gold . . . the heart of one's beloved was a lace of delicately programmed electric charges and they were dancing eagerly to my every desire. We were definitely an Item.[13]

The technobliss Green enjoyed in this love affair with his computer derives from the perfection he sees in the computer's performance: "When the human intellect glimpses the razzle-dazzle perfection of its electronic counterpart, it just about loses it. 'Awesome!' cry the synapses; 'At last,' echo the neurons, 'here is the precision we've but dreamt of!' Technobliss: Stimulating the brain by *electronically simulating* the brain."[14]

Spending full days at his computer in the attempt to achieve "pixel perfection" of his graphics, Green observes the effect on his thinking:

> The digital undertow was altering my feeling and sensibilities most drastically . . . with all creative decisions reduced to on or off, the allure of achieving Ultimate Order and Perfection became so strong that I eagerly compressed this vast and inexplicable human consciousness down to the level of shifting little black squares around a luminous screen for hours each day. A tour-de-force of technological mesmerism.[15]

It is not that the technocentered person has some deep personality problem, according to Brod; rather the work and the computer environment themselves create the problem. People who have been sociable, relaxed, and caring before becoming technocentered regain those qualities after leaving computer-related jobs. Brod cautions that the technocentered person is not just the valued obsessive-compulsive Type A personality who succeeds in high-pressured jobs; computer work, he says, "invites a dangerous transformation" of the glamorous model of the hard-charging young executive:

> Achievers may bring to any job the desire to perform well, but if the nature of the job is not based on a perfect machinelike ideal, any obsessive-type characteristics are softened and the workers retain their basic humanity. The special demands of working with computers exacerbate those obsessive-compulsive qualities without allowing for humanizing influences, such as ample social contact with other workers or a relaxed and informal milieu. The overspecialized character that results from high performance in technical work is destined to become the norm of the electronic culture.[16]

The problems of the technocentered individual are by-products of Western culture's highly developed technology, technology that reflects our worship of efficiency, speed, and perfection.

## LONELINESS AND DEPRESSION

Perfectionists who are as critical of others as they are of themselves— who researchers have labeled *other-oriented* perfectionists—are prime candidates for feeling lonely.[17] They have difficulty forming lasting friendships because they are too critical of others to establish the mutual bond necessary for the relationship to work. The other-oriented perfectionist always finds something wrong with the other person as an excuse to avoid closeness. (In chapter 11 we will see how this dynamic operates in love relationships.)

Loneliness can often be accompanied by depression. The perfectionist may try to drive away depression by the frantic pursuit of work or hobbies, activities often undertaken alone. Many perfectionists have secret fantasies of being appreciated for their skills and talents. They believe others have not given them their due credit. They would rather be by themselves with their fantasies of recognition, waiting for the day when they will finally be appreciated by others, than form the imperfect but real human relationships that could satisfy some of their needs for intimacy. Some prefer to become "legends in their own minds" rather than risk proving themselves to others. They fear they will be misunderstood and unappreciated. Instead, they may choose to submerge themselves in their projects or their collection of "perfect" objects, and do without much social contact.

If the perfectionist slows down and begins to understand the meaning behind the drive to keep busy, he may find himself in what psychologists call an agitated depression. In this state, surface anxiety covers an underlying depression. The research literature is replete with indications that the shame and guilt perfectionists feel in their inability to live up to their expectations are enough to bring on episodes of depression.[18-21]

Some perfectionists fight the awareness of loneliness or depression by assuming a stance of righteous indignation or one-upmanship. For example, Rhonda maintained that "if others don't meet my expectations, I simply don't get involved with them. It is more frustrating for me to start a friendship with someone who is going to continually frustrate me by having lower expectations of himself than I do of myself." She spent a lot of time by herself, collecting antiques, writing poetry and short stories, and reading voraciously. Given her difficulty in forming friendships, she had made a reasonable adjustment to coping with being alone without feeling too lonely. She kept herself at arm's length from depression. But her needs for "an audience of more than one" went unfulfilled because of her perfectionistic standards.

## WORKING WITH THE CONCEPTS

Have you ever gone on an eating binge? If so, what kinds of feelings led you to begin overeating and made it easy to continue once you got going? Did all-or-nothing thinking have any part in your allowing the binge to continue? Or did you feel the matter was out of your control and you made no conscious decision to indulge? Without judgment, notice what kinds of feelings are present when you consider indulging in any kind of binge eating, even if it is not serious enough to qualify as an eating disorder.

Notice what you are feeling when you decide to have an alcoholic drink or indulge in any kind of mood-altering substance. Often, we experience some anxious moment that brings up uncomfortable thoughts or feelings from the past or stirs anticipation of what may occur in the near future. We may wish to escape the present anxiety by changing our consciousness through alcohol or drugs.

When you notice a desire to change your mood, question what it is you want to avoid. Do you feel out of control? Do you notice any sense of being not-enough that propels you to want to change your present state through a mood-altering substance? If you can identify something that is disturbing you, see if you can hold onto the thought or feeling long enough until it passes on its own. Realize that you can tolerate momentary discomfort created by thoughts and feelings without having to do anything to change them.

How do you experience stress in your life? What forms does it take? Can you see the difference between the types of stress that can make you stronger (the challenge toward excellence) and the kind of stress that weakens you and causes vulnerability to physical illness (the striving for perfection)? Do you experience technostress? If so, how do you notice it? Remember that you are not to blame for the pressures of technostress.

# PART TWO

# How
# We Get
# Ensnared

# FOUR

# A Society Devoted to Perfection:
## *The Cultural Roots*

*The late 20th century has become an advertising executive's dream come true: Life-style has become a product that sells itself, and the individual has become a consumer who seeks, desperately, to buy.*
PHILLIP CUSHMAN

OUR SOCIETY VALUES THE pursuit of excellence in all we do, and this striving can easily cross the line into the pursuit of perfection. In this chapter we will look at how our society helps push our thinking and behavior into the perfection trap.

### FACING THE PERFORMANCE CRISIS

One of the lessons we learn early in our socialization as children is how competitive our world is. After an initial, blissful period of receiving undivided love and attention as infants, we may learn that we must compete with siblings for the satisfaction of our needs. We may begin to learn that we must *do something* to earn love, approval, and admiration. For most, this is the first cruel awakening to the realization that love is no longer freely given as our birthright, the beginning of a continuing education about competitiveness.

We may begin to believe that we don't really deserve love and attention simply because we are unique and lovable just as we are. We learn that we must not only do something but must do it well. For many, this early programming gets twisted into the dictate that we must perform perfectly.

In an indirect form, the seeds of pursuing the perfection path are planted as early as infancy. The infant learns very early what it takes to gain attention from parents. Before the baby has words or concepts, he learns instinctively that when he does certain things he receives smiles and attention. The infant is continually validated and sustained by the ongoing feeding, care, and attention provided by the mother. The baby begins to understand that certain acts lead to smiles and attention more quickly than others. During the first few years, the child learns more and more ways of gaining attention. While this development is healthy and necessary, it nonetheless begins the conditioning of the infant to please his parents.

The early seeds begin to sprout in the elementary school years. As a child is expected to take on work assignments (schoolwork, homework, chores), she is faced with judgment of her performance. Instead of the blissful infant experience of getting attention just by making the right sounds or simply because she is the apple of her parents' eyes, the child learns that the rules are changing. Suddenly the stakes in the game of being loved and accepted are raised.

The child faces the developmental crisis of realizing that if she isn't able to master the skills to produce "good" work, she has failed to measure up. Her flawed and imperfect work may lead her to feel *she* is flawed and imperfect. The message becomes clearer that she may no longer be loved just as she is; parents' love and teachers' and friends' approval are now conditional upon performing up to a high standard. In addition, she begins to think of her self-worth not as something that resides *within her* but something that is bestowed upon her by significant others.

All children are forced to confront this developmental crisis. What is crucial is whether the child learns that, while doing his best in school is important, it is not the only or even the primary thing that determines his acceptance and the admiration of his parents. Parents who are able to make their child feel loved regardless of his school performance will be creating a solid sense of goodness to help the child sustain disappointments in school projects. Parents face the difficult task of balancing unconditional love and acceptance with teaching the child to feel pride in doing his best.

By preadolescence, after self-control has been mastered, the child has clearly learned the rules of the game: he strives to please parents and teachers by producing quality work. To produce only average work will not get the desired response. If self-esteem apart from his work has not been cultivated, he may become overly sensitive to imperfection and may develop psychological and physical problems by adolescence.

Sometimes, children reveal an inability to cope with anything less than perfection by attempting to lie and cheat in order to win at games. Or they may fly into a rage and quit when they realize they may not come out ahead.

Under stress, self-control breaks down. The gorge-and-purge sequence of bulimia may be one result as the adolescent strives for a new level of commitment, control, and perfection. The recent high incidence of eating disorders among teenagers and young adults has a clear relationship to the need these kids feel to look perfect and to be perfect.[1-4]

Strong efforts at self-control and the compulsive pursuit of perfection may reveal an underlying feeling of never quite measuring up to the expectations of parents and society. This never-enough mentality can be further complicated if the parents' values are distorted in their own idealization of perfection. (In chapter 7 we will return to the problems inherent in parents' attempts to shape the perfect child.)

The pressure to be perfect that we may have experienced through our socialization at home and at school forms a foundation that is reinforced, amplified, and exploited by many other facets of our culture as we grow older. In subtle and not-so-subtle ways, we are encouraged to conform to an image of perfection in many areas of life having nothing to do with academic performance. Nowhere are these influences more evident than in the advertising media.

# Smile if you're perfect.

## What? No smiles?
## Well, nobody's perfect.

But now, with porcelain veneers we can create picture-perfect smiles. Change your smile from dull to dazzling. Porcelain veneers can repair chips, cracks, breaks, or worn areas of teeth. Straighten or close spaces without braces.

Porcelain veneers have transformed thousands of smiles from self-conscious to self-confident. And they can give you a whole new self image.

Dress to the teeth, no matter what you're wearing!

Now you can have something to smile about!

*Figure* 4-1

## Selling the Image of Perfection

We strive to be a "10" and will do whatever it takes to measure up to the image that has been repeatedly drummed into our heads by the advertising media. The above fictional advertisement is an example of how we are taught to think about imperfections in our society. While this ad is supposed to be an eye catcher and perhaps provide light humor, the message is that, indeed, we should do whatever is possible to rid ourselves of physical imperfections. Cosmetic dentistry and surgery can do the trick. It is no wonder, given the influence of advertising, that we have come to view the pursuit of physical and performance perfection as a virtue.

To measure up to the perfect image, we are told to "dress for success" and to surround ourselves with material goods that signify we have made it in the competitive game of life. When we have acquired enough of these goods, we can use them to continually reaffirm to ourselves and those around us that we have made the grade and are therefore valuable and worthwhile persons. Of course, this pattern can lead to the compulsive need to acquire more and more status-conferring goods. We are easily seduced into the materialistic more-is-never-enough trap.

For some the image of living the "perfect life" reaches its zenith in the desire to be featured in a popular lifestyle magazine showing off their perfect furniture, in their perfect living room, dressed in the perfect clothes, with the perfect smile of success, standing next to the perfect partner. The motto is, "If you've got it, flaunt it" (but graciously). This is the message promoted by advertising in our image-conscious culture. It is a message not lost on those whose greatest concern is what others think of them and whether they will be approved of by the "right" people.

## "You're Only as Old as You Look"

We allow influential segments of our society to define the "right" way to look and dress and, like lemmings, many of us follow the lead set by a small group of fashion designers. We gawk with envy at those fortunate few who can afford haute couture and are quick to buy knock-offs of clothing and accessories that resemble the real thing. If "thin is in," we will do anything to make the grade, including starving ourselves and risking a serious eating disorder.

We are too quick to give up our own judgment as to what styles fit with our own body shape and personality. Instead, we try to ride the fashion crest of the moment, to surf the trendy waves of style that peak and ebb. The irony is that the fashion statement that we make and which sharpens our personal image is almost always a statement not of our own creation.

Our social values are reflected in the popularity of cosmetic surgery. Thighs a little too heavy? Have the fat sucked out. Nose not quite perfect? Smooth out that bump and give it an upturn. Little paunch in the stomach? No problem—have a tummy tuck. Sagging gobble-gobble under the chin? A little nip and tuck will take off 20 years. Breasts not in keeping with today's full-bosomed fashion? Choose from the wide array of larger cup sizes the one that satisfies your fantasy.

It is not unusual for psychologists and cosmetic surgeons to see women and growing numbers of men who are willing to take out large loans to pay for surgery to make themselves more physically appealing. In most cases, the feature they want altered is fine just as it is, but, in their eyes, not perfect. For example, a woman who has a slightly receding chin may go through a painful operation in which her jaw is broken and reset in order to create a "more appealing" square-jawed look.

The controversy regarding the dangers of silicone gel breast implants highlights the degree to which some women are willing to risk their health to measure up to society's image of sexual desirability. Before the recent evidence of the risk of cancer and other serious disease, why did so many women refuse to entertain the possibility of complications of the operation itself and its future consequences on the body? Why did they not take more seriously the possibility that anything foreign to their bodies might very well create future problems? Why did they put so much faith in the word of a cosmetic surgeon who makes his living by fulfilling their dreams to look perfect? And why have they unwittingly allowed themselves to be ruled by the predominate male image of the *Playboy* centerfold body as the epitome of female sexual desirability?

We can't really blame plastic surgeons for our pursuit of the perfect shape and our desire to look forever young. It is the societal pressure to measure up to our ideal of youthful appearance and to rid ourselves of perceived imperfections that are responsible for spawning the cosmetic surgery industry to begin with.

## SUPERWOMAN: HAVING IT ALL

Beyond just striving to have the perfect body which never ages, many contemporary women further spiral into the perfection trap by believing the media hype of the superwoman. These high achievers want to "have it all," hoping to reach the impossible dream of being everything to everyone. They feel pushed to juggle their time, trying to maintain a successful career, an exciting and passionate marriage, and an ideal family life—in other words, to play all of the roles perfectly.

The superwoman image is partly a social phenomenon due to the lack of institutional support for working women who must also be primary care-givers. Not having been primary care-givers, men have been spared the added pressure that many women now experience in trying to juggle these roles at the same time. Growing numbers of working women feel they must be superwomen just to survive and make ends meet.

Reinforced by the advertising media's image of the perfect woman, these women strive to be the perfect nurturing mother, who is attentive to her child's needs, while at the same time able to successfully perform at work, be the perfect lover for her husband, maintain friendships, handle all housekeeping chores, and contribute to her church or charity group. These women are not content to excel in one role only. In striving to have it all, they believe they are aiming for the perfect life, where nothing will be omitted.

A few women do seem to be able to juggle various roles without ending up stressed beyond tolerance. But even these women sooner or later realize that the only way to make their life work is by compromise: child care is necessary; friendships have to be curtailed;

working late means less time with one's mate, a diminished sex life, and less quality time with the kids.

It is not surprising that most who try to play superwoman end up depressed, angry, frustrated, and feeling like they have failed. They are trying to live up to an impossible image. Like the few women who appear to juggle all the roles successfully, these women end up learning they must give up their unrealistic fantasy of being everything to everyone, accept their limitations, set priorities, and focus more on limited quality rather than unlimited quantity in their lives. But first they must face their bitter disappointment at falling short of their image of perfection.

## Men as Success Objects

What does it mean to be a man? This is the central question being asked by growing numbers of men coming together to address the constrictions they feel about their roles in our society. In recent years, writings and workshops probing the meaning of masculinity have given birth to what is referred to as the men's movement. The issues raised seem to have struck a nerve; books focusing on men's need to heal the wounds of childhood, especially with their fathers, have reached best-seller status.[5]

In some gatherings, men camp out in natural settings for weekend workshops to learn to relate to each other in more emotionally intimate ways. Through psychological exercises and ceremonies that have been influenced by the American Indian heritage, these men discover the deep camaraderie and self-healing that are possible when emotional barriers are dropped and the artificial constrictions of our stereotypes of masculinity are penetrated. These constrictions include the traditional image of the harsh, dominant and competitive man who is limited in his capacity for intimacy and who avoids coming to terms with his deep personal wounds and human limitations.

The men are provided a supportive environment and encouraged to let out their "wild man"—an expression of both pain and rage

at their father's absence in their youth. The "wild man" is characterized by a spontaneity preserved from childhood; a capacity for de-
cisive action, a positive, non-exploitative sexuality; a consciousness of
a personal wound; and an affinity with the wildness of nature.[6]

The absence of the father is traced to the social change that took
place as a result of the Industrial Revolution. The battle over resources
and profits served to intensify competitive relationships among men
and made male camaraderie and friendship more difficult. In addition, there was a physical separation between a man's physical place of
work and his family life. When fathers are striving for financial success, they are forced to spend more time away from their families.
This resulted in a diminished presence of the father in the family and
had a negative impact on the bond that could be forged between a
father and his sons. Fathers were not available to guide their sons
through the developmental trials and tribulations of growing up.

As a result of an economic system and social values that encouraged them to compete successfully against their peers in the market
place, men became "success objects." Significantly, it is the driven,
perfectionistic father striving for unlimited power, status, and financial success at any cost who is now being called to task by the men's
movement (see chapter 9).

## EVERYONE EXPECTS PERFECTION

A client, Kevin, tells me about his job frustrations. As an architect, he
is responsible for planning and supervising work on the projects designed by his company. It is his responsibility to make sure the job is
completed according to the drawings. He has been doing this work
for about ten years and always has the same complaint.

> Everyone expects perfection. They think they have a right to
> have it perfect. If there happens to be a small problem many
> years later, they band together as a homeowners association and
> sue the architectural firm that built their homes.

So I end up having to "mop up" projects that we designed and built seven years ago because someone isn't happy, and they sue us. And it's not just with my business. People seem to have the idea that all professionals should be perfect or "we will make them pay." Doctors are sued if there is the slightest hint of malpractice. And attorneys encourage everyone to have this attitude.

Angry parents sue the doctor if their baby doesn't come out absolutely perfect. We blame the doctor. We think he should guarantee us a perfect baby. I don't blame all those doctors who don't want to take on patients who have a history of suing people.

Kevin is able to tell the difference between holding professionals responsible for their actions and expecting them to be perfect and then blaming them when they fall short. His perception reflects a common pressure that all those with high-level responsibility feel: the fear that they may be taken to court and forced to defend themselves should they not perform up to the expectations of those they serve.

## Winning Is All That Counts

Our society is obsessed with coming out on top, whether in sports like the Olympics, professional sports teams and the fanatical fans they represent, megacorporations competing for market share, or individuals striving to be the most talented and highest paid in their jobs.

We learn it early in life and we learn it well: the person who comes out "Numero Uno" is the only one who matters, the only one who is remembered. Second place means little.

Many of the moral and ethical beliefs we learned as children are later challenged by widespread evidence to the contrary. The old slogan of sportsmanship and fair play that I was taught as a child ("It's not whether you win or lose but how you play the game that counts") was challenged, as I got older, by the reality of in-your-face competition.

Who got the attention? Winners. They got the applause, the trophies, the praise, their names in the paper. Losers might be good sports but not much else. "Nice guys finish last." And how does one get to be a winner? By practicing, of course—"practice makes perfect."

Sooner or later we begin to feel, from real-world experience, that that old slogan should be: "It's not how you play the game that counts, but whether you win or lose." This, we learn, is how our society decides whom to reward and whom to call an also-ran, a wanna-be, or just another has-been.

Everywhere in our society we find examples of the high pressure to come out on top, where any means is justified by the end of "making it." Here are some everyday examples.

*Politics.* Candidates may lie about their academic credentials to impress voters. Political campaigns often focus on making the opponent look bad rather than proclaiming what the candidate believes in and intends to do if elected. Public relations firms help candidates put the proper "spin" on their statements. Candidates learn how to say as little as possible, how to make themselves look as good as they can, and how to please as many segments of the voting public as possible. Too often it is the image that is important, not the substance.

*Business.* Fast-talking salesmen may say anything in order to make a sale. Insider trading on Wall Street, blatant lying, cheating, and deception are all part of the reality of business in corporate America (and, of course, throughout the world). When the "bottom line" (a favorite expression of the greedy '80s) is all that matters, anything that seems to enhance profit is okay.

In Donald Trump we have a good example of the extent to which a man will go to try to impress others and yet, despite power and riches, be unable to get the respect he desires. He is also a good example of the perfectionist's fear and expectation of failure.

"There is in Donald a genuine need to self-destruct," a person who knows him well is quoted in a popular magazine as saying. "In order to feel real and whole, he had to exceed himself constantly, make more money, build bigger buildings. Underneath there's despair: *'Nothing I do is enough, and it never will be.'* And you can't outdo yourself forever, so you have to screw it up and start all over."[7]

In discussing his financial downfall, the same article points out, "Many who know him believe that Trump's reach exceeded his grasp because he was striving for something his new money could never buy: acceptance by New York City's high society."

> Says a close personal and professional acquaintance: He's *very* insecure. He'd tell about when he first moved to New York he was shunned by a lot of people—hardly any invitations to the Hamptons for the weekend and all that. Although he claims he doesn't care, you know deep down it bothers him. . . . He thought they would accept him if he built the tallest building or if he owned the most important landmarks. The tragedy is they never wanted to accept him, and the harder he tried the more they laughed at him after they left his parties. He doesn't see that he has had everything a man could hope: a beautiful wife, three perfect kids and enough money to last them all their lives. Unfortunately, he's just out to impress.

"Money was never much of a motivation for me," Trump has said, "except as a way to keep score." A man working on a documentary about Trump says, "The minute he gets out of bed in the morning, it's important for him to say, 'I'm the best, I'm the greatest.' He can't say that now."[8]

*Sports.* We see Olympic athletes use steroids to gain an advantage, even if doing so jeopardizes their health, personal integrity, respect by peers, and the dignity of their country.

Baseball pitchers doctor the ball, and batters do the same to the bat. Every little bit makes a difference—the difference between success and failure. A newspaper article on cheating in baseball gives the opinion of former major league manager Dick Williams that "cheating will forever be a fixture of baseball." The article points out that, "These days another season in the big leagues can mean another half-million dollars or so in the bank. Faced with the option of fracturing a few rules or selling aluminum siding, what do *you* think a veteran will do?"[9]

> The same article quotes Joe Torre, manager of the St. Louis Cardinals: I have no problem with cheating. Whatever you can get away with, I mean, we're not going out and robbing stores or anything. And anyway, what about football? Holding, now that's illegal but they get away with it.
>
> Or how about pro basketball? You get six fouls. In other words, six chances to cheat. Or how about pro hockey? You grind your stick into an opponent's thorax and you get, what, five minutes or so in the penalty box? Golf is the only game I know where you call a foul on yourself.

"I did anything I could to win," proclaimed Don Drysdale, the legendary Dodger pitcher. In admitting that he threw a spitball, Drysdale said,

> Oh, I doctored it every now and then. Sure I did. Mine was a little personal war with the hitter and the other club. I didn't give a _____ about you and I didn't expect you to give a _____ about me on that particular day. We got paid on winning. We didn't get paid on losing. I knew what hitters did to bats but I never worried about that.[10]

The final word on sports cheating we give to Chilli Davis, noted baseball philosopher and ex-Angel outfielder: "If you ain't cheatin', you ain't tryin'." And he meant it.

*Education.* The *Los Angeles Times* has proclaimed "an epidemic of college cheating," catching our attention with the following example.

> James relaxed in his dorm room, drinking beer and boasting to his friends of the 'A' he would earn. He knew how to beat the system, he told them. He was going to shave his arm, scrawl

notes on it and sneak glances while the professor absentmind-
edly read the newspaper. Hours later, James had his high score
and the respect of a small group of friends.

"It's kind of funny to see people banging their heads as they
try to remember the material they've crammed in a few hours
before," James says. "If they resorted to my method, they would
wind up with great grades."[11]

James had achieved a 3.2 cumulative average by cheating on 75
percent of his tests and papers. "I really don't feel any remorse," said
the student athlete. "I feel satisfied and happy that I've done well. I
look at it this way: Grades depend on your ability to utilize more resources than the average person, so I'm able to do better." The article
went on to say,

> Recent studies suggest that students nationwide follow similar
> dishonest practices to ensure academic success. The Carnegie
> Foundation for the Advancement of Teaching recently released
> a survey on campus life, which reported that an estimated 40 to
> 90 percent of students cheat on exams or papers, and that 43
> percent of faculty believe students today are more willing to
> cheat to get better grades.

Ernest Boyer, president of the Carnegie Foundation, is quoted as
saying that "College for many students has become a credentialing
exercise. It's not seen as a serious intellectual quest. . . . The aim is to
figure out what you need to do to get through the system."

The article continues:

> Those who have studied academic dishonesty believe that other
> than sharing an everybody-does-it mentality, cheaters have little
> in common. They include athletes sometimes too immersed in
> the rigors of competition to study; those trapped by internal
> and external pressures to excel; and others caught in the whirl-
> wind of social life and outside activities.

At the faculty level, young college teachers, under pressure to "publish or perish," fudge the statistics in their research projects, hoping to impress colleagues with their results and earn further funding.

Even well-known, high-level physics researchers with impeccable credentials get caught in the pursuit of fame and fortune. Eager to obtain large grants for further research, in addition to publicity, two physicists created a worldwide stir recently by claiming they had succeeded in producing cold fusion. If true, this discovery had monumental implications for the production of energy for the world.

When their results could not be replicated by other labs and they were unable to answer technical questions regarding their experimental methodology, they were shouted down by their colleagues at professional meetings and shamefully admitted they had jumped the gun with their claims.

All of these examples of striving to come out on top reflect how perverted our attempts may become to satisfy our deepest yearnings to excel, to stand out from the crowd. Some will risk their reputation, fortune, security, dignity, and self-respect.

In the free-spirited tradition of our society, we learn to "go for it" and let the chips fall where they may. We are taught that to be Number 1 is to come close to perfection. We are often reminded that "anything worth doing is worth doing right" (that is, perfectly). The goal of striving for excellence becomes distorted until we no longer rationally weigh the consequences of our actions. In cheating, true excellence certainly falls by the wayside.

## Working with the Concepts

How often do you let yourself be sold by advertising on TV, radio, and the print media? For the next three days, make a mental note each time you find yourself strongly desiring something that you see advertised. Do these desires come and go? Or do they linger, invoking fantasies about what it would be like to possess the objects?

Without judging yourself, simply notice how many different products capture your interest enough for you to think, "I want it." Notice what products, large or small, trigger the thought, "I want it *very* much." How strong a hold does advertising exert on you in deciding the image you want to project to others?

What is your attitude toward cosmetic surgery? Have you had it done or thought about it? Imagine what part of your body you might like to change if you decided to have cosmetic surgery. How do you imagine your life would be different with this feature changed? How much of your self-worth have you invested in your body image?

Try this exercise: Stand nude in front of a mirror, preferably a full-length one, for 10 minutes. See if you can be accepting of every body part, even if you don't think it is perfect. Say out loud, "Although my thighs are not perfect, they are good enough." Or: "Although my stomach is not perfect, it is good enough." If there are parts of your body that you cannot accept, think about whether you care enough to do the work to change these features, if they can be changed. What would it take for you to feel good enough about each and every part of your body?

To what degree is your sense of self-worth dependent on the accumulation of material goods? Imagine what it might be like to give up your 10 most prized possessions. What would be gained or lost in the process? How would the change affect your feelings about yourself?

# FIVE

# The Perfectionistic Mind:
## *The Psychological Roots*

*It is through Art and Art only
that we can realize our perfection.*
Oscar Wilde

*Almost invariably a woman addicted to perfection will view herself
as a work of art, and her real terror is that the work of art, being so
absolutely precious, may in one instant be destroyed.*
Marion Woodman

What are the psychological roots of perfectionism? How can we make sense of the thinking and actions of the person for whom good enough is never enough? No simple formula, no single psychological theory or concept can adequately account for the various complicated aspects of perfection-seeking. In this chapter we will survey diverse points of view, each of which has something to offer, none of which contains the whole truth. Together, these concepts and theories can help us understand the perfectionistic mind.

This chapter consists entirely of theory, with no case histories or prescriptive exercises. In later chapters, we will see practical applications of some of these concepts.

## The Archetype of Perfection

What is the origin of the image of perfection? The idea of perfection was thought by Carl Jung to be one of the collective templates, or archetypes, of the unconscious mind. Archetypal forms are unconscious, universal images that are part of the inherited nature of the psyche. Appearing as metaphors in art, literature, world mythology, and psychoanalysis, archetypes express common human needs, instincts, and potentials. Examples of archetypes are the Hero, the Good Mother, and the Wise Old Man.

Such eminent psychologists as Jung and Freud believed that we have an intuitive and instinctive knowledge of the perfect and the flawed.[1,2] We use our archetypal image of the perfect form as a yardstick with which to judge physical forms in the everyday world. For example, young children hold an idea of the perfect rabbit or cat and judge the rabbits and cats they find in the real world according to the mental picture.

It is partly because of this intuitive sense of the perfect form that, as indicated in chapter 2, we so easily mistake our ability to *conceive* of the perfect with our ability to *achieve* it. While the image of the perfect is thought to be part of our collective storehouse of unconscious contents, this does not mean that perfectionism in behavior is inherited in human beings. We need to keep in mind the distinction between mental images of perfection versus socially and culturally learned perfectionistic behaviors.

## Psychoanalytic Theory

Not satisfied to accept the conscious intentions to which people attributed their actions, Freud and his early followers were interested in discovering what unconsciously motivates human behavior. Thus, in order to make sense of the interpretations that come from psychoanalysis, we must be willing to accept the idea that much of what motivates our behavior lies outside our own awareness. Repeatedly in my psychotherapy practice, I have observed that many people who are not psychologically oriented find this a very challenging idea to accept.[3] They find it difficult to believe that something far beyond their own awareness and far different from what they consciously believe to be their own motivation could possibly account for their impulses and actions.

The concept of unconscious motivation is especially disturbing for the perfectionist. To accept this idea, perfectionists, who are striving to be perfectly in control, are forced to acknowledge that they have much less control of their own thoughts and feelings than they would like to believe.

It is in this powerful idea of unconscious motivation that I base my interpretation that addictive behaviors and the desire for perfection are partially a defense against the unconscious fear of being out of control of one's own thoughts and emotions (see chapter 3). This theory is based on watching how often clients (perfectionists in particular) report fear of what they may discover in psychotherapy. They are afraid of realizing how little they are able to control their own moment-to-moment thought processes, feelings, and behaviors.

Rather than viewing perfectionism as a defense against the unconscious fear of loss of control, psychoanalysts tend to focus on early developmental stages and the mental conflicts accompanying them. We all know that children tend to demand the immediate release of physical tensions. As an infant becomes a toddler, mother demands the delay of gratification of anal urges. The child begins to understand that there is a time and place for everything, and learns that a good performance is as easy as delivering a bowel movement at the proper time. Prematurely pushing the child to learn sphincter control during toilet training is thought by traditional psychoanalysts to lead to the later development of anal-retentive (uptight and withholding) characteristics that form the compulsive personality, which, as we shall shortly see, includes many perfectionistic characteristics.[4]

Early psychoanalysts believed that the pursuit of perfection begins as a child works to resolve the Oedipal conflict. That is, the boy resolves what Freud believed was the universal, unconscious boyhood desire to possess his mother and kill his father, so he can be the "main man" in his mother's life. For girls, the same dynamic operates against the mother; this is called the Electra complex. The resolution of the Oedipal period was viewed as crucial to the formation of the child's personality and sexual development. (The child's vulnerability and openness to parental seduction during the period will be further explored in chapter 7.)

As the child makes peace with his Oedipal feelings, the moral conscience begins to develop. The values and character of the same-sex parent are taken in and made the child's own. Instead of plotting the overthrow of daddy so he can possess mommy for himself, the boy makes daddy his ally and hero and uses him as a model for his behavior.

From these dynamics with parents, the child develops the idea of what is right and wrong and what it takes to be good or bad in the eyes of his parents. From positive instructions about what is right, children begin to develop the emotions of pride and self-esteem for accomplishing goals. If the child is given love and approval *only* for a good performance, the lifelong pursuit of perfection may be set in motion, because the child will begin to equate one with the other. As we mentioned in the last chapter, this hunger for approval becomes prominent as children begin to be judged for their work in school projects and chores at home.

The conscience represents the negative instructions on morality: don't sin, *don't pursue pleasure,* and so on. When the don'ts are violated, the guilt that ensues signals a threat to psychological survival.[5] It is important to remember that because of the power and influence of the parents in the child's life, and dependence upon them the child feels, he is unable to evaluate his actions independently of their judgments. Thus parents hold tremendous power to shape the child's behavior. It also creates an unconscious resentment in the child that may, in later years, be expressed in refusal to take advice from the parents, or in oppositional and rebellious behavior.

Freud's overall view of human beings was basically pessimistic. It implied that the most we can hope for in life is to control and rechannel to more acceptable expression (sublimate) the raw human instincts of destructiveness and sexuality.[6] Because of this pessimism and for many other reasons, psychoanalysis is currently out of fashion in its classical Freudian form. However, Freud's views are important to our understanding of perfectionism in at least two ways. First, they give us a systematic theory to understand how hidden, unconscious inner motivations may cause us to behave in certain ways. They explain how different psychic structures within our minds may compete for control, and how these internal struggles find outward expression in behavior.

Secondly, some of the well-known traits that characterize the perfectionist were originally identified in the work of early psychoanalytic theorists. The concepts of the obsessive-compulsive personality and of the narcissistic personality are vital contributions from psychoanalytic theory; in overly simplified form, they have made their way into the everyday vocabulary of today's popular-psychology culture. Many social and personal problems are related to these personality types, as we saw in chapter 3.

## THE OBSESSIVE-COMPULSIVE PERSONALITY

It is considered a truism among psychotherapists that obsession is the chief sign of perfectionism. This follows from observation of clients and from psychoanalytic theory. Therefore, a closer look at the dynamics of the obsessive-compulsive personality will help us understand how the perfectionistic mind operates.

As briefly defined in chapter 1, an obsession is an idea, emotion, or impulse that repeatedly forces itself into consciousness even though it is unwanted. We all know what it is like to have a jingle or part of a song come to mind again and again. Normal obsessions of this type tend not to last long, are not harmful to our functioning, and often can be amusing or entertaining.

The pathological obsessions that the perfectionist may suffer from, however, are not so innocent. They tend to last for long periods of time and may end up torturing the person and greatly disturbing mental functioning. They are out of conscious control and seem to have a life of their own, no matter how the person tries to rid himself of them. And the universe of things around which obsessions may form is as unlimited as the variety of thoughts a person may have.

Most common obsessions appear as ideas that are charged with emotion. They tend to fall into three broad categories. The first type of obsession is of an intellectual or existential nature, featuring preoccupation on religious or spiritual concerns regarding the purpose or meaning of one's life, ultimate destiny, death, suffering, or evil. Brooding, depression, and pessimism may accompany this type of obsession.

An example of an existential obsession may be seen in the character Woody Allen has often portrayed in his movies: the brooding, anxious, fearful, but creative intellectual who is fixated on the ultimate meaning of life, death, and suffering. The best image that comes to mind is from his film *Stardust Memories,* in which he plays a well-known movie director and writer (in other words, himself). On the living room wall of his fashionable New York apartment hangs a large art piece. It is a life-size blow-up of a late '60s newspaper photo in which a blindfolded Vietnamese peasant is about to have his head blown open by a soldier who holds a gun at him at point-blank range. With this kind of message to greet him upon awakening in the morning, who wouldn't be obsessed with death and suffering?

A second type of obsession is the inhibiting variety, including various phobias that paralyze our actions. An example of an inhibiting obsession is the refusal to fly in an airplane because of a persistent fear of crashing. Another example is the irrational fear that any food that one has not personally washed three times is unclean and must be avoided. Other examples of inhibiting obsessions include the inability to enjoy sex because of strong feelings of guilt and the inability to tolerate being the focus of attention at a party because of an obsession with being perfectly dressed.

A third form is the impulsive obsession, which leads to actions that we can't control. These are called compulsions. They are repetitive actions that tend to be stilted and often trivial behaviors. Although we don't like the action, we feel we *must* do it or our anxiety will increase and we imagine that something terrible will result. Performing the action gives us temporary relief from anxiety. Being obsessed with sex, for example, may lead to the compulsion to search for frequent new sexual partners or to masturbate many times per day. *Compulsions are obsessions in action.*

Obsessive people have developed an overly severe, self-punishing moral conscience. They use the psychological defense of *reaction formation* (doing the opposite of their unconscious impulse) to protect themselves from further guilt at recognizing unconscious aggressive and sadistic impulses. If, for example, a child unconsciously desires to kill his father so he can possess his mother, he can block these impulses, keeping them from awareness. He focuses instead on being very hard on himself and becoming overly moralistic, uptight, and a "good little boy," as close to perfect as possible. In this way he counteracts his thoughts of sex and aggression from reaching conscious awareness, and therefore does not have to worry so much about losing his parents' love. He may also use this "good-boy" behavior to manipulate his parents to get what he wants from them. This has prompted psychiatrist Fritz Perls's statement, "Behind every good boy is a spiteful brat."[7]

## Obsession as Fixation

In discussing the role of the obsessive-compulsive personality as it relates to perfectionism and eating disorders, Jungian analyst Marion Woodman believes that the messages that bombard us from the news and entertainment media contribute to the development of compulsive behaviors related to the body. These include compulsive dieting and exercising, eating habits based on oversuspiciousness of the harmful effects of food ingredients, and a catastrophizing reaction to disease, injury, and physical accidents. Continually confronted by destruction—wars, airplane crashes, auto accidents, rape, murder, cancer, AIDS, pollution, radiation—we feel that our bodies could be annihilated at any time.

Coupled with the threat of physical extinction is the tendency for compulsives to live in the future rather than the present. Since they can't cope with the present, they dream about, as Woodman puts it, "what they could be, should be, or were meant to be in the future. The gap between reality and dream is often filled with obsession."[8]

In line with psychoanalytic thinking, Woodman views obsession as the chief symptom of the pursuit of perfection. Energy that ought to be distributed among various personality parts is instead focused on one area of the personality to the exclusion of everthing else. She puts it like this: "Obsession is always a fixation, a freezing over of the personality so that it becomes not a living being but something fixed, like a piece of sculpture, locked into a complex."[9]

Because of this fixation, in Woodman's view, the perfectionist rejects life as it is and substitutes compulsive addictions for unmet spiritual needs. Woodman focuses especially on the Great Mother, the unconscious connection to God in feminine form, that is missing for many women who are out of touch with their inner psychological worlds. The literal mother herself rejects her own feminine spiritual consciousness and passes this rejection down to her daughter. "The mother who rejects her own feminine consciousness cannot see her child in its becoming; she cannot allow it to live its own imperfect humanity in its own imperfect world," Woodman asserts.[10]

Woodman sees the mother-daughter connection as crucial because, when it fails, the daughter is taught to be a thing or machine, without meaning or love, manipulated by her mother toward a high level of efficiency. The daughter undertakes spiritual striving and excessive discipline to achieve a goal (becoming perfect to please her mother) that has nothing to do with her. The daughter is not allowed to be human and make mistakes—mistakes would mean disappointing her mother. In Woodman's words:

To strive for perfection is to kill love because perfection does not recognize humanity. However driven it becomes, the ego cannot achieve its perfectionist ideals because another Reality is within. Nor can it accomplish the task of loving. Only by opening ourselves to inner Reality do we open ourselves to possibility of the gift of love.[11]

## The Compulsive's Payoff

When an obsessive-compulsive personality is not too extreme, it can bring rewards. Our society does not necessarily label the obsessive-compulsive mentality a problem, an illness, or a disorder but often considers it a virtue. In its less severe forms, an obsession, such as the desire to practice and excel at tennis, can foster dedication to a single-minded effort toward high-level performance.

It is necessary to consider *how* the obsession is put into action. If the desire to excel at tennis does not lead to the compulsion to play tennis to the exclusion of everything else in life, and if the person is able to derive enjoyment from dedicated practice, this interest takes the form of a healthy concentration of attention. It would then be viewed as a positive striving for excellence.

People who become workaholics to get ahead, or persist at a project until it is completed, or keep their houses extra spic-and-span, are all applauded by our society. Obsession is usually considered a problem only when we can no longer cope with the consequences of our obsessions and they lead to out-of-control compulsive behaviors.

Obsession also causes problems when it involves behaviors that society does not condone—for example, drug or gambling addictions, compulsive masturbation, or exhibitionism. Other compulsions are considered relatively innocent and do not carry any social stigma; in fact, they may be the subject of envy (for example, compulsive clothes shopping, compulsive womanizing by the rich playboy, compulsive exercising or dieting). The fact that our society values aspects of the obsessive-compulsive personality does not mean that people do not pay a heavy psychological price for their inability to practice moderation. Because our society sanctions so many compulsive behaviors, some in the recovery movement have gone so far as to label our whole society "addictive."

## Adler's Drive Toward Superiority

Alfred Adler was one of the inner circle of original Freudians. He was the first of Freud's disciples to break away and form his own line of research. His thought matured from an early focus on the motivation to overcome inferiority to a later emphasis on the positive striving for power and perfection.[12] He believed there was an inherent biological instinct to achieve competence and growth; he called this instinct "a striving for superiority." Striving for perfection was viewed as the motivation that guided the healthy personality.[13]

How can we determine if the striving for perfection is a neurotic urge for self-security through personal superiority, or a healthy, positive goal? Adler and Abraham Maslow (whose work we will consider in a moment) both answered this question with the concept of *transcendence*. The healthy personality is motivated by a transcendent concern, not so much by personal survival and security as by what Adler termed "social interest." This means that the person is interested in contributing to his society.

For Adler, striving for perfection had religious aspects and could represent either a personal disturbance or personal potential. In the case of a disturbance, the compulsive neurotic strived for godlikeness by overcoming the anxiety of an inferiority complex. Adler believed that

> The compulsion neurotic endeavors to overcome this anxiety and tries to represent himself in the form to which he originally aspired—*as a demigod, who exalts himself above humankind and who depreciates everyone else and puts them in the shade.* He covers over his inferiority complex with a superiority complex.[14]

On the personal potential side of the equation, Adler views the idea of God as an expression of the goal of perfection. The healthy individual recognizes that salvation comes through divine grace, not human works, and that the degree of God's perfection is humanly impossible. In his words:

> Man as an ever-striving being could not be like God. God, who is eternally complete, who directs the stars, who is the master of fates, who elevates man from his lowliness to Himself, who speaks from the cosmos to every single human soul, is to date the most brilliant manifestation of the goal of perfection.[15]

The phrase "the most brilliant manifestation of the goal of perfection" seems to imply that we do not seek perfection in order to be like God; on the contrary, because we seek perfection, we need to imagine it in the perfect form of the concept of God. Adler's view is an example of placing the psychological motive above the spiritual in striving for perfection.

Adler answered the question of whether striving for perfection was pathological or healthy by focusing on social interest and the recognition of human limits. He believed that in a healthy religious individual the motivation is to serve others, to assist them to become more perfect. This person does not achieve superiority at the expense of others and does not confuse God's absolute omnipotence with human weakness and powerlessness.[16]

In its emphasis on helping others become "more perfect," Adler's concept of social interest values perfection as a goal to be achieved. Therefore, despite its altruistic elements, this concept still invites competition with others and the inevitable shame, guilt, and regret that result when one is unable to measure up to one's goal.

It is interesting to consider whether Adler, if he were writing today, *might* endorse striving for excellence in place of striving for superiority. The excellence concept *perhaps* fits more neatly with his focus on social interest. In addition, in viewing striving for superiority as a biological instinct, Adler was clearly influenced by the biological orientation of medicine. He *may* have failed to distinguish between the inherent and *possibly* biologically based ability to *conceive* of perfection (superiority) and the socially learned motivation to *achieve* it.

## Maslow's Self-Actualization

Abraham Maslow is considered the father of humanistic psychology, which served as the scholarly arm of the popular human potential movement of the 1960s and 1970s. His motivational and transcendent perspective was similar to Adler's but more encompassing. Maslow believed that personality is motivated by biologically- and security-based D-needs (deficiency needs) arranged in a hierarchy beginning with the most basic. Higher needs are recognized and become one's focus only when lower needs have been satisfied.[17]

The focus of the deficiency needs is personal and ego-centered. These would include, for example, "I need food and shelter," "I need to belong," "I need your love," "I need self-esteem," and, at a higher level, "I need to actualize myself." Satisfaction of D-needs brings into awareness higher-level needs, termed meta-needs or B-needs (being needs). Being values transcend personal survival and security to encompass cultural and spiritual values like truth, beauty, goodness, and perfection.

Maslow viewed both the deficiency and being needs as instinctual but only unfolding into awareness one step at a time. As each lower need is satisfied, it recedes to the background and the next higher need makes itself felt. Of course, should a natural catastrophe or other emergency threaten survival, the higher needs drop back until the most basic needs are again satisfied. So, for example, if you pull off the road to take in the visual splendor of a sunset (meeting a B-need for beauty and the perfection of nature), and then you notice in the distance that your house is on fire, suddenly your concern reverts to your needs for shelter and security.

In this way, your primary needs at any given moment may shift from B-needs to D-needs and back again. So, while you might not maintain a steady state of B-needs, these higher values would eventually become the primary focus of your stretching for growth toward perfection.

At the higher levels, Maslow believed that people have a need to become the most that they are capable of becoming. He called this a "self-actualizing tendency." To self-actualize means to experience something "fully, vividly, selflessly, with full concentration and total absorption."[18]

When viewed as a process leading toward a goal, self-actualization refers to those who are motivated by higher-level needs to continually press to bring out the very best they have to offer in all they do. Maslow put it like this: "If you deliberately plan to be less than you are capable of being, then I warn you that you will be deeply unhappy for the rest of your life."[19] This need to push oneself to be one's best is what I am considering the healthy desire to strive for excellence.

Maslow wrote of peak experiences—ecstatic moments when we realize that "what 'ought to be' is, in a way that requires no longing, suggests no straining, to make it so."[20] Such moments are often experienced as mystical, religious, or transpersonal. Although they are transient in nature, we long to have more peak experiences because when we are in the midst of one, everything seems as perfect as it can possibly be. The emotional reaction in the peak experience has a special flavor of wonder, reverence, humility, and surrender. Often during peak experiences, perception is ego-transcending, self-forgetful, or egoless.

In relation to perfectionism, peak experiences offer a glimpse of the possibility of experiencing ourselves and our world as perfect just as it is. For a brief time we are able to let go all need to judge ourselves and others, experiencing ourselves as uniquely perfect in a perfect world where everything fits. For Maslow and Eastern philosophy, this is the richly fulfilling experience of the perfection of our essence that we so long for. It must clearly be contrasted with our misguided efforts to perfect our behavior.

It is worth noting that while Maslow's theory of B-needs is labeled by some a "psychology of perfection,"[21] Maslow himself was quick to point out "the dangers of unrealistic perfectionism," especially in naive social and political forms. As if he were speaking directly to the well-meaning but idealistic sentiments expressed by the 1960s counterculture "love generation," as well as to the tragic abuses of authority by religious leaders and cult groups in the '70s and '80s, Maslow wrote:

> I assume that perfection, that is, assuming that ideal or perfect solutions may be demanded, is a danger. The history of Utopias shows many such unrealistic, unattainable, non-human fantasies. (For example, let us all love each other. Let us all share equally. All people must be treated as equals in all ways. Nobody must have any power over anybody else. Application of force is always evil. "There are no bad people; there are only unloved people.")[22]

The common sequence of perfectionistic thinking did not escape Maslow: unrealistic expectations leading to inevitable failure, leading to disillusionment, leading to apathy, discouragement, or active hostility to all ideals. He wrote: "Improvability has often been thought impossible when perfectibility turned out to be impossible."[23]

Despite his own awareness of the dangers of perfectionism, Maslow's influence on the human potential movement of the '60s was partly responsible for today's pop-psychology thinking that we all have unlimited potential. Striving for self-actualization and the desire to be the best that we may be has been distorted to mean that we must strive for perfection and that the sky is the limit.

## Cognitive Approaches

Like those who hold the psychoanalytic view, theorists who focus on our inner statements (self-talk) also emphasize the role of the conscience in perfectionism. They believe that behavior can best be altered by first altering these self-statements enhanced by experimenting with new behavior. These theorists fall into what is called the *cog-*

*nitive* school. Cognitive theories emphasize the role of erroneous thinking processes in human disturbance. They interpret perfectionism as resulting from an overly moralistic self-evaluation.[24]

## Horney's Search for Glory

A combination of psychological and social perspectives is prominent in the work of Karen Horney, who maintained that the perfectionist is plagued by what she called "the tyranny of the shoulds."[25] This view has much in common with Freud's concept of the overly stern superego. In both the cognitive approach and classical psychoanalysis, the perfectionist's lowered self-esteem is viewed as the result of a harsh conscience.

Although trained as a classical analyst, Horney replaced the Freudian motives of sex and aggression with anxiety and hostility. Anxiety and hostility originate in the child's life when parents are seen as inconsistent, indifferent, and interfering. Hostility, Horney believed, stems from a sense of injustice at treatment by manipulative parents.

Because children need to feel a sense of security about their survival, they repress this hostility. To allow themselves to feel hostile directly toward parents would put them at odds with their source of security and survival—a dangerous position. Hostility and a sense of being unwanted manifest as feelings of helplessness, powerlessness, desertion, endangerment, and insignificance.[26]

For Horney, the core of identity is the "real self," a subjective image of one's true potential for realization. But feelings of helplessness and hostility force the formation of another image, the "despised real self," as children turn their hostility inward because it is unsafe to turn it outward. Because they feel hostility toward the world, they see the world as aiming this same hostility back toward them. The result is a negative self-image in which children see themselves as having characteristics deserving of this perceived hostility.

To compensate for and defend against anxiety, the child forms an idealized self, which, like the despised real self, is one of distortion and fiction. This idealized self is the image of what the child thinks she should be to gain love, affection, and approval.

Our relationships as Horney viewed them are frequently strained by neurotic needs related to underlying unresolved anxiety and hostility. She believed that neurotic needs were common to everyone and became pathological only when expressed indiscriminately, irrationally, persistently, and rigidly. Of the neurotic needs that Horney identified, she placed major importance on the neurotic need for perfection—the desire to be infallible and to gain superiority over others. Motivated by this neurotic need, we pursue perfection relentlessly and are quick to judge ourselves and others for possible flaws. We also feel superior to others and dread criticism.[27]

The idealized self and the need for perfection together lead to what Horney called the search for glory. The coping strategy used when there is a neurotic need for perfection is to move against others. We seek to reduce our anxiety by aggressively expanding our control and influence over the self, the world, and other people.

Unlike some theorists, Horney believed that pursuing perfection in itself is not abnormal. (What she thinks of as good perfectionism is what I have labeled striving for excellence.) The desire for perfection becomes neurotic when one becomes more concerned with projecting an image of having attained an end-state of absolute perfection than with striving for continued accomplishment. The fear of guilt for deviations from the strict moral standards dictated by the conscience increases one's anxiety and only serves to heighten the neurotic need for perfection.

### Ellis's Rational-Emotive Theory

The rational-emotive philosophy and therapy of Albert Ellis is also cognitively oriented. This theory contends that it is important for people to realize how they create problems by "accepting or inventing absolutistic demands for themselves, for others, and for their environment."[28] It asserts that people need to identify the unconditional "shoulds" and "musts" with which they disturb themselves. These "shoulds" represent exactly the kind of thinking (all-or-nothing absolutism and self-demands) that is characteristic of the perfectionist.

Ellis outlines categories of irrational thinking that we can directly apply to the perfectionist. These include the following:

*Demand statements.* Statements of demand imply absolute necessity or need. People who make such statements believe they *must* have what they want. They must come out on top or they can't stand it. They rigidly dictate the way their worlds must operate. As Ellis puts it, "People typically demand approval, recognition, perfection, success . . . the irrational demanding belief is evident when someone believes that he absolutely must have that which is likely preferable."[29]

*Catastrophizing statements.* This is the process of making "mountains out of molehills." An event is magnified until a typical hassle is seen as a horror. For example, inconveniences are labeled as "awful" and pains as "tragedies."[30]

*Intolerance statements.* Ellis maintains that irrational beliefs of intolerance exist when people "strongly insist that they 'can't stand' something or that it is 'too' hard or difficult. People most commonly feel intolerant of frustration, discomfort, and other people."[31] Ellis aims to modify such beliefs and show that while something might be difficult, it is not too difficult or impossible. The perfectionist's intolerance of the frustration of learning a new game, for example, makes her turn away from new experiences just because she can't play like an expert.

*Rating statements.* At the core of the belief system of the perfectionist are self-rating statements and evaluations of others. Ellis maintains that

> It is irrational to measure an individual's total human worth on the basis of some trait, behavior, accomplishment, or other at-

tribute. The rational alternative is to help people to see that their human worth is independent of their actions or achievements. It makes no sense to say that one's value as a person is contingent upon any extrinsic measure.[32]

While certain traits do make some people more adept at certain tasks, this does not make them better people. For example, good social skills can be an advantage in many situations and may make a person more desirable for many jobs. But this does not mean that one with good social skills is an inherently more valuable person than the person who lacks them. The ability to run fast makes a person more valuable to a track coach, but does not make the fast runner a more valuable person.

Unfortunately (as demonstrated in chapter 4), our culture does not promote the view of intrinsic human worth. The perfectionist has learned well that the person who exhibits a stronger, more attractive body, a quicker mind, and the money and possessions to live the "good life" is held to be of greater value than the individual who lacks these attributes.

This is partly why the perfectionist keeps up the struggle: he truly enjoys the feeling of (false) superiority, of having higher standards, morals, or values. Just as the religious fundamentalist needs to believe he is more righteous than the next person, the perfectionist needs to believe he or she is more perfect than others.

So, although Ellis and many others in psychology, religion, and philosophy encourage a nonjudgmental, nonrating attitude toward ourselves and others, in the everyday reality of our culture *having* more makes us feel we *are* more. The rational-emotive therapist faces a tough job convincing the perfectionist that self-rating and other-rating is destructive.

### Seligman's Attribution Theory

Another example of the cognitive model in understanding perfectionism can be found in the work of Martin Seligman, who has written about psychological pessimism. According to Seligman, psychological pessimists make three attributions (or interpretations) when a bad event occurs: internal, global, and stable. An internal attribution is one in which the person blames himself for the outcome of an event. A global attribution overgeneralizes from one experience. A stable attribution assumes that things must always remain as they are now.

Imagine that you're a student who has done poorly on a biology test. A psychological pessimist might say, "It's all my fault [internal]. I'm a bad student, I mess up everything I do [global]. And I'm always going to be like this [stable]."

With this self-blame, you ignore many other possible reasons for your poor performance (you may hate biology, or the teacher wasn't very good, or you had too many other courses). You feel hopeless, good-for-nothing, and unable to change for the better. The psychological pessimist lives with a pervasive sense of unhealthy guilt: "No matter what I do, it's [I'm] never good enough."[33]

As perfectionists, we take on more than our fair share of unhealthy guilt. When we are unable to perform up to the unrealistic standards we have set, we feel guilty, unable to question the process by which we have set such impossible standards. Since we are bound to fall short of the mark, guilt may become a constant companion.

## THE TWO FACES OF GUILT

Psychologists tend to view guilt as either healthy or unhealthy. In healthy guilt, we realize that we have done something harmful to someone else and we feel bad about it. The positive way to deal with healthy guilt is to take responsibility for what we did, make amends where possible, and then forgive ourselves and let go of the guilt. If we can do this, healthy guilt teaches us compassion. But if we hold on to guilt, it turns into an internalized source of shame, a basic feeling of unworthiness, that can remain with us for the rest of our lives. We will go into more detail regarding the role of shame when we discuss self-psychology and the work of Heinz Kohut below.

Unhealthy guilt is intimately related to shame and comes from fear. It is the feeling, based on the experiences of childhood, that we won't be good enough to get the love we so desperately desire. When we carry unhealthy guilt, we project our sense of unworthiness in our interactions with others. We tend to be overly apologetic for things that are not our doing, to take on excessive responsibility even for things totally out of our control, and to have trouble accepting compliments. We don't believe anything we do is ever good enough to deserve a compliment.

In the addiction recovery movement, this type of unhealthy guilt is called "toxic shame." Shame cuts to the core of our identity. As we grow up, all the parts of ourselves that have not been affirmed and loved by others end up being denied, disowned, and projected onto others. We see others feeling toward us what we are actually feeling toward them (anger, for example). The result is that our identity is a fragmented construction in which we are aware of only those parts of ourselves that have not been tainted by shame.

It now becomes more apparent how the fear of failure motivates the perfectionist's driven pursuit of accomplishment. If your identity is based on shame, you have a tremendous fear that unless you appear perfect, you will not be loved. Your whole life becomes organized around the avoidance of fear rather than around the attraction of love or the healthy pursuit of the joy of accomplishment.

## The Empty Self

A growing number of theorists speak of "the empty self," brought about in part because of our sense of loss of family, community, and tradition.[34] As psychologist Phillip Cushman puts it, "It is a self that seeks the experience of being continually filled up by consuming goods, calories, experiences, politicians, romantic partners, and empathic therapists in an attempt to combat the growing alienation and fragmentation of its era."[35]

With an empty self, people always think they need more. This is what Ram Dass means when he says that when we are ruled by our desires (out of a sense of emptiness), *more is never enough.* As perfectionists, our driven need to accomplish is due in part to this sense of psychological and spiritual emptiness that permeates our basic identity. Mounting one accomplishment upon another, we try to fill, at least temporarily, this sense of emptiness.

It is not just that we want to be loved, admired, and recognized. When we have learned that our basic identity and sense of worth as individuals is something that is largely given to us from outside ourselves, it is but a short step to feeling empty and needing desperately to be filled up by the outside world. The heart of the matter is this: if we cannot be filled up with a sense of personal worth, self-acceptance, and integrity, then we will settle for whatever else may give us a temporary sense of being soothed and fulfilled.

Inner emptiness may be expressed in many ways. These include an absence of personal sense of worth; the absence of personal values and convictions; the compulsion to fill the emptiness with food or to embody the emptiness by refusing food (eating disorders); the compulsion to seek chemically induced emotional experiences (drug abuse); the chronic consumerism of shopaholics ("receiving" something from the world); and the drive to produce incredible accomplishments. Inner emptiness may also take the form of a wish to be filled up by the spirit of God, by religious truth, or by the power and personality of a leader or guru (see chapter 6).[36]

## The Empty Self and Narcissism

The "empty self" has become such a prevalent concept in interpretations of our culture that much psychotherapeutic theory is devoted to its treatment. Related to this sense of emptiness is another of the key personality traits of many perfectionists: narcissism. *Narcissistic disorders* have become prevalent diagnoses.[37]

Basically, narcissism refers to a preoccupation with oneself to the exclusion of everyone else. One analyst has said that "the narcissist becomes his own world and believes the world is him."[38] Narcissists present various combinations of intense ambitiousness, larger-than-life fantasies about what they can accomplish, hidden feelings of inferiority, and overdependence on external admiration and acclaim.[39] They need to be the most attractive, best dressed, smartest, most admired, most courageous—the "most" everything. They have, in other words, a need to be perfect and to have others view them as perfect.[40]

In many cases, narcissistic persons can claim numerous achievements and seeming success, for they are able to create a polished surface impression and often get along well in the world of power and money. But the narcissist is trying to fulfill a false self-image.

The psychological dynamics of the narcissist include a great deal of repressed rage. This rage is unconscious but comes through in the way the narcissist uses other people as objects to meet his own needs and in his inability to empathize with others or to feel a deep commitment to social or political causes.

Because the narcissist does not truly love herself but has a false and empty self to fill up, she always needs the approval and admiration of others. This is a never-ending process—the applause from others is only short-lived, and the narcissist then returns to feeling empty.

Narcissistic people tend to become overinvolved with their self-images. On the physical level, for example, they do not exercise just to feel good but are concerned with shaping the perfect body. This is why the narcissist is a prime target for advertising promoting the perfect body image. Instead of toning his muscles, the narcissist might go to the extreme of using weight training to build massive, overdeveloped muscles.

The narcissist hides feelings. While his ego grandiosity and bravado may give the outward impression of self-confidence, the narcissist hides his inner emptiness and insecurity. The outward puffed-up image does not represent how the narcissist truly feels about himself. It is as if his self-image must continually be inflated by others, like a balloon, or it will collapse into depression.

## Kohut's Self Psychology

Heinz Kohut developed an entire theory and treatment based on the empty, fragmented self. In the theory that he called *self psychology,* he attempted to explain how the self is developed and to offer methods by which to lessen the effects of emptiness and fragmentation.[41-43]

Like the reasonably healthy person, the neurotic person has a clear and stable sense of self. A rejection by a lover, for example, does not threaten the cohesiveness of this person's core identity. Since the conscience is fully developed in the neurotic, the threat of expressing forbidden wishes is experienced as a moral violation and arouses feelings of guilt.

In contrast, the emotional and relationship difficulties of the narcissistic personality, according to Kohut, concern primarily the poorly differentiated self. The narcissist's sense of individual, separate I-ness is not cohesive or stable. She experiences anxiety as a result of a realistic appraisal of her vulnerability to identity fragmentation. Her self-esteem is crippled, inconsistently shifting from false grandiosity to severe shame. Kohut has helped clarify the difference between the neurotic's guilt and the narcissist's shame.

Kohut calls the people in the narcissist's world selfobjects. Failing to sufficiently differentiate others from his own self, the narcissist uses them as objects to maintain that self. It is the loss of the *admiration* (as opposed to loss of love) of these self-objects (such as parents) that can result in a blow to the cohesion of the self and the sense of self-esteem. Such a loss may cause feelings of overpowering shame.

Kohut believed that in normal development, the child establishes a grandiose image of himself and thinks, "I am perfect." He also establishes a grandiose image of his parents and thinks, "You are perfect and I am part of you." According to Kohut, this stage replaces the perfection enjoyed by the infant at the beginning of life when he is the center of his own and his parents' world. In Kohut's view this grandiose image is a transitory phase and a necessary condition of healthy development.

As the child comes to recognize the parents' normal shortcomings, this grandiose self-image is gradually toned down. The new modified self-image is integrated into the child's existing mental structure and works constructively to supply ambition and motivation for activities. The idealized parent image becomes internalized as ideals and morals. This positive but not grandiose self-image also works to regulate healthy self-esteem relatively independently of external factors.

The narcissistic parent may be unable to mirror back to the child the message that the child is deserving of admiration. This failure, called narcissistic trauma, impairs the development of a mature, cohesive, and stable feeling of self. The child never experiences the sense of being perfect that is necessary in early development. As a result, the person continues to strive for ultimate perfection or for merger with a perfect parental selfobject.[44]

### Neurotic Versus Narcissistic Perfectionism

The distinction between shame and guilt, as well as Kohut's distinction between neurotic and narcissistic disorders invite us to view perfectionism in at least two different forms.[45]

For normal and neurotic people, perfectionism is a reaction to the demands of a harsh conscience acquired as a result of learning and as a result of repressed hostility. Seen this way, perfectionism is a defense against inner conflict related to feelings of guilt around issues of morals and ideals. Failure to live up to these ideals creates lowered self-esteem. Instead of expressing hostility, the perfectionist pushes it out of awareness and strives to be perfect.

In the narcissistic personality perfectionism is an attempt by the individual to live up to an inflated self-image in order to avoid humiliation, shame, and the loss of admiration of important selfobjects. A perfectionistic view of self and selfobjects is necessary for the narcissist to develop a cohesive and stable sense of identity.

While the various cognitive styles mentioned earlier (all-or-nothing thinking, overgeneralization, and so on) apply to both forms of perfectionism, the way of thinking about one's behavior differs for each form. For example, the "tyranny of the shoulds" of the narcissistic perfectionist focuses on the self ("I should be perfect"). The failure to live up to the dictates of the "shoulds" evokes thoughts of "I am worthless" and "I am a nobody" (shame).

And finally, in the neurotic personality, the focal point of perfectionism is not on the self but on one's *actions* ("I should never get angry.") The failure to live up to this expectation evokes feelings of guilt. The shame-prone person would be obsessed with the question, "How could *I* have done that?" The guilt-ridden person is more likely to wonder, "How could I have *done that?*"

## HIGHLIGHTS

In this chapter we have briefly examined many concepts and theories related to perfectionism. In review, these are the key concepts you will find highlighted in future chapters in our examination of the perfection trap and how to transform perfectionism to excellence.

1. Universal, archetypal images of perfection should be differentiated from socially and psychologically learned and reinforced perfectionistic behavior. *Conceiving* of perfection does not mean *achieving* it.

2. Unconscious motivation is important. Perfectionistic behavior can be a defense against the unconscious fear of being out of control of one's thoughts and emotions.

3. The Oedipal conflict contributes to perfectionism. The lack of resolution of the unconscious urge to gain the favor of the opposite-sex parent while doing away with the same-sex parent can influence later sexual and personality development and encourage the conditions for perfectionistic striving.

4. Obsession is the chief sign of perfectionism. In the unconscious dynamic of the child fighting aggressive and sexual impulses left over from the Oedipal conflict by the defense of reaction formation to keep these impulses from outward expression, overly perfect or rigid behavior may result.

5. Psychodynamic and cognitive approaches agree on the importance of the parents' injunctions of right and wrong. The child is unable to evaluate his behavior or his self-worth independently of his parents' judgments.

6. According to Maslow's concept of the self-actualizing tendency, we desire to excel at the highest level possible and to find expression of an innate desire to become the most we can be. In peak experiences, those mystical and highly satisfying moments, everything seems perfectly in place, "as it should be," self and world are in perfect order and harmony.

7. In Horney's theory, the child's anxiety and hostility are created by inconsistent, indifferent, interfering, manipulative parents. To ward off this anxiety and hostility and to ensure necessary security through parents' love and approval, the child develops a fictitious *idealized self.*

8. We can alter our feelings about our behavior and self-worth through our self-talk—what we tell ourselves. The perfectionist's thinking is characterized by irrational statements including demands, catastrophizing, intolerance, and ratings. The psychological pessimist lives with a pervasive sense of guilt.

9. While healthy guilt is expressed and then let go, unhealthy guilt is turned inward in the form of shame.

10. The narcissistic personality is characterized by extreme self-centeredness, surface-level grandiosity, and overconcern for self-image, attention, and admiration. The nar-

cissist seeks a perfect image to cover up shame, inadequacy, and fear of self-fragmentation.

11. Neurotic perfectionism is based on guilt and focused on issues of harsh conscience, morals, and ideals. Narcissistic perfectionism is based on the avoidance of shame and humiliation, the strong need for love and admiration, and the need to develop a stable sense of self.

# SIX

# Looking God in the Eye:
## The Religious Roots

*When the eyes of the soul looking out meet the eyes of God looking in, heaven has begun right here on this earth.*

A. W. Tozer

*The eye with which I see God is the eye with which God sees me.*

Meister Eckhart

## Western Religion and Perfectionism

The term *perfectionism* has both positive and negative connotations in theological thinking, as it does in psychological theories. The positive use of the term implies a moral and spiritual ideal for the Christian that is thought to be realizable in this life.[1] This ideal is attained through spiritual knowledge, special inspiration and insight, vigorous moral education and discipline, mystical experiences, or gifts of the Holy Spirit.[2]

Religious environment is a potent force in psychological development and functioning. The psychological dynamics of perfectionism are amplified and aggravated when the religious heritage emphasizes conscious, deliberate, and willful pursuit of the perfect. The dynamics that arise in one's relationship to God and those who act as God's authoritative intermediaries (priests, rabbis, religious teachers) are similar or identical to those involved in the psychological stages of child-parent relationships. The common element is the desire to be approved of and loved—both by our all-powerful and all-knowing parents and by our conception of God. These common psychological dynamics contribute to the susceptibility of spiritual seekers to cults, as we will see later in this chapter.

### Christian Perfection

In American religious history, perfectionism as a theological doctrine and religious tradition began with the writings of John Wesley (1703–1791). His work on Christian perfection became a dominant feature of both English and American Methodism; perfection, holiness, and sanctification were to become cornerstones for the 19th- and 20-century holiness movement.

In a book written by J. A Wood in 1885 interpreting Wesley's teachings, Wood explains that:

> To Wesley, Christian perfection was defined as: a renewal in the image of God, in righteousness and true holiness. To be a perfect Christian is to love the Lord our God with all our heart, soul, mind, and strength, implying the destruction of an inward sin; and faith is the condition and instrument by which a state of grace is obtained.[3]

In Wesley's view, perfection was more an inner attitude and motive than a behavioral compliance with an absolute standard of perfection. He explained: "By *perfection,* I mean *perfect love,* or loving God with all our hearts, so as to rejoice evermore, to pray without ceasing, and in everything to give thanks. I am convinced every believer may attain this."[4] Christian perfection in the life of the believer, according to Wesley, was not to be confused with an absolute, infallible, sinless perfection attributed to God.

Successive alterations of Wesley's doctrine over the years by overly zealous followers of his thinking ultimately led to various teachings advocating a sinless or absolute perfection on the part of human beings—exactly the opposite of what Wesley and other careful scholars had taught. It is, of course, this concept of "sinless perfection" that survived and has been largely responsible for the perception by fundamentalists of God as a "spiritual terrorist" who will hold us accountable for our sins when we die.

## Perfection in the Bible

*You . . . must be perfect, as your heavenly Father is perfect*
MATTHEW 5:48

In the Bible, God and his law are described as absolutely and sinlessly flawless.[5] But when the term *perfection* is applied to people it is always clearly differentiated from God's perfection.[6] One biblical scholar, interpreting the Gospel of Matthew, viewed perfection this way:

> A man is perfect if he realises the purpose for which he was sent into this world. . . . It is in the holy teaching of the Bible that we only realize our manhood by becoming godlike. The one thing which will make us like God is the love which never ceases to care for men, no matter what men do to it. We enter upon Christian perfection, when we learn to forgive as God forgives and to love as God loves.[7]

In contrast to the teaching quoted above, for many Christian perfectionists, their relationship to God is based on how well they perform. They are drawn to faith in God by an awareness of their badness, and their day-to-day solution is to try harder to do things perfectly. This tendency has led some mental-health professionals to hold that perfectionism is the most disturbing emotional problem among evangelical Christians.[8]

Cathy was a delicate 26-year-old graduate student in literature and a born-again Christian. Shy and vulnerable but very determined, she showed signs of anxiety in the quick, birdlike movements of her arms and in playing with her long blond hair. She needed to be urged occasionally to speak up so her soft voice could be heard. Cathy led a Bible study group at her college and, like many "born-agains," spent much of her time "in the service of the Lord." For her, this meant total absorption in the Bible and charity projects.

She came to see me in hopes of understanding her ambivalent feelings toward men and the meaning of recurring sexual dreams. She was having trouble concentrating on her graduate studies. Although these issues were her stated admission ticket through the consulting room door, it became apparent that Cathy's main problem was her out-of-control compulsive personality.

Cathy carried her Bible with her everywhere, including her psychotherapy sessions. She read it obsessively, to the point that her graduate studies suffered because she couldn't tear herself away from her Bible long enough to read her literature assignments. Cathy would underline particularly important passages in her Bible with a yellow marker. She set a rigid requirement for herself of reading a minimum of 10 pages per day. Bible reading was the first thing she did when she awoke at 5:30 each morning. To make sure she understood everything she read, she imposed the further requirement that she had to reread the same 10 pages by 6:00 each evening. If for any reason she was unable to complete her rereading on time, she felt terribly guilty and had to make amends by requiring a second rereading of the same pages before she would allow herself to eat dinner.

Cathy told me that she had denied herself dinner on 46 days of the past year because, even though she had completed her third readings, she still felt too guilty to allow herself to eat. Cathy used this guilt as a rationalization to periodically starve herself, and she was close to being anorexic. She confided in me that she hoped to become thin enough that "someday maybe the light from God's Being would shine right through me." She also believed that if she were a "perfect

Christian as God wants me to be," one of her rewards would be to be able to "exist on fruit, seeds, sunlight, and the strength of Christ."

When I asked her if she thought perhaps she was overly demanding and punishing herself, she smiled and said, "Punishing myself? Oh no, Doctor—actually, I'm letting myself off easy. When I let God down, nothing is too much to do to get back in his good graces. I must double my efforts to put things back in order."

Doubling of effort is common thinking among perfectionists. They live with the dictum that if a little of something is good, then a lot more must be better. More discipline, more practice, stricter controls—the perfectionist believes they will all lead to the desired outcome of being more perfect.

Cathy kept detailed records of a number of her activities. In her daily record-keeping and list-making she used designated pencils that she kept in a ceramic container on her desk. Each day when she sat down to make or add to a list, she performed the ritual of sharpening all six pencils. She knew exactly how many times she had attended church in the past year, how many times she had read (and reread) various Bible verses, how many hours she had spent in prayer, and most of the food she had bought during the past two years. In addition, she kept a special journal that she titled "Next to Godliness," in which she recorded those experiences that, as she put it, "made me feel close to Christ."

Cathy had dreams in which a six-winged angel would fly down to meet her while she was frolicking innocently in beautiful green pastures filled with lilacs. The six-winged angel (and Cathy's obsession with the number six) derived from her identification with the story of a vision said to have occurred to Saint Francis in 1224 at Mount La Verna. A crucified Christlike figure with six wings appeared to the saint one day as he prayed. During the vision he received stigmata wounds in his hands, feet, and side identical to those suffered by Christ. In Cathy's dreams, the angel served a different purpose: he would, as she put it, "spiritually infuse me with the spirit of God." When I asked her exactly how the angel managed to do this, she looked away, blushing and stroking her long hair nervously.

After about a minute, she looked back at me and said shyly, "Doctor, they have spiritual intercourse with me. They deposit semen into me that makes me radiate with the energy of a goddess. After this, I am ecstatically happy and blissful in my dream and when I wake up, I share my joy with others." Cathy was looking for perfect sexual union with Christ, a union that not only made her sexual impulses acceptable but elevated them to saintly status. She desired a spiritual purity that could not be tainted by earthy sex with real men in the real world.

Over time, Cathy learned to let go of some of her more compulsive behaviors without having to give up her religious beliefs. As she gained insight as to how her early childhood beliefs about sex and religion created guilt and powerful inpulses to overcontrol much of her behavior, she gradually became less rigid.

Her obsessive-compulsive behaviors gave her a surface-level feeling of control and were a defense against recognition of a deeper anxiety and emptiness that her religious beliefs were unable to fill. They also protected her from addressing a terror of catastrophic illness and death that she had never consciously acknowledged. After prolonged therapy, she adopted a more nourishing diet and was even able to engage in a sexual relationship with a real man in place of the angels in her dreams. Cathy is an example of how the Western religious heritage can amplify the psychological dynamics of perfectionism.

Martin, a 29-year-old carpenter and handyman, was tall and muscular. He favored jeans and work shirts and had a dark, close-cropped beard and imposing manner that exuded confidence and commanded attention. His appearance and demeanor camouflaged the nagging guilt and insecurity that were his constant companions. On the surface, Martin wanted to please people and could not tolerate the thought that he might not be liked by everyone. But no matter how hard he tried to be accommodating to others, Martin felt guilty.

Like Cathy, Martin wanted to be as morally perfect as possible so he would be "worthy of Christ's love." But he continually fell short, in thought and in deed, of living up to his standard of moral perfection.

His feelings of guilt, shame, and unworthiness were the price he had to pay for his inability to meet this standard. Unable to reveal his sexual shame and embarrassment to his minister, he came to see me. In his words:

> How can I be a worthy Christian when my thoughts are lustful? I can't stop lusting after women at the beach and at strip joints, nor can I hold myself back from masturbating when I get home—I'm so turned on after looking at them that sometimes I even jerk off in the car on the way home. I hate myself when I do it but I just can't stop. If I were morally perfect, I wouldn't have any need for sex. I would view all women from a spiritual plane—not from the dirty level of desire and pleasure. I feel sick and out of control.

Martin could not accept that his lustful thoughts were normal, that everyone has thoughts of sexual desire for those they feel intimate with, as well as occasionally for friends, acquaintances, and total strangers to whom they might be physically attracted. Following church doctrine, Martin believed the thought was as bad as the deed. Like Jimmy Carter, he had "lust in his heart." And when that thought and desire led to frequenting strip joints and to the deed of masturbation, Martin felt totally consumed by his sexual needs. So he played a little game with himself:

> When I masturbate, I don't think about the women at the beach or dancing on stage who turn me on. I only use them to get an erection. But once I get it up, I think about God and direct the pleasurable sensations as a gift to him. Sometimes when I come, I feel like I've become one with Him.

Before entering psychotherapy, Martin was unable to understand how his early religious programming about the sinful nature of the pleasures of the body related to these more recent beliefs about masturbation as a "gift for Christ." Nor could he see that attributing a heavenly purpose to his masturbation was a coping mechanism that allowed him to continue this highly pleasurable activity without feeling even more guilty than he already did. It also gave him a way to be close to, even merge with, the object of his perfectionistic striving; in orgasm he felt momentarily "perfect, as your heavenly Father is perfect."

Despite his desire to be liked and his strong shame and guilt in not measuring up, Martin was nevertheless rigid in his ideas about how others should think and live. His idealized self was accommodating and placating to others, while his true self felt superior to them, despite the burden of guilt he carried for his thoughts, impulses and "sinful" actions.

In the safety of the consulting room, his true opinions and absolutist thinking became evident. For Martin, there was only one correct view on abortion. There was only one right answer to the economy, the homeless, and homosexuals with AIDS. Those who didn't hold his views were "inferior." Martin needed to pretend the answers to difficult social and political issues were simpler and more absolute than they really were, in order to attain a false sense of security and a feeling of self-righteousness.

In Martin, we have a good example of the need to feel and act superior on the outside, while feeling terribly inferior and guilty within. He was a man who, as Adler put it, "exalts himself above humankind and who depreciates everyone else and puts them in the shade." Over the course of psychotherapy, Martin began to examine his need to feel righteously superior, learned to accept his sexual impulses as normal. He slowly became more able to direct his sexual and affectional needs toward a woman and cut back on his compulsive masturbation.

In the Jewish faith, one of the fundamental rules of ethics is related to the matter of perfection. It states, "It is not incumbent upon you to complete the work, yet you are not free to desist from it."[9] This means that it is not obligatory for anyone to complete the work of life, to think of the self as being perfect, yet the awareness of imperfection should not result in inaction. One should strive, within reasonable expectations, to reach toward perfection in whatever manner possible. This teaching is aimed toward balance—not expecting too much but continuing to strive for perfection.[10] And yet, here again we see the conscious and intentional pursuit of perfection as part of the Judeo-Christian ethic. Guilt has always played a central role in the Jewish religion, as it has in Christianity.

Biblical scripture and its interpretation suggests that for some people, the Bible can be used to reinforce neurotic perfectionism. For example, some obsessive-compulsives seem magnetically drawn to a legalistic literal interpretation of scripture rather than metaphoric one and to a religious scrupulousness that is overconcerned with the externals of faith. They tend to be rigid in outlook, judgmental of others and of themselves, guilt-ridden, unable to love, and conforming to the approval and disapproval of others.

As in the examples above of Cathy and Martin, their religious beliefs make their lives more difficult rather than more comforting. The way they understand and live out their religious beliefs only intensifies the psychological pressure to be perfect. Such people fill the consulting rooms of mental-health professionals and pastoral counselors when they suffer from their inability to live up to their interpretation of scripture and their unrealistic perfectionistic standards.

A broader question arises here: Are the core, mystical teachings of Christianity and the other major Western religions (Judaism and Islam) aimed at increasing people's guilt over not measuring up to God's expectations? Or is it simply that imperfect humans bring to the spiritual realm their psychologically based perfectionistic tendencies, and therefore distort and misinterpret religious literature to fit their own psychological needs?[11] Could their striving for perfection to measure up to God's expectations be a substitute for something else that they want but can't quite understand and that Western institutional religion fails to offer?

No matter what religious tradition it may be grounded in, our conception of God and our feelings about living up to God's perfectionistic expectations are related to our own psychological development and maturity, as well as to the culture in which that development takes place.[12]

Our image of God is based mostly on what we were taught as children by our parents and religious institutions. Many of us never seriously question this image but only reinforce it (or rebel against it) as we become adults. Our involvement with institutional, organized religion meets valid social and psychological needs, as well as offering a deepening faith in our particular God-concept. But our ideas about God are basically a matter of belief and faith, not based on *our own personal experience.*[13] Our psychological tendencies toward perfectionism may exert an unconscious influence on our beliefs and faith.

In the Eastern view of spirituality, our striving for perfection to measure up to God's expectations is a pale substitute for our own deeper desire to actually experience our own Godlikeness—not just to believe in a transcendent God who is separate from us.

## THE EASTERN VIEW: AWAKENING TO PERFECTION

> *We should find perfect existence through imperfect existence. We should find perfection in imperfection. For us, complete perfection is not different from imperfection.*        SHUNRYU SUZUKI

In the Western religious view, man falls from grace by turning his back on his spiritual sources and thereby making God an absent, "transcendent other." God then reenters human experience in the form of the holy, an immense force that is not part of the self. The holy appears to derive from a completely transcendent source and affects the self in overpowering ways.

In contrast to this idea of an outside force, one of the basic tenets of Eastern philosophies is that spiritual development is really an awakening to what one already is. Through progressive psychological and spiritual development, one uncovers one's true nature, a nature that is inherent in the psychic structure of each person. One awakens to one's true nature as ultimate consciousness, absolute self, or oneness with God. To put it simply, "Every conscious being, precisely as he or she is, is a perfect embodiment and expression of the Ultimate."[14]

In the Hindu version, for example, the divine spirit (*Brahman*) that is manifest in the external world is viewed as the same spirit as our true inner self (*Atman*). Although we first take our true inner self to be our conscious ego, the deeper insight induced by Hindu teaching is that our true self is not the self-conscious ego at all. Instead, it is much larger, so much larger that it cannot be described or defined but only pointed to by metaphors. At the moment of highest insight, the true inner self (*Atman*) is seen to be identical with the life essence of all the external universe (*Brahman*).[15]

## Wilber and the Atman Project

In a creative synthesis of Western psychology, religion, and Eastern philosophies, theoretical psychologist Ken Wilber argues persuasively that we are consciously or unconsciously striving for this oneness, or unity with God. He shows how we create various substitute gratifications in our attempt to satisfy this desire. He calls this striving for perfection, for unity with God, the "Atman project."[16]

The soul intuits its true Atman nature from the start and seeks to actualize it as a reality, not just as potential that is inherent in all people. Wilber quotes from Dante: "The desire for perfection is that desire which always makes every pleasure appear incomplete, for there is no joy or pleasure so great in this life that it can quench the thirst in our Soul."[17] This thirst is the desire for perfect unity with God.

The problem, according to Wilber and Eastern philosophy, is that we have forgotten our true nature at birth and have not sufficiently developed our consciousness to be able to regain awareness of our own godliness. We must go through various developmental stages of expanding consciousness before we realize our own true original nature.

It is only in the final fruition of psychological and spiritual growth (which most people never attain) that we are able to actualize our true nature as Atman. But this does not mean that we are not already God—it only means that we are unable to fully realize it. This "always already" nature of our own perfection distinguishes Eastern spirituality from the Western religious view. The Western teachings of sin and redemption find no place in Eastern thinking.

Because we are unable to actualize our desire for unity at lower stages of growth, we set up various substitutes. These substitute gratifications are also part of what Wilber considers the Atman project. Hungering after enlightenment and unity, the psychologically and spiritually empty self instead seeks all sorts of alternative gratifications, or surrogate God-projects, that don't really satisfy the longing for ultimate unity.

It is the separate ego-self that creates the boundary between itself and oneness. We maintain this boundary out of our fear of giving up our sense of separate identity. As a result we feel like subjects viewing an objective world. Without at least temporarily transcending our separate sense of self we cannot, according to Wilber (and Eastern thinking) experience our wholeness. From this perspective, the rediscovery of our infinite and eternal wholeness or perfection is our single greatest need and want. Yet we also fear and resist it, for we are unwilling to risk losing our own ego, our personal identity, our subjectivity.[18]

Our compromise solution is that we take our own ego to be God. We substitute our ego for true Atman. If we can't *be* perfect, then we will at least *act* like we are perfect. We then believe ourselves to be central to the cosmos, all-embracing, all-significant. Instead of being one with the cosmos, we desire to possess the cosmos (in the form of material goods, power, food, knowledge, fame), which we "imbue with infinite worth or infinite desirability."[19]

Wilber's notion of the Atman project helps explain the push toward perfection in its many neurotic and narcissistic forms. Take, for example, the extreme acquisitive nature of Donald Trump, Ivan

Boesky, Michael Milken, and many others who, no matter how much they have, are never satisfied.[20] In their efforts to find their own original perfect nature they get lost in various substitute gratifications that never quite do the job. Recall Trump's friend who said, "In order to feel real and whole, he had to exceed himself constantly, make more money, build bigger buildings. Underneath there's despair: *'Nothing I do is enough, and it will never be.'*" Trump seemed to make a god of his own ego, with the name Trump emblazoned on his homes, office buildings, casinos, airplanes, and yachts. Of course, no wealth will ever be enough because his unconscious desire to find his own perfect nature can never be fulfilled this way. You can't buy your way to perfect oneness!

## The Perfect Guru or Teacher

If we can't find our own perfect nature, we may seek it in someone else who claims to have found it. Whether it be an evangelical minister who claims to be speaking to God, or a guru who promises to show us the Way, we are always hoping to find the real item. We look for models, people whom we think to be perfect or close to it, and we often get caught in the trappings that surround those who claim to have "found it."

We are all too ready to find the Good Parent (or God-Parent) who will finally give us the good-enough soothing and attention we didn't get from our own parents. Armed with various psychological defense mechanisms such as denial, rationalization, and projection, we wholeheartedly immerse ourselves into spiritual groups with leaders who promise to deliver all the soothing we always wanted but couldn't get from Mommy, Daddy, and the family.[21]

Numerous recent examples in both Western religious evangelical groups and Eastern spiritual groups show us the dangers of blind obedience and idealization of authority figures who promise to lead us to spiritual fulfillment and closer to perfection. We have seen, for example, the marketing of God by televangelist ministers Jim Bakker, Jimmy Swaggart, and others. They put themselves up as models, only to have their private sexual sins exposed; they then ask our forgiveness, claiming to be just imperfect men with feet of clay. In the name of doing God's work and helping others become more perfect, many of them prey on the desperation of their flocks, collecting large amounts of money to further aggrandize their own egos.

We have witnessed the mass-suicide tragedy of Jim Jones's Jonestown, where Jones was cast as the God-Parent who could do no wrong. His adherents blindly followed him even into death. Geographically isolated in the jungle, Jones convinced his followers that his paranoid and delusional view of the world was reality.

Nowhere near as tragic a story nor as crazy a leader, but still a good example of pathological group dynamics, is the mystic guru Bhagwan Shree Rajneesh. His community leaders in Rajneeshpuram were willing to go to extreme lengths to gain political superiority in their small Oregon county, while the guru claimed to have no knowledge of what was occurring.

According to a psychiatrist and disciple who lived in the commune and researched the group, Rajneesh was "brilliant and funny when he spoke about organized religion and politics. He would say and do absolutely anything to expose the foibles, absurdity, and pomposity of priests, politicians, and pundits." But, ultimately, he couldn't avoid falling into the same traps he criticized: "As the group grew and its achievements became more impressive, he became intoxicated with his own power. He began to believe all the incredible things his disciples attributed to him. The disciples in turn became more impressed with their specialness and their mission."[22]

Although members of the group knew something was wrong when they saw other members carrying guns and taking bizarre actions (like placing toxic bacteria in 10 salad bars in a local city), they believed "it had to be done. Otherwise, their survival wouldn't have been guaranteed. Their survival was preeminently important because without it there would be no model of an ideal society."[23]

Repeatedly, seekers of models of perfection are painfully forced to learn this lesson: Anytime you put someone else up as an embodiment of the perfect, he or she is bound to let you down. Both through the teacher's own ego inflation and the followers' neediness to be led by a perfect example, seekers fall in love with an image—the image of the perfect.

Once they have idealized the leader as perfect, they will psychologically do whatever is necessary to keep him there. But at some point their efforts usually come tumbling down. From perfection, there is nowhere else for their leader to go but down—falling into the everyday world of the imperfect and taking disillusioned disciples with him.

Rather than see this happen, devoted followers will often ignore abuses of authority. They ignore inherent contradictions in the group belief system or personal idiosyncrasies of the teacher, minister, guru, or therapist. They refuse to listen to outsiders who tell them something is wrong, just as they fail to heed to their own inner voice that warns them something needs to be questioned.[24]

They may not take their inner voice seriously until the damage has already been done. For how can their leader, the one who is perfect, be wrong? They rationalize that others just don't understand their leader and that with more faith, everything will be fine. They block out their own good judgment and are unable to utilize what I have called the "discriminating mind."[25] Through the psychological mechanism of projection, they attribute to the outside world all the evil they are unwilling and unable to recognize in their own group.

Often they fall in love with a smooth voice, a certain twinkle in the eyes, a cadence of speech or graceful movement. Allured by a charismatic personality, they are entranced as the leader strings words together like pearls. They savor the warm feelings that come when they narcissistically bond with the leader and receive soothing love and acceptance from him or her and other group members. They cling to the hope that some of what the leader has will rub off on them. They go for *perfection.*

# PART THREE

# FORMS
## OF THE
# TRAP

# SEVEN

# THE PROMISE OF SPECIALNESS:
## *Shaping the Perfect Child*

*The promise of specialness is the seductive lure put forward in the parent's effort to mold the child into his or her image of what the child should be.*

ALEXANDER LOWEN

### FAST-TRACK KIDS

Infants are shown flash cards of everyday objects before they are able to utter a word. Children are put on the ski slopes and into swimming pools as toddlers and are taught everything from violin to foreign languages before they enter the first grade. They are expected to know how to take care of themselves at an early age; if they can't, they are viewed as lagging behind their peers in development. They are not allowed to pass through childhood at a leisurely pace; instead, they are molded in the image of the adult—an image of perfected skills and abilities.

In many cases, the parents of these fast-track children work hard for the payoff of achievement. This achievement is commonly measured in earnings that provide for a house, cars, school tuition, babysitters, and an endless array of lessons and activities. What are the consequences for the children of these busy parents?

On the positive side, some experts believe that many of the children of superachieving parents become the independent thinkers and leaders of their generation. The few studies available indicate nothing intrinsically wrong with having affluent, hard-working parents, even if these parents tend to leave much of the chore of child-rearing to schools and domestic help.

On the negative side, however, "some of these children are falling off the track before they even get on."[1] Some show the same psychological symptoms of children of the very poor: lack of self-esteem, initiative, and imagination; inability to relate; depression; and in extreme cases, thoughts of suicide.

Time is one of the major issues in family life. Parents worry that they don't spend enough time with their children. Some try to compensate by trying to schedule too many activities for their children's free hours. The time the family does spend together is often devoted to activities that do not best meet the child's needs. In many cases the parents come from families in which parental roles were more sharply differentiated, where father worked and mother was home with the children. These high-achieving parents therefore have had no role models to show them how to shift gears smoothly between family and work.

Andree Aelion Brooks, author of *Children of Fast-Track Parents,* defines "fast track" as a "high driving, get-rich-quick attitude" where achievement is the only thing that matters. Fast-track parents, according to Brooks, typically work more than 40 hours a week, consider possessions one mark of success, and put as much pressure on their children as on themselves to achieve great things. Being first in one's class, becoming chairman of the board, and making a six-figure income before reaching age 30 are the kinds of achievements that are meaningful to fast-trackers. Brooks claims, "When they became parents, it wasn't a question of whether their children were sweet, kind, and affectionate but, rather, whether they could read before they were two, could spout Shakespeare by five, that sort of thing. Life was a numbers game."[2]

Brooks says that fast-track parents transmit their highly competitive attitudes to their children, with "terrible repercussions." For example, nursery-school teachers report that some three- and four-year-olds come to school with trembling hands or facial tremors from too much pressure at home. "No matter how much they achieve," Brooks says, "some children will never be able to measure up to their parents' accomplishments."

Self-esteem may be at risk when parents are frequently away, no matter how worthwhile the reason for the absence. Children begin to assume that the parent's absence is a sign of disinterest, that the parent always has better things to do than be with them.

"Many children aren't even allowed to be children," says Joyce Grief, director of development for the Chandler School, a private elementary and junior high school with over four hundred students. "They're so programmed with lessons after school that they have no free time just to play and be kids. There has to be an emotional toll."[3]

While it is difficult to make generalizations about fast-track parents or the consequences for their children, many of these parents exhibit characteristics of perfectionism. Perfectionistic parents are more interested in the product than the process. They look to the end goal rather than the means of getting there. They are less concerned with exactly *how* they raise their children than with the end product, a successful child. Of course, this orientation comes through loud and clear to their children, who are only too happy to do whatever is necessary to earn their parents' approval.

## "First Born, Perfect Born"

Steven, age 10, is a tall, good-looking child with shaggy brown hair. He smiles and laughs easily, has a vocabulary beyond his age, and chooses his words carefully. His mother does not need to remind him to pick up his toys or to make his bed—he keeps his room tidy without a word from his parents. Steven yearns to be the perfect child. He wants to be favored, to get more attention than his two younger sisters. He hopes that by behaving perfectly he will make his parents proud of him and thus earn their admiration. He believes that it is his role to be as perfect a child as he can be. He exclaims proudly, "First born, perfect born!"

His mother brings Steven to see me because, as she puts it, she "can't believe he is for real." She is overly polite and proper in dress and manner. The orderliness of my desk and office impress her. Has her own perfectionistic behavior influenced her son? Initially she doesn't see the connection and wonders why Steven, at only 10, is on the compulsive side. He keeps his shoes lined up in the closet and polishes them regularly. His dress shirts hang neatly in the closet. His toys are carefully arranged on shelves according to personal value and weekly usage.

Steven says with assurance, "I like everything in order. I know where to find my stuff without a hassle. I like looking around my room and knowing everything is perfect."

In his clothes drawer, he arranges casual shirts and sweaters from top to bottom, with the newer garments on the bottom so they will be "protected." His few most cherished shirts get special treatment. They are individually placed in plastic bags and kept in a drawer that is opened "for inspection only." Steven explains it this way: "They are too good to wear—I know it sounds crazy but I think if I wear them they will be ruined. A few times a month, I love to open the drawer and look at them. This is enough for me. Maybe on a special day, like my birthday, I will wear one. But not yet."

But there is a darker side to Steven. He flies into a fury if his sisters disturb his toys or enter his room without permission. When playing games of skill with his friends or parents, sometimes he cheats to be sure he comes out on top. He reacts stubbornly when he loses and feels guilty when he doesn't perform well at everything he tries. Although he has little trouble making friends, he confides that he often prefers spending his play time alone, building complicated futuristic space stations of plastic blocks or playing educational games on his parents' personal computer.

Through consultations with Steven's mother, I help her realize that his compulsive orderliness is the natural outcome of her and her husband's desire to have him be the perfect child. He is simply doing his best to mirror what he sees his parents doing and what he thinks they want. Seeing their perfectly ordered closet, he imitates them; seeing his father keep the garage and car spotless, he learns that neatness is valued.

### "Give Me a Break!"

Jonathan, 11, has blond hair and wears typical California beach-style clothes. With a scowl on his face, he appears distressed and mildly depressed. He wishes he had time to relax. In addition to his demanding classes at a private accelerated school, he has a lineup of extracurricular activities that would exhaust any parent responsible for schlepping him around. Yet his parents are the ones who have committed him to so many activities. And they push him to excel in each and every one.

After classes from 8 A.M. to 3 P.M. Jonathan takes karate lessons on Mondays and Thursdays. On Tuesdays and Fridays he practices soccer with his local team for two hours in preparation for the Saturday morning game. On Wednesdays he takes piano lessons and practices for one hour afterward. He practices piano on Sundays for one more hour. To top it all off, he does his homework or reads each evening for at least an hour. With various substitutions, depending on the sport in season and changing interests, he has been involved in this rigorous program of activities since the age of 8.

More recently, his schedule includes visits with me once a week before soccer practice. He has been creating problems at school by interrupting and challenging his teacher, telling her she is "wrong." He also complains of severe stomach problems that his family physician believes are stress related.

In confidence, referring to his parents, Jonathan says, "I know they want me to try a lot of stuff. I know they want me to be the best. I like the soccer and the karate, but the piano lessons and homework suck. Sometimes I wish they'd give me a break and just let me relax for a while."

I ask him why he interrupts his teacher. Without a blink, he looks directly at me and asserts, "Sometimes she doesn't know what she's talking about. I know she's wrong and I can't just sit there and listen to her be wrong. So I say something."

Jonathan doesn't like it when his teacher isn't perfect. But more than this, his drawing attention to himself in class is his way of indicating that he is unhappy with all the structure in his life. Without having to confront his parents directly, it is his way to say, "Stop pushing me so hard!"

## PERFECT SONS AND DAUGHTERS

As chapter 4 and the sections on Horney and Kohut in chapter 5 pointed out, children learn perfectionism from interaction with parents. Children want to earn their parents' love and admiration. The love that ought to be given freely becomes a bartering tool for parents to satisfy their own emotional and psychological needs, as well as a way to shape and control their offspring in ways the parents believe are best for their children.

If there is a family system in which parents have been forced to prove themselves in order to receive love and acceptance from their own parents, this mode of operation is often passed down to the next generation. The common perception is that all children must compete strenuously to achieve the honors and awards that will ultimately gain them entrance into the best schools, the best jobs, and the best social situations. If they lag behind, they lose out.

From their own experience of the harsh realities of the world, parents learn that if they want their children to make something of themselves, they had better instill in them that perfectionistic edge. This means good enough is never enough—nothing less than striving for perfection will fortify the child's ego with sufficient compulsive drive to push beyond the disappointments of life.

So the children discover that, rather than being loved and admired *as they are,* love and approval are exchanged for doing good work and behaving like a perfect child. And the ante can always be raised to a new, higher level: what constitutes acceptable performance may be refined over time to more exacting standards. In this way, children are shaped to strive continually to exceed their previous plateau of achievement. *The result: We never get all the unconditional love we need as children. And we never get all the love and admiration we want as adults.*

There never seems to be enough love, attention, security, or admiration, no matter how giving our parents might have been. As adults, we rarely experience as much respect from others as we'd like, or feel sufficient power to control our environment. When we don't get the necessary parental love and admiration as children, we are more likely to compulsively seek it from peers and elders as we become adults. And yet, since our basic self-image is formed in childhood, nothing we get as adults seems to compensate adequately for the basic lack that we experienced as children.

At birth, we are torn from the oceanic bliss of swimming inside mother's womb.[4] As children, we unconsciously long for the intra-uterine bliss of this perfect oneness with mother. If we're lucky, the trauma of birth is tempered and soothed by the love and devotion shown in the powerful mother-infant bond. We are showered with an all-encompassing devotion to our every need that we wish would last forever. We are forced to relinquish this oneness with mommy as we begin to mature psychologically and become separate from her.[5] Psychologists believe it is in part the unconscious memory of these earlier heavenly conditions that makes the love we receive as we grow up seem never quite enough.

Finally, as growing children we are forced to confront the imperfections inherent in the relations between parent and child. This intrinsic limitation is why child psychologists talk about children needing "good-enough" parenting rather than perfect parenting.

Perfectionism and striving for excellence affect not only those who are compulsively driven to accomplish. As we said before, the dynamics of perfectionism affect, at least to some degree, everyone who is subjected to the values of hard work, progress, success, individualism, and the social status that goes with material accumulation. In addition, we are propelled to strive for excellence by our psychological needs for love and respect and our desire to conform with and yet to stand out from the crowd.

Even those who are hopelessly buried in shame and humiliation, who have given up trying to accomplish anything, have been heavily affected by these same values. They have simply dropped out of the dash for glory. They become the unfortunate "losers" who are left behind by a society that has room at the top only for the best and the brightest, where being average is often viewed as just a notch above failure. And when one is labeled a "loser," it is impossible not to be continually reminded of it, both by one's own self-talk and by the disgrace felt in response to treatment from others.

## Family Patterns

Children may develop neurotic perfectionism from two different kinds of family environments. One is an environment of nonapproval or inconsistent approval; the other is an environment of conditional approval. In the first case, the child never learns to please the parent or is given approval without any apparent rhyme or reason. In the second case, parental approval comes only when the child does the "right" thing.[6]

With regard to the second kind of environment, psychologist Alice Miller noted that clients who were given praise and love primarily for performing activities well as children developed a depressive narcissism in adult life when they did not meet their own standards of perfection. They were capable of giving and receiving love only when they were productive.[7]

In the first type of family setting, we find the roots for what later becomes the deep sense of shame and humiliation that is experienced as a lack of self-worth. The child internalizes the message, "If I am unlovable and unacceptable to my own parents, I must not be worth a damn to anyone else. Therefore, I must be despicable." This shame is believed to be fundamental to many of the common substance addictions and self-destructive behaviors that we try to unlearn as adults. It is this shame and humiliation that we are trying to heal when we try to "love the injured child within."

## Shaping Pigeons and Children

With inconsistent parental approval, children are on a schedule of what psychologists call *intermittent reinforcement*. To use an experimental comparison: A pigeon pecks away with wild abandon at a food-releasing bar, waiting for a pellet of food to drop randomly. Sometimes food might drop three times in a row; other times it doesn't come even after 30 pecks at the bar. Because the reward follows no regular schedule, the pigeon is at a loss to figure out the rules of the game. He doesn't know what it takes to win. So he just keeps pecking away, always hoping the next attempt will deliver the goods.

Such studies teach us that the pigeon will peck much longer with random reinforcement than if it learns that food comes after a precise number of presses of the bar. This knowledge translates into real power to control the pigeon's behavior. But the main thing these studies teach us is that *a little positive reinforcement goes a long way.* With regard to shaping the behavior of perfectionistic children, it is easy to see the power of positive reinforcement in general and intermittent reinforcement in particular. If, for the very same behavior or performance, parents offer approval one time and not the next, or inconsistently give approval unrelated to performance, the child ends up confused, unable to determine the meaning behind the random pay-off schedule. But, like the pigeon, he will try for a long time to figure it out.

Alternatively, if love and approval are given only for a good-enough performance (conditionally), the child will be more inclined to repeat the desired behavior in hopes of getting more emotional nourishment. In both cases, it is the power of the reinforcement itself (love and approval or punishment) that strengthens or weakens the desired behaviors. For the child baffled by inconsistent approval, the lifelong script may be to figure out *what it takes to finally get it right*. For the child caught in conditional approval, the script may be to *finally do it often enough and well enough (perfectly)*.

The child who *never* gets approval eventually learns that the effort is a losing proposition and, in exhaustion and despair, finally gives up. This giving up leads to a learned helplessness and the psychological pessimism we mentioned in chapter 5.

### Approval by Any Other Name

The majority of patients seeking psychotherapy harbor deep, unfulfilled needs to finally "do it right" or "do it often enough" to earn their parents' love. It is not surprising, then, that many writers focus on this central dynamic, each seeing a particular aspect of the need for love and approval as the cause of perfectionistic behavior.

One book, for example, focuses on the problems women have in gaining love from their mothers as infants and adolescents and how this lack of emotional feeding relates to eating disorders and the desire to be perfect women.[8] Another book tells us how important it is for daughters to be loved and accepted by their fathers and cites a high incidence of alcoholism among "perfect daughters" who don't get what they need from dad.[9]

As we mentioned in chapter 5, many other books in the popular recovery movement talk about "healing the child within" or "healing the shame that binds you."[10] No matter what terms are used or what the particular variation may be on parent-child dynamics, the message is the same: *With inconsistent and/or conditional love, adult children will end up looking for more love, seeking some sort of parental "Good Housekeeping Seal of Approval." And most of them will never get it.*

Most parents are influenced by their own fears, needs, hurts, vulnerabilities, and misinformed programming, such as the belief that too much love will spoil the child. Since the unconditional seal of parental approval is nearly impossible to obtain, various permutations of perfectionism inevitably result. This is why almost nobody is completely free from the deep need to be a "good little boy or girl" and to perform perfectly. This need, combined with our spiritual and cultural pressures for perfection, pushes us into the perfection trap. And, as the next section shows, there are yet more factors in this conspiracy toward perfectionism.


## SEDUCTION AND THE PROMISE OF SPECIALNESS

For narcissistic perfectionists, the experience of deep humiliation in childhood is common. Using power as a means of control, parents may use their superior physical strength to control their children, at times by spankings and physical abuse. Children may be criticized in a manner that makes them feel worthless, inadequate, and stupid and serves to prove their parents' superiority. Parents act in a humiliating fashion with their children because this is the way their parents treated them. Children are the easiest and most available objects upon which parents can vent their frustrations and resentments.

After being humiliated, the narcissistic perfectionist is often seduced into seeing himself as special in the eyes of one parent. Seduction may be defined as the use of a false statement or promise to get another person to do what he or she would not otherwise do.

For example, when the relationship between the parents is unfulfilling, mother may turn to her son to supply what her husband cannot give her. She may induce her son to play a role that offers her the excitement of romance; she may subject him to special glances, smiles, and subtle sexual teasing in exchange for a special relationship

that carries a promise of closeness. This promise is a powerful draw
for the child, as he did not receive sufficient intimacy from her in infancy. If he had, he would not be so willing to give up his sense of self
in exchange.

The promise is made when the boy is between the ages of three
and six, during the Oedipal period when his interest in the parent of
the opposite sex is believed to be strongly sexual. The mother ties her
son to her through various subtle suggestive sexual gestures and behaviors. She may allow the boy to watch her dress, or she may treat
him as a confidant and share private feelings and thoughts with him.

To the boy, to be in a special relationship means to be the preferred one, more important than father or brother. The boy knows
his mother needs him, which gives him a grand sense of importance.
This dynamic may operate just as strongly between father and
daughter.

Through the seductive promise of specialness, parents are able to
mold children into their image of what the child should be. Most parents want or need something from their children. Here is how psychiatrist Alexander Lowen puts it:

> For some parents, a child has to be successful in the world, often
> to compensate for the parent's own sense of failure. For others,
> the child has to be outstanding, to achieve some recognition
> that will make the parent feel proud. Too often, parents turn to
> their children for the affection and support they did not receive
> from their own parents and are not getting from their
> spouses. . . . many parents have a need to be superior to their
> children—to make up for the inferiority they felt when they
> were young and from which they still suffer unconsciously. Par-
> ents tend to identify with their children and to project onto
> them their own unfulfilled longings and desires.[11]

A parent's most potent weapon is rejection, or the threat of it.
The child believes that his rejection must be the result of some fault
or failure in himself. Out of a desire to avoid rejection, and drawn by

the lure of specialness, the child complies with his parents' efforts to control and shape him.

Acceptance by the godlike parent boosts the child's ego to the same godlike status, as the child identifies strongly with the parent. (This is an example of Kohut's idea of merging with the perfect selfobject, as we discussed in chapter 5.) The resulting grandiosity is not toned down and incorporated into the child's self-image, as in healthy development. Therefore, this grandiosity still requires strong outside support and, as an adult, the person continues to strive for ultimate perfection (approval).

In adults, this childhood sense of specialness leads to feelings of omnipotence ("I can do anything"), omnipresence ("I am visible everywhere"), omniscience ("I know everything"), and "I am to be worshiped."[12] In other words, the adult feels he or she has the attributes of a god. It is exactly these narcissistic attributes that we find in the messianic leaders of spiritual and religious cults, a variation on the theme of the Atman project (see chapter 6).

These attributes are clearly the stuff of the narcissistic perfectionist, who teeters between surface grandiosity and the fear of exposing a deeper sense of emptiness and shame. Narcissism is a like a dragon with many heads. It shows up in another form in teenagers striving to measure up to their image of perfection.

## COSMETIC SURGERY FOR TEENS

A 1990 news story reported that cosmetic surgery for teenagers in the United States is up 200 to 300 percent in the past two years.[13] Nose jobs are the most popular operation for teens, followed by breast surgery and liposuction. The increase in teenage cosmetic surgery was attributed to a more accepting attitude toward surgery, the role models provided by celebrities, and the increase in advertisements by cosmetic surgeons.

A segment on the TV show "20/20" also looked at the trend

toward cosmetic surgery for children and teenagers. The adolescents and teens seem to think nothing of taking growth hormones. High school girls discuss in detail how operations are performed, having taken the time to analyze the procedures and compare good results with bad. One teen proudly displays the results of her recent breast enlargement, which she received as a high school graduation gift from her parents. She says, "Why not look as perfect as I can?"[14]

As early as junior high school age, teens go in for eye jobs, ear jobs, and chin implants. Many have watched their parents undergo various procedures in an effort to look more attractive. They have naturally decided that what was good for their parents must be good for them. The parents are often supportive or even encouraging of these cosmetic improvements, in keeping with their own narcissistic desire to create the physically perfect family.

Although the show reported that some surgeons turn kids away and suggest psychotherapy instead, there are plenty of surgeons willing to accommodate teens striving for a look that is closer to their image of perfection.

A psychologist, Rita Freedman, was briefly interviewed, sharing her concern about these kids striving for perfection. She views many of them as preoccupied with cosmetically altering minimal physical flaws instead of learning to accept themselves as they are. She asks, "How will these kids feel about their decisions down the road?" The interest in "designer faces," she says, is "pushing kids into a small world as to what is acceptable physically."

## TECHNOSTRESS IN CHILDREN AND TEENS

Technostress (see chapter 3) has been witnessed even in young children. Many computer-involved children and teens suffer from the same mental strain, alteration of time sense, and tyranny of perfectionism experienced by adult computer users.[15] Because parents think that computer skills are advantageous for their children, they often approve when their children are lost in a computer time warp.

They are unaware of the problems children may experience in learning how to shift contexts and relate to family and peers when they come away from heavy computer involvement.

The speed and intensity of computer work heighten the child's sense of engagement. External sensory experience is reduced, the outside world fades, and the child becomes locked into the machine's world. We can see this phenomenon clearly with video games, as they suck the child or teenager into their fast-paced excitement.

For some children, as for some adults, computer use changes inner standards of perfection. They want to measure up to the computer's own standards of perfection and feel frustrated and unhappy when they are unable to. When computer involvement is heavy, the distortion of time and the drive for perfect performance may be unlike any experience young people have had before. Here are some comments from teens involved with computers:

> Don (age 14): Not everything I talk about is about computers. But a lot of it is because my friends know what I'm talking about. I don't have to drag things out a lot with them. But in school, my teachers talk too much. They could say half as much and be more efficient.

> John (age 16): When I write out a program, I can't stand it when I have more than one or two mistakes. I end up feeling like maybe it's not worth going on. Maybe the whole thing isn't worth it.

> Tara (age 15): I hate making any errors. I try getting around it, because sometimes making a mistake destroys what I've done up to that point. I feel like I want to have it come out perfect.

> Danny (age 16): Sometimes it's hard to switch over from programming to being with my family. Work with the computer is like being in a bubble. Once my bubble is broken all the liquid flops out and then I can be outside again. I shake once or twice and I'm back in the real world again, trying to function like normal.

Until the effects of computer overinvolvement have been fully acknowledged and parents take precautionary measures to ensure that kids understand its influences, technostress in children is sure to be an ongoing contributor to perfectionism.

## PERILS OF TEEN PERFECTIONISM

We have already mentioned in other chapters the eating disorders that are associated with children who get caught in the perfection trap. Besides bulimia, anorexia, and overeating, adolescents and teenagers who are used to performing at high levels are prone to various psychosomatic disorders, such as irritable bowel syndrome, colitis, skin problems (including severe acne), and nail biting.

Explosions into anger and rage, overwhelming guilt and shame, nightmares, drug and alcohol abuse, fear of abandonment by parents, and anxiety disorders may all be common symptoms of the underlying pressure to measure up to unrealistically high expectations of performance. When children striving for perfection disappoint themselves or those significant people around them, social withdrawal and depression may easily follow. Severe disappointment and feelings of failure, combined with high frustration, guilt, and a devastating sense that there is "no way out," may lead to suicide attempts, either as cries for help from family and friends or as serious attempts to end one's life.

Many teens express the pressure of their own and their parents' high expectations for accomplishment.

> Gina (age 14): I thought I was hot [at competitive junior tennis] until I started going up against girls who were two or three years older. When I began losing to them, my confidence sank and I felt like a total failure. Even though I knew I was pretty good and had won a lot of tournaments and stuff, I couldn't handle losing to them. I would cry after matches and want to

give up halfway through when I was losing. I got mad if I didn't win every point and I hated myself for not winning every match. So, sometimes I would get drunk with my friends at parties to relieve the pressure. When I was drunk, I could accept losing easier, at least for a while.

Gregory (age 17): I first started drinking beer and vodka and smoking pot at 14 when it suddenly hit me that I would never be as good a surfer as my father. He was really "bitchen" on a board when he was my age and still knows how to do "rad" maneuvers that I can't do. I wanted so much to have him tell me I was good and be proud of me. And all I would get from him was, "Keep tryin'—maybe someday you'll be as good as the ol' man."

Jennifer (age 19): I was totally depressed for months after I didn't get into Stanford. Even though I got into some other good schools, for my parents it was like I had failed. And it rubbed off on me. At one point, I began eating a lot and gained about 20 pounds. But then I got rid of it. I was really miserable. For a while, I felt like maybe they would disown me as their daughter for not making it into the same school they went to.

Ethan (age 18): I won everything in sight in my age group [in competitive junior golf] for a while. Then I started growing and it screwed up my timing—I didn't have the same feel. I got so discouraged that I thought of giving up. I started getting really bad stomach cramps, feeling sick all the time. I knew I was putting a lot of pressure on myself to win, but I just couldn't stop doing it. I got so frustrated I gave up golf for six months and saw a sports psychologist. I learned how to deal with all the pressure I was putting on myself by trying to hit every shot perfectly. Now I feel ready to start playing in tournaments again.

These vignettes suggest the tremendous pressure teens feel to measure up to the expectations of their parents and authority figures as they internalize the perfectionistic thinking of their parents and the larger society. With the degree of stress teens feel—both to be accepted by peers and to please their parents—it is not surprising that growing numbers of them seek temporary relief through drug and alcohol use, sexual experimentation, and various risky behaviors that offer a sense of rebellion and freedom.

The stress of performance pressure also helps us understand why teens begin to question their parents' values even as they try to fit into an adult world, and how easy it is for them to feel alienated when they don't measure up. In an effort to avoid being overwhelmed and smothered by their demanding elders, they search for group rituals and symbols that proclaim their separate identity. The struggle to forge a sense of individuality and uniqueness becomes a paramount need as teens begin to think for themselves in young adulthood.

## Working with the Concepts

Were your parents perfectionistic, demanding, and stingy in their approval-giving? If so, were they inconsistent, nonapproving, or conditionally approving? If you received approval periodically regardless of your performance and could never figure out why you received it some times and not others, you received inconsistent approval. If you received approval only when you performed up to your parents' standards, you received conditional approval. Most deprived are those who *never* received approval, no matter what they did. How do you think your parents' style of approval-giving affected you while growing up? How does it affect you today? How often do your actions aim at winning approval from friends, colleagues, or family? What form does this approval take when you get it? When you don't receive approval after a job well done, how much does your reaction resemble the way you used to feel with your parents?

As a child, were you ever treated as special by one of your parents? If so, how do you think this special relationship affects you today? Often, children who were treated as special by one or both parents end up believing the world ought to treat them the same way.

Is this true for you? If so, what form of entitlement does your specialness take? Do you feel you deserve special privilege from others?
How do you react when you are not accorded this special treatment?
What fantasies do you have of receiving special treatment from the
world? In what ways do you feel unappreciated for your skills, talents, knowledge, personal qualities, or accomplishments? How do
you imagine your life would be different if you were getting all the
acknowledgment from others you believe you deserve?

As a parent, are you overly perfectionistic? To avoid perfectionism in parenting, practice the following.

1. Give consistent and unconditional approval for small and
   large tasks accomplished by your children regardless of
   their level of performance.

2. Tell your children often how much they mean to you and
   how much you love them. Assure them that your love for
   them is not dependent on what they accomplish. Follow
   through with congruent behavior. If you withhold affection or approval when your children do not excel, they will
   not believe your words.

3. Encourage them to do their best and gently push them to
   learn new skills, have new experiences that will help them
   grow, and gain new knowledge that will increase their self-
   confidence, body image, and optimism about the world and
   their future in it.

4. Support their projects by showing interest and encouragement regardless of how skilled or unskilled they may be.

5. Participate in their projects. Show them that you care
   enough to become involved in what is of interest to them.
   In doing so, you demonstrate that the process of sharing the
   activity means as much as the end goal of completion or
   any judgments as to level of expertise.

6. Don't expect your children to master the same skills you have, and don't show disappointment if they choose not to follow in your footsteps.

7. Don't continually criticize your children for every small mistake or imperfection. They are already berating themselves for any perceived shortcomings, and they don't need you on their backs in addition to the burden they are already carrying.

8. Don't give inconsistent approval based on whim or conditional approval based on performance.

9. Don't use your children to live out your own unfulfilled dreams and fantasies of greatness, fame, or fortune.

10. Don't manipulate your children to make up for your own perceived character flaws or inadequacies. Allow them to focus on taking care of themselves.

11. Don't believe the nonsense about giving children too much love or praise, especially in their early years. They can never get too much, nor can they be spoiled by real love and affection.

# EIGHT

# ADULT CHILDREN OF PERFECTIONISTIC FAMILIES:
## *Beyond the Approval Game*

*My love she speaks softly*
*She knows there's no success like failure*
*And that failure's no success at all.*
BOB DYLAN, "Love Minus Zero/ No Limit"

IN THE LAST CHAPTER we saw how perfectionistic parents, using the child's powerful needs for love, acceptance, and admiration, control their children through the promise of specialness, the threat of rejection, and inconsistent or conditional approval. We will now look more closely at the consequences of this early behavior shaping on family relationships of the adult child.

How do adult children of perfectionists relate to their parents? How do they relate to their siblings? What can they do to gain control of their desire to please their parents? How can they move from feeling dependent, needful of approval, and vulnerable to their family's judgments to feeling like secure, independent, and self-possessed adults?

## WHY THE ADULT CHILD LABEL?

Ascribing the label of "adult children" to those distressed by a particular problem has in recent years been prevalent in self-help literature, especially that of the 12-step recovery movement. The term refers to people suffering from a common set of psychological problems caused originally by the behavior of their parents. The popularization of the adult child label has spawned a host of spin-off groups, some of which assume clinical problems where none exist. Therefore I use this label cautiously, not wanting to generate yet another recovery program, this time for "Adult Children of Perfectionistic Parents."

Nonetheless, when it comes to hard-core perfectionism, the label of adult children is accurate and valuable. To reiterate a main point from the last chapter: The single emotional need or desire that most pervades the minds of children—especially perfectionistic children—is the unmet need for love, approval, and admiration from their parents. For most of us, the love and acceptance we received was based conditionally on performance; it was not given often enough simply for our intrinsic goodness and uniqueness. Because of this, those who do not escape from the perfection trap continue the unending pursuit of the perfect performance, with the hope of finally receiving the ultimate, unconditional approval.

Because the desire for parental approval is so strong, we refuse to accept the evidence that we just aren't going to get it. In my consulting room, I hear the same scenario repeatedly. As adults, we have learned through arduous psychological and emotional work to value ourselves, overcoming the inadequacies we experienced as children. As we mature we gradually gain self-acceptance, self-worth, and a growing independence from our parents. We make our way in the world financially and psychologically. We may raise children of our own. And yet, when we visit our parents' home, we find ourselves in much the same place of emotional need as when we were children. As our parents unthinkingly begin to criticize, all our hard-won independence, security, and self-worth begin to weaken. In the face of our parents' sometimes subtle assaults on our personhood, we find ourselves fighting merely to maintain our sense of adult identity. We feel under attack and struggle to avoid either passively withdrawing or impulsively lashing out in self-defense.

That is how we become adult children of perfectionists. We become the next generation of perfectionists, trying to measure up to those who have shaped us and taught us how to play the game.

## Social and Economic Family Status

In addition to the conditional and inconsistent parental approval-giving identified in the last chapter, the family's social and economic background may contribute to motivations toward perfectionism. In lower-middle- or middle-class upwardly mobile families, the emphasis may be on striving for more but never quite making it. In upper-middle- and upper-class families, perfectionism is expected to lead to high accomplishment, and success is the status quo. In this group the next generation may be viewed as insurance, expected to consolidate gains already made and further entrench the family's social and economic power.

In the case of the upwardly striving family, adult children of perfectionistic parents represent the hope of breaking through the social, cultural, educational, and economic barriers that their parents could not fully penetrate. Adult children are expected to have it better than their parents did, and each generation is viewed as pushing the extended family toward greater economic comfort and higher social status.

Adult children from this type of background learn that it is never enough merely to duplicate their parents' efforts. They are expected to surpass them, building on the foundation provided by their parents, who have sacrificed to provide their children material comforts. The image typifying this scenario might be one of adult children standing on the shoulders of their parents, who in turn stand on the shoulders of *their* parents. This progression, with each generation expected to outdo the former, continues until relative prosperity, social status, and cultural freedom are attained—and even beyond, becoming the perfectionism of the upper class. The push beyond excellence toward perfection is viewed as the extra effort necessary to compete with the more advantaged.

In the upper-class scenario, adult children of perfectionistic parents are not so much expected to stand on the shoulders of their parents but to stand alongside them, shoulder-to-shoulder. These families have already made it and don't want to lose any ground. Adult children are viewed as possessors of superior intellectual, creative, or anatomical genes who are expected to carry on the family's good name in the business, professional, and social worlds. They are expected to make good use of the splendid opportunity provided by the hard work and/or inheritance of their cultured and established parents.

## RELATING TO PARENTS

Regardless of socioeconomic background, perfectionistic parents tend to be highly critical of their adult children. When they are with their parents, adult children are often overly cautious in what they say and do in an effort to avoid criticism. At the same time, they may try to do whatever they think will gain their parents' approval. As they become aware of both their cautiousness and their desire to please, adult children soon find themselves feeling fearful and exasperated, just as they did as children. They are fearful of the criticism they have come to expect and exasperated at their inability to get more than token approval.

For example, Lenore, 35, is a marriage counselor, an accomplished pianist, and happily married with one child. She is a physically striking woman with big brown eyes and auburn hair. She comes to me with concerns about her relationship with her perfectionistic parents. She says she "falls apart" when she visits them.

When I walk through the door I'm in control. But it doesn't take more than a few minutes before one of them is picking at me for something. Too much this or not enough that—they always find something to start harping on. I'm successful, feel good about myself, strive to do my best, and obviously have attained a level of accomplishment in my life. But it's like I become an insecure kid all over again. If it's not "you're a little overweight" it's "why don't you buy some new clothes? You're looking a little shabby." What—I don't look good enough? I can't walk down the street without men doing a double take and making lewd comments when they see me! Yet, never can my parents just tell me they think I'm beautiful, accomplished, and that they love me. I get so frustrated I either end up screaming at them or feeling terrible and withdrawing. Either way, I end up miserable and want to leave. And then, to top it off, my mother wonders why I don't call or visit more often!

As the adult child of perfectionistic parents, Lenore bears both the emotional scars and the accomplishments of being pushed to be the best. Knowing she looks good and that her weight is not a problem, she has long since learned not to take her mother's words regarding her weight seriously. She has also learned not to take seriously her father's criticism of the wide latitude she allows her own child in diet and dress. But Lenore is unable to control her reactions to her parents when she walks back into the house in which she grew up. Guilt over not being good enough is reinforced by the old setting with which it was originally associated.

In Lenore's work with me, we concentrate on helping her feel more in control in her parents' home. She is learning to limit the amount of time she spends there, to not feel guilty in refusing to visit when she is not up to it, and to refrain from discussing with her parents certain issues that can only lead to argument. She learns that saying "no" need not be associated with someone else's judgment or disapproval—and that even if it is, she need not worry about it.

We discuss ways for Lenore to respond to her parents' criticisms from the perspective of an adult rather than that of an injured child.

This last issue is crucial for adult children. They must be able to maintain their emotional strength and reinforce the hard-won knowledge that they need not measure up to their parents' demands, rather than become overly identified with their injured, guilty, and humiliated child who only wants parental approval.

Warner, 42, loves to laugh. He is an attractive man who finds humor in the absurdities of everyday life. He comes from a wealthy, old-money family. His parents were overly formal, demanding, and emotionally distant; they entrusted his early care to a series of nurses and nannies. Meals were taken in a formal dining room where the children were expected to dress up and relate in a stiff and stilted manner. Warner's parents had unrealistically high expectations as to how well he ought to do in the private schools and colleges he attended. Never a high achiever in school, Warner saw his more academically oriented brothers and sisters receive what little recognition his self-involved and emotionally withholding parents had available.

Warner learned that if he couldn't earn his share of attention by measuring up to his parents' high standards, he could get it another way—by failing. He consistently received failing grades in each prep school he attended and ended up on probation. This would create an uproar with his parents, who blamed either the teachers or headmaster for their son's poor performance. When blaming didn't work, they would entice the administrators by making a contribution to the school in hopes of buying Warner a reprieve from expulsion. Despite his promises and cursory efforts to improve, Warner continued getting kicked out of various prep schools and colleges.

Like many children—rich or poor—whose attempts for recognition are thwarted, Warner consciously decided he would get attention from his parents any way he could. He learned that "there's no success like failure," as a Bob Dylan song puts it. But the resulting attention came in such a disgraceful form that Warner ended up feeling uncared for by his parents and with little self-confidence or self-respect. And, as the next line of the song continues, "failure's no success at all."

Because of the family wealth, Warner did not have to worry about making a living. He claimed not to think or care about his family's wealth during his early years of school failures. Never having lived up to his parents' expectations or gained their approval, Warner lacked any desire to push for success as an adult. Beyond managing to complete military service, he had few accomplishments of which to feel proud. After the service, he dropped out of college just before completing his degree. After receiving his inheritance, he invested in a number of marginal business ventures that brought him little personal satisfaction. He had every advantage that money could buy but was unable to find direction or set goals in his life.

As an adult, he still hoped to please his father. But after numerous attempts met with rejection and disappointment, Warner eventually distanced himself from his father and gave up trying. Then, through long-term psychotherapy, he gained the courage to personally confront his father and tell him how he felt neglected. After this confrontation, Warner felt stronger and much less needy of his father's attention. He could be with his father on occasional visits without wanting anything from him. Because of his early economic independence, the fact that he was not a perfectionist himself, and the insight gained from psychotherapy, Warner became an exception to the usual cycle of adult children of perfectionistic parents continuing forever to strive to please their parents.

## RELATING TO SIBLINGS

Compounding the difficulties of relating to their parents, adult children of perfectionists must also relate to their often perfectionistic siblings. The normal sibling rivalry that is found in all families, especially between children close in age, is intensified in families with perfectionistic parents. The competition to be the best-performing child in the family, in hopes of winning the lion's share of parental approval and admiration, often creates bitter rivalries that may overshadow more loving, cooperative, and supportive feelings. Usually the oldest child is expected to outperform the younger ones and is set up as the model to emulate.

I can remember my father pitting my brother Timmy, one year younger than I, against me in swimming races. We were both fairly fast swimmers, and my father wanted us to go head-to-head to continually improve our speed. We would often compete in short sprint races until we were exhausted, or swim 15 laps to see who had the best endurance. When we weren't racing against each other, we were taking turns diving to catch red dice that my father would toss into the deep end of the pool. The object was to come up with the dice before they hit the bottom. He would complicate the game by making us wait before diving in, until there was just enough time to swoop up the dice before they landed. When I beat my brother in these contests, I felt I was doing what was expected. When I lost, I felt I hadn't measured up. Too much of the time, it didn't feel like friendly competition. Instead, I felt like I was competing with my brother for our father's attention. As a reminder of those days, I kept the red dice. I still have them today, more than 30 years later.

## Jealousy and Envy

The core issues for perfectionistic siblings are the unrelenting competitiveness, jealousy, and envy that color relationships as the children become adults. Who has the most education, the highest income and job status? Who is married to the best-looking and richest husband? Who wears the most expensive and fashionable clothes? Who has the fanciest home, nicest car, smartest children, or takes the most exotic vacations? These are the yardsticks by which competitive perfectionistic siblings measure who's on top in the family hierarchy.

Siblings may compare the price of material goods purchased, quibble about the quality of possessions, or criticize the good fortune, recognition, or advantage gained by a sibling. Envy blocks the sibling's ability to feel sympathetic joy for what another accomplishes. *When one sibling gains in status, the competitive sibling experiences diminishment of himself.*

Among perfectionistic siblings, behavior expressing the need to feel superior and gain favor in the eyes of parents can take rather vicious forms. For example, there is a clear psychological need in many perfectionistic families to carve down to size the sibling who gains too much attention for an accomplishment. Initially, siblings may genuinely identify with and praise the sibling receiving recognition. However, should the achiever appear to feel too good for too long, family members (including parents) often become uncomfortable with the enhanced status and attention the achiever is enjoying. This leads to unconscious resentment and envy. They may then begin to pick at the achiever, to find her flaws and weaknesses, reminding her that she really isn't so special after all. Of course, no one is in a better position to attack the soft underbelly of one's deepest feelings of inadequacy than those who know her best—her family. The one who stands out too far above the family will not stand out for long. Competitive family members will always find a way to bring her down from her elevated status and thereby reestablish the balance of family power.

## BEYOND THE APPROVAL GAME

As adult children, how can you go beyond the desire to win your parents' love and approval? How can you begin to stand on your own feet, independent of your parents' critical, never-enough judgments?

*You must give up the hope that you will ever receive unconditional love and approval.* If you retain the fantasy that your parents are withholding their love until you perform perfectly, you will continue to be disappointed. This does not mean you must give up the *need* for love. You can hold the need but at the same time realize it will never be fulfilled by your parents. Staying in touch with the need for love will enable you to seek its satisfaction from others in your life, including yourself. *We can learn to give to ourselves much of the unconditional approval that we seek from others.*

You must come to a deep understanding of this unfortunate truth: *Your parents simply don't have the capacity to unconditionally express love and approval.* To really comprehend this means to shift the focus from earning from your parents what they don't have, to learning positive ways of giving to yourself and getting from others who *do* have the capacity to give.

As part of this understanding, you must realize that as an adult, your self-esteem and self-worth are no longer dependent on whether your parents express love and approval toward you. It is not your fault they are unable to express unconditional love and open their hearts to you. If you recognize this, you can then sever the internal connection between your performance and winning their approval. You must realize that you are a unique, valuable, and lovable person even if your parents are unable to reaffirm this to you.

*You must give up any guilt and regret you may feel for not winning parental approval.* As a child, you interpreted the withholding of love as an indication that you were unworthy or undeserving of love. You never questioned whether your parents *had* love to give—you assumed they did. Thus you felt guilty for your unworthiness and made unremitting efforts to perform perfectly to win their unconditional love. Now, in realizing your parents were unable to show such love, you can let go of any guilt for what you believed was your unworthiness. This, in turn, makes it easier to give up the need to prove yourself to your parents. Typically, the initial progression goes like this, each step leading to the next.

1. Frustration of the child's normal need for parental love (given inconsistently, conditionally, or not at all), accompanied by parental criticism of the child's efforts.

2. Feelings of badness, unworthiness, guilt, frustration, and confusion.

3. Intensified efforts by the child to perform perfectly to become good and win approval.

4. Continued frustration and confusion at the parents' lack of response, inconsistent response, or conditional response to the child's performance efforts.

5. A deep sense of shame and regret at never proving oneself as good enough; continued hope that striving for perfect performance will win unconditional love and approval and thus establish self-worth.

6. The adult child's continued reaction to parents as if still a vulnerable, dependent child, filled with regret, resentment, and self-doubt.

In moving beyond the need for parental approval, the progression goes like this:

1. The adult child's deep realization and acceptance that parents cannot or will not give unconditional love and approval.

2. Giving up hope that perfect performance will ever lead to the payoff of unconditional love and approval.

3. The insight that the failure to gain love and approval occurred not because one was bad or unworthy but because the parents were unable to show love.

4. Giving up feelings of badness and accompanying guilt.

5. Giving up the compulsive need to prove oneself through striving for perfection.

6. Establishing inner self-worth based on a deep realization of one's inherent uniqueness and worth independent of external accomplishments.

7. Striving for excellence and self-actualization to enhance feelings of self-integrity and inner strength.

*Find others who can reaffirm your lovability, goodness, and self-worth.* These may include a marriage partner, lover, friends, colleagues, children, siblings, grandparents, in-laws, or parent substitutes like bosses or mentors whom you respect and who have a genuine interest in you.

Since we have been conditioned to unconsciously express our needs for love and approval through performance, it is not easy for adult children of perfectionists to consciously, openly, and verbally express needs to others. It is important to begin experimenting with asking directly for what you need, no matter how threatening this expression may feel initially. To lessen your fear of rejection, choose people who you think are willing to play this part in your life and are capable of openly expressing love and approval. Otherwise you will only repeat the same disappointing experience you had with your parents.

*Continue to develop inner strength and self-approval.* Nurture your own goodness, uniqueness, and value. Honor both your inherent worth as a person and your accomplishments. Continue to strengthen the realization that, while gaining recognition for your projects can make you feel proud and enhance self-esteem, it is not necessary in order for you to feel your inherent value. Whether or not you receive recognition for your projects, your very existence in this world is inherently meaningful.

These suggestions for moving beyond the need for parental approval do not tell us how to relate to perfectionistic parents and siblings as an adult. Of course, even when we realize that we are not going to get unconditional love and approval from family members, we still may want to relate to them. Our realization will serve to put our relationship on a more adult-to-adult rather than parent-to-child basis, since we will not be as cautious, fearful of criticism, or needy of approval. We will be more able to be ourselves, without the need to be calculating or manipulative.

### Relating to Parents and Siblings: Strategies

*Feel in control, act in control.* Do not give in to your parents' or siblings' conscious or unconscious efforts to provoke childlike, impulsive responses. Parents' critical remarks may be attempts to gain control by stimulating old dependency feelings. Siblings' critical remarks may be aimed at reviving competitive feelings. You will always be vulnerable to feelings and behaviors that reflect defensiveness, a sense of inadequacy, or lack of control. Remember that you do not need your parents' and siblings' approval for anything you do, and so there is no need to revert to defensive behavior. With this realization, they can say whatever they want without provoking a defensive response on your part.

*Defuse insulting or cruel remarks.* Should a parent or sibling purposely taunt you, you can assert yourself. You might say, "You seem to want to put me down. Why?"

Suppose your mother says, "You need to lose some weight." You can say, "Thank you for your concern about me, but if I lose weight it'll have to be for myself, not for you." Show your mother you will not be provoked by her taunt and that you can even agree with her, while making it clear that any effort at change will not be due to her remarks.

Realize that in their own misguided way, many perfectionistic parents are trying to show their concern through critical remarks they hope will "improve" you. Many families have never learned to relate in a more complimentary, compassionate, and direct manner.

Sometimes, when defusing will not do the job, it is necessary to directly confront insults from parents or siblings by telling them in a firm voice that you will not listen to any more. You can demand that they stop berating you, or choose to leave their company if they persist. You must decide in each case what the most appropriate response might be. Sometimes direct confrontation is the only way to take care of yourself. Be aware that this setting of boundaries may meet with resistance from family members who have come to expect a more passive response from you. In chapter 12 we will discuss in detail the setting of boundaries in relating to perfectionists.

*Resist pleasing and placating behavior; try self-assertion.* To defuse insulting or cruel remarks does not mean to offer pleasing and placating responses in hopes of gaining approval. Placating responses are phony and often make you feel like a child, whereas defusing is an adult response that implies a refusal to become ensnared in a trap that is being set with the bait of provocative remarks. Pleasing and placating are characteristic of self-denying or self-hurtful tendencies that often lead to pessimism and depression.

*Resist withdrawal and avoidance; stay engaged and confront your discomfort.* For some adult children, the preferred mode of self-protection to criticism is withdrawal and avoidance. Withdrawal is exemplified most clearly in those who cannot tolerate raised voices and will immediately leave the room if there is an argument or if they feel slighted. Avoidance behaviors may be aimed at staying away from parents and siblings altogether.

Avoidance usually leads to further deterioration of family relationships. When feelings of hurt remain unexpressed, anger and resentment build, and the triggering incident may be magnified in memory. This may lead to eventual explosion out of proportion to the original incident. At its worse, avoidance may lead to complete breakdown of all communication. You may lose all interest in resolving resentments with family members, or you may wish to punish them by silent treatment.

Although there are times when complete avoidance is warranted (for example, if your parents inflict violence or you are the victim of incest), avoidance is often an attempt to sidestep the responsibility to face the unpleasant feelings that surface in working through family emotional difficulties. Guilt and regret often result from prolonged avoidance.

*Resist blaming and attacking behaviors; preserve your integrity and the integrity of the other.* Unless you are prepared for direct confrontation with parents, try not to fall prey to blaming them or attacking them, no matter how much they may provoke you. Blaming and attacking only lead to further animosity, chronic anger, and bitterness. Standing up for yourself does not have to mean blaming the other, nor does assertiveness require attacking the other. This is one of the hardest areas of behavior for adult children (if they are not the pleasing and placating type) to control. It is very tempting to lash out at your brother after he has poured out his own venom at you. Staying at the adult ego level means firmly holding your own without indulging in the same childlike behavior.

You might say, "I have listened to you lash out at me for five minutes now and don't like what you are saying. I don't know why you are trying to hurt me and I'm doing my best not to get sucked in by your taunts. But I will not continue listening to you if you can't talk to me with more respect."

*Resist controlling and conniving behaviors. Be honest and direct, and control only yourself.* Attempts at controlling others through manipulative, deceptive maneuvers will not help you to feel the integrity and true strength you are looking for. You do not need to be clever or cunning in order to outfox your parents' or siblings' critical judgments. You need to realize that your own self-worth is not dependent on their (or anyone else's) evaluations. Following this realization, you can drop much manipulative behavior.

*Give plenty of genuine compliments to parents and siblings.* Model healthy interactions for them. Give compliments freely, rather than being emotionally stingy. Demonstrate that it is possible to give compliments without feeling lessened because you helped someone else feel *more.* Give compliments especially for good-enough behavior, showing that perfect performance is not required for the payoff of a compliment.

*Stay alert to subtle invitations to move the relationship to a deeper level.* Sometimes, in families where direct messages of need and vulnerability are too risky, members offer subtle and indirect invitations that allow windows of possibility for deepening the relationship. An invitation to take a walk to the market may be your mother's way of saying she wants to make a more intimate connection with you. A brother who invites you to a basketball game may be saying he misses you and wants to share more with you. Be aware that many families of perfectionists send such indirect messages, and be open to deciphering them.

*Don't expect too much; be satisfied with small positive changes in family relationships.* Remember that family dynamics have taken a lifetime (and often longer) to create and are not likely to change radically. Be satisfied with small indications that parents and siblings are treating you with more respect, have gained more awareness of your hard-won boundaries, and are somewhat less competitive, envious, or jealous. Modeling an acceptance of your parents' and siblings' psychological and emotional hang-ups might make it easier for them to do the same for you.

If you can begin to let go of the need to be superior to your siblings and, at the same time, can allow your parents simply to be the limited and imperfect people they are—*whether or not they can do the same for you*—you can transcend the approval game that has dominated family dynamics. It doesn't happen overnight. But with growing awareness, you can modify your automatic reactions with family members. Identifying with your strong and capable adult self that is not dependent on parental approval, you can respond in ways that enhance self-respect and integrity. You can escape the adult child's never-ending search for love and approval.

Over the long term, your own self-knowledge, self-caring, and self-forgiving will enable you to be less defensive and more able to accept parental and sibling relationships for what they are. Part of maturity and self-healing is learning to appreciate whatever you *can* get from your family members and not focusing so much on what you *can't* get.

It seems to be a simple truth that the better you feel about yourself, the more understanding and compassionate you can be of perfectionistic family members. Realizing how hard you have been on yourself and learning to forgive yourself gives you more compassion for those you care about, who must also deal with their own perfectionistic demons. You might reinforce this with the following affirmation: "I am not perfect and my family is not perfect. I can be loving and accepting of their imperfections and they can be loving and accepting of mine." Or, as the Zen master Suzuki Roshi put it, "Find perfection in imperfection."

# NINE

# Climbing the Ladder of Success:
## *The Perfectionist at Work*

*Act without doing; work without effort.*
*Think of the small as large, and the few as many.*
*Confront the difficult while it is still easy;*
*Accomplish the great task by a series of small acts.*
Tao Te Ching

## Work: The Perfectionist's Proving Ground

As perfectionists, we view work as the proving ground for how we compare to others. It is within the arena of work that we hope to stand out from our colleagues and competitors who are less perfectionistic and less dedicated. Our competitive drive is often welcomed and positively reinforced in the work world. Through our dazzling performance, we hope to gain self-esteem, recognition, financial reward, status, approval, and admiration from others.

As in all other areas of perfectionism, we have unrealistic expectations as to what we should accomplish at work. We feel guilty and regretful if we don't measure up. Blaming our own inadequacy, we try harder and work longer. Because we are driven by the belief that doing a perfect job will bring us the respect and admiration from others that we long for, we are willing to sacrifice ourselves in all sorts of ways before the god of perfection.

As we saw in chapter 3, we may suffer burnout, various stress-related diseases and disorders, addictions, and poor work relationships in our undivided pursuit of reaching the top of the ladder of success. We may give up much or all of our free time, devoting our lives to the job, if our dedication promises to bring us the hoped-for satisfaction of being viewed as the best. We may allow our personal relationships with family and friends to deteriorate through neglect in our drive for work achievement.

### Fueling Work Perfectionism: Anxiety and Fear

Andrew was a highly successful perfectionistic executive who headed a Fortune 500 corporation. He had moved up the management ladder for over 20 years. His dedication, political maneuvering, striving to get ahead, and willingness to give up much of his personal life to work-related travel had ultimately paid off. He commanded a salary of over $300,000 per year along with various stock options and company perks. He had tickets on the 50-yard line for the Los Angeles Rams and corporate seats to watch the Los Angeles Lakers. He was a member of an exclusive private country club, where he played golf. He drove a $70,000 customized car. He traveled with his wife every year—to Europe or anywhere else they wanted to go.

Andrew's name was listed among the benefactors on a wall of honor at the local performing arts center. His wife was a well-known socialite who donated time and large amounts of money to various charities. By anyone's standards, Andrew had made it into that small circle reserved for the "movers and shakers" of the corporate world. He had everything in the way of material comforts and possessions that anyone could want. He was healthy. His children were on their own and doing well.

And yet, at age 57, just at the point in life when he thought he should be reaping the benefits of all those years of hard work, Andrew was not satisfied with his accomplishments. He came to see me because he didn't feel he was enjoying his life the way he ought to. Although he had all the material things he had ever wanted and a life that most people could only dream of, his success didn't give him the sense of joy and deep satisfaction he had hoped it would. Many of his social activities felt empty and phony. He put it this way:

> I never really seemed to be focused on where I was in my race to the top. I was always looking forward, to the next big deal or next promotion. As soon as I reached one plateau, I couldn't stop and enjoy it; I had to go like hell to outdo myself and everyone else around me. That became the game—to outdo myself no matter what it took. When I look back on it, I can see how afraid I was of not making it; I can see how anxious and driven I was and how much I was willing to give up just to get the glory of making it to the top. I was always afraid of not having enough money, of struggling like my father did just to take care of the bills. And I was afraid that my life wouldn't amount to much if I didn't strive to be the best. Excellence for me was taken for granted—I wanted everything to be perfect.

As we worked together, Andrew began to face his fear that the bottom would drop out of his motivation to be productive if he gave up seeking perfection. He had used the goal of being the best to keep him moving forward for so long that he couldn't imagine letting go of it. In his words:

> I get anxious when I think of giving up the goal of perfection. Even though I don't think I'm feeling the joy in life that I ought to, it scares me to think of not having that end goal to shoot for—the goal of being perfect. I know that I can't achieve complete perfection but I still use it as the target. I have used it pretty well, I believe. Without seeking perfection, what would I use as the goal to keep me productive, to keep achieving more?

So, don't ask me to stop striving for perfection unless you've got
something better to replace it with.

That "something better" became the pursuit of personal satisfaction and happiness beyond making more money or obtaining more
power. It was not until Andrew understood that being productive was
no longer what he really needed that he began to entertain giving up
perfection-seeking. He began to see that business productivity and
success did not necessarily lead to his feeling any happier. Once he
made a clear-cut decision to change, he began to enjoy donating time
to groups that needed help with business management. He was able
to use the same focused concentration he had applied to business to
seek deeper personal satisfaction.

He also began pursuing hobbies, like the study of history and
sailing, that he had neglected for years. He began to play golf more
often during the week. He got more and more comfortable with the
image of himself as semiretired, even at his rather young age. While
he didn't give up his position as CEO, he drastically cut back on the
amount of time he spent at the office. He learned to delegate more
responsibility to other executives and to enjoy more of his time in
non-work-related activities. He learned how to feel good about himself without having to chase a goal.

## Other Examples of Work Perfectionists

Bill, age 36, comes to see me because he feels disconnected from others and suffers from insomnia. He sleeps only five hours per night.
He sells microcomputers to corporations. He has set himself a quota
of selling at least 15 computers per week, and feels like a failure if for
any reason he does not meet it. He prides himself on being able to sell
companies more computers and more elaborate peripherals than
they really need. He speaks of his clients as "fools" for not understanding the technical aspects of the product. He reveals gleefully
how he will lie, if necessary, to make a big sale.

Elaine, age 38, when not on her car phone, listens to self-help tapes while driving because she has no time to sit down and read the books on which they are based. She works for a large company that sells copying machines. She prides herself on winning the Hawaii vacation prize each year for the highest gross sales. When colleagues criticize her for being too aggressive, she takes offense and feels misunderstood. Privately, she admits to feeling like she could "fall apart at any minute," but she always presents a polished facade to customers and colleagues. While successful at her job, she fears that she is unable to love a man and complains that she expects too much from all men. She fears becoming married to her work.

Corina, age 33, manages a legal office. She can't stand to see anything in the office the least bit out of place. She spends much time in therapy complaining about having to check the work of secretaries, file and refile legal folders, pick up after sloppy attorneys, and make sure the waiting room is spotlessly clean. When these tasks are not performed to her exacting specifications, she gets anxious and angry at her co-workers. She believes she should be working at a job with more prestige, not "playing mother to immature attorneys," but lacks the training for the kind of work she would like. Her husband, who suggested she seek therapy, struggles to tolerate her obsessive-compulsive neatness and her bossing him around.

Mitch, age 43, is a marriage counselor who believes he ought to be highly respected by his colleagues and appreciated for his "outstanding mind." Mitch complains that he can't get any respect from peers. He writes articles that no journal will publish and offers workshops that no one attends. His papers, which he brings for me to read, are not of the high quality he imagines. He barely makes ends meet after many years of struggle in private practice and feels terribly bitter that so many therapists who are, as he puts it, "inferior to me in brains and talent" are able to develop successful practices. A clear tone of envy comes through when he criticizes the business practices and ethics of his peers. He is a self-professed perfectionist who never comes close to measuring up to his ideal but is always quick to blame others for his misfortune. His perfectionism has created chronic frustration, self-pity, regret, and depression.

Frank, age 39, is a consultant who owns a small firm that deals with taxes and real estate. He boasts how much money he earns and how he often works more than 50 hours per week. He has trouble relating to women and has never married. He enjoys arguments but dreads hearing criticism. Frank prides himself on being an expert at most of his hobbies, and drives a sports car fast and recklessly. He spends his money on technical gadgets, clothes, and art. He considers it a virtue to "live for today" and makes no plans for the future. In fact, he is not sure he wants to live to old age. Below the surface, he has strong resentments and anger that he won't express; he gets depressed easily and sometimes turns to drugs.

The above examples show some of the consequences of perfectionism in work. Let's look at the contrast between perfectionism and the pursuit of work excellence.

## PERFECTIONISM VERSUS EXCELLENCE AT WORK

*Motivation.* Striving for perfection at work is usually motivated by fear and anxiety, even when actual performance may be high. Those perfectionists lacking self-confidence often view work as the arena in which they will at last be found out as insufficiently competent. They are fearful of being judged by superiors. Being held accountable for their efforts brings up memories of rejection by parents and other authority figures. Because of their all-or-nothing thinking, perfectionists know that the odds are they will fall short of their self-imposed mark. They often dread the actual performance of work tasks, even though they may be skilled at them.

Excellence-strivers, in contrast, enjoy the challenge of performing at a high level and are motivated by pride and satisfaction in a job well done. They view feedback from superiors as an opportunity to validate their competence as well as to learn how to improve their performance. They usually enjoy the actual performance of work tasks. They are motivated by pride, integrity, and a desire for accomplishment in addition to the rewards of money, status, and peer respect.

*Relationships with co-workers.* The work perfectionist often feels threatened and thwarted by peers and colleagues, whom he fears may outperform him. He fears that co-workers may take away something that he feels he rightly deserves—the bonus, the perks, the promotion, or special recognition by the boss. He tends not to identify himself with the company or team, preferring to put his energy and attention into self-promotion and individual productivity.

For the work perfectionist, competitive feelings are strong, and he may cover his anxiety and envy with ridiculing, backbiting, and being sharply critical of peers. Scheming to make others look bad may be a ploy of the desperate perfectionist. It is difficult for the perfectionist to engage in cooperative tasks with peers and co-workers. Lack of communication and teamwork result in decreased productivity and enjoyment of work.

Another form this competitiveness may take is the denial of errors. The perfectionist may lie to himself and to others when he does make mistakes. He may try to hide his errors to avoid appearing inadequate or being reprimanded. When we feel pressure to deny or hide our mistakes, we are unable to learn from them. When we cannot acknowledge our mistakes, we lose the benefits of honest and open self-disclosure that contributes to team-oriented problem-solving.

High achievers striving for excellence, fueled by a more genuine sense of self-confidence and ego strength, are far less threatened by co-workers. While they may at times feel some envy of those who perform at a higher level, this envy only serves to bring out their best to meet the challenge.

Their personal relationships with peers are more positive, less critical, and more cooperative. They know how to join forces and share ideas and skills with co-workers to accomplish the required task. They are able to appreciate the skills and ingenuity of peers. They are less suspicious and paranoid of the motives of others, able to share their mistakes more openly, and therefore form more satisfying work relationships.

In the pursuit of excellence, competitive feelings tend to be expressed more in good-natured joking and teasing with peers rather than in the perfectionist's hostile put-downs or scheming. Workers striving for excellence compliment peers for a job well done and have learned that getting along with others is more likely to further their own careers than going it alone or creating enemies. On a company level, when the emphasis is on excellence rather than perfectionism, the competitive impulse is directed toward other companies rather than dividing the company against itself. Productivity is increased, employee turnover lessened, and morale enhanced.

*Holding grudges.* Anxiety-driven work perfectionists are compulsive score-keepers. They know exactly who has blocked the way on their climb to the top and they won't forgive these people easily, nor will they forget! Actual or perceived slights are experienced as assaults to their self-worth and may be blown out of proportion, leading to overreaction. Resentments act as fuel to ignite revengeful actions if the opportunity arises. Although often insensitive to the effect their words have on others, perfectionists are quick to tune in to any suggestion of criticism by others. They are especially attuned to comments relating to their standing in the company pecking order.

Strivers for excellence, because their entire sense of self-worth is not on the line when others gain recognition, are less likely to hold a grudge or become vindictive. They do not view peers, co-workers, and superiors as enemies. They can feel sympathetic joy for a co-worker who may have outperformed them. They are appreciative of the skills required for good performance and don't magnify disagreements or minor slights.

High achievers are more likely to compete with themselves than with co-workers, just as they are more likely to assume responsibility for their unskillful performances rather than blame others. They are also more willing to acknowledge their own good-enough performance even though they may not be the one who wins the competition or makes the sale. Their good-enough performance may even strengthen their ego and help them perform better the next time. Unlike perfectionists they are not caught in the paralzying bind of all-or-nothing thinking.

*The ends justifying the means.* Perfectionists tend to think primarily in terms of the end goal. Some will do virtually anything necessary to reach that goal, including, at times, breaking moral, ethical, and legal constraints. "The ends justify the means" might be a fitting work ethic for the most driven perfectionist, tempered only by a sense of guilt to stop him from doing whatever it takes to reach the goal.

If the threat of being caught is strong enough, the perfectionist is less likely to violate legal constraints. For the neurotic perfectionist, guilt may be strong enough to prevent him from transgressing moral and ethical barriers. The narcissistic perfectionist is not inhibited by guilt so much as by the fear of shame and humiliation. Nevertheless, some perfectionists will override both internal moral prohibitions and the external constraints of the law if the payoff seems worth the risk.

Despite a focus on the end goal, the more obsessive-compulsive perfectionist may get bogged down with annoying details in the process. These details serve more as obstacles than as careful steps toward a more thorough finished product. Preoccupation with details is part of the obsessive-compulsive style. Too much attention to detail may cloud the perfectionist's ability to see the larger picture. Focus on obsessive detail may also be an excuse to procrastinate, to avoid the fear of digging into the heart of a project.

In contrast, excellence-strivers may cut corners when it seems appropriate but usually will not risk their reputation and integrity for the sake of reaching a goal. For example, they may use a personal connection to cut through bureaucracy and red tape to accomplish a task more quickly. Or, they may do everything ethically possible to get a scoop on a news story, to get the best judge to hear a case, or to gain the upper hand by flattery or artful ingratiation. But they are keenly aware of ethical and legal boundaries and are more careful than the driven perfectionist to observe them. They are more appreciative of the step-by-step *process* of a project and less dependent on having to reach the goal. They feel much less of the driven anxiety that is the life-blood of the perfectionist, and their self-worth is more dependent on their personal integrity, which they are less willing to risk by breaking moral, ethical, and legal boundaries.

While excellence-strivers may also get bogged down with obsessive detail, they are less likely than perfectionists to procrastinate. They know that they must initiate a task despite anxiety or apprehension regarding its outcome, or else they will not become outstanding in the work environment.

*Workaholism versus balance.* Work perfectionists take their work too seriously. They are likely candidates to become workaholics, never having learned when enough is enough. They don't know how to disengage from their compulsive work track and channel energy in other directions. Because work is the arena most closely linked with performance, productivity, achievement, and success, it is the obvious vehicle for proving their self-worth to themselves and others. Once they get a taste of the intoxicating feeling that achievement brings, they throw themselves headlong into the pursuit of perfection.

For the compulsive work perfectionist, work seems to hold the greatest promise of proving self-worth and receiving admiration— more than marriage, family, friends, religion, sports, or hobbies. Sports often runs a distant second. Spouse and family may help to satisfy needs for love, sex, security, and companionship. But making one's mark in the world is deeply ingrained in the Western you-are-what-you-accomplish mentality. It is admiration, even more than love, that the narcissistic perfectionist is looking for. This is why work is so enticing to him.

For the work perfectionist, the love of spouse, children, or extended family never seems to be enough. What the work perfectionist wants more than anything else is to prove himself in the arena with the gladiators.

Those who have managed to avoid the perfection trap have a more balanced attitude toward the place of work in their lives. While work may be very important to them, it is not their primary vehicle for self-definition, self-worth, or personal satisfaction. Their values are more likely to be expressed in the slogan "Work to live, don't live to work. But if you must work to live, do the very best job you can."

They are aware of the trap of becoming a slave to a career, and realize that work is just one meaningful activity among many in life. Because they derive enjoyment and satisfaction from family, friends, hobbies, political or moral causes, religious or spiritual practice, and the natural world around them, they are more able to achieve a healthy balance in their commitment to work.

## THE PERFECTIONISTIC BOSS

A perfectionistic boss can make your work life hell. Often, it isn't easy to determine initially whether your boss is firmly pushing you toward excellence, with high but achievable expectations, or is a hard-core perfectionist for whom nothing you do will ever be good enough. How can you tell the difference? Signs that your boss may be a perfectionist include the following:

1. rarely or never gives direct compliments for work well done
2. constantly nags you regarding deadlines and/or office policies
3. is picky, always wants your work to be just a little bit better; makes you repeat tasks until perfect; often focuses on insignificant details
4. tends to change task requirements in the middle of projects and fails to inform you of the changes—then may act outraged that you are not a mind-reader
5. motivates by fear and threats rather than by making you feel good about yourself and your work projects

6. pits you against other employees, creating rivalries rather than fostering honesty, trust, openness, communication, and teamwork

7. displays typical Type A behaviors: often in a hurry, feels the pressures of time and impending deadlines; nervous mannerisms; speedy speech; sharp, tension-filled body movements; emotionally high-strung; competitive in most areas of life; needs to be in control at all times; can't relax

8. displays moderate to severe obsessive-complusive behaviors in work style and relations with employees

If it becomes painfully obvious to you that your boss is indeed a perfectionist, the following strategies may help you deal with your boss.

*Get your boss to be very clear with you on exact expectations.* Make sure your job description as a whole, as well as individual projects and tasks, are described clearly, preferably in writing, and preferably with measurable objectives. This will save you from the frustration, misunderstanding, and friction that result when it is not clear whether you have met a goal.

*Make sure you understand these expectations and feel you are capable of meeting them.* If you don't understand them or don't believe you can fulfill them, don't agree to them. Make it clear that you think too much is being expected, and express what you believe would be more appropriate. Do this in a firm but nonconfrontational, conversational tone without hostility or defensiveness. Your alternative is to passively accept the unrealistic expectation without saying anything, and then resentfully (and therefore, probably poorly) try to pull off the task, berating yourself when your boss is unhappy with the result. Of course, how well you know your boss and what your position is in the company will influence how you voice your objections. But there is almost always room for questioning expectations and for asking that they be made specific.

*Realize that your boss's perfectionism is his or her problem and does not mean you are inadequate as an employee.* While you may need to find creative solutions with your boss to keep relations on a positive basis, you are not forced to accept judgments or criticisms based on unrealistic expectations of perfection. Don't let criticism make you feel inadequate. If your employer seems to be sufficiently open to communication, try to suggest how she can best get across her desire for you to do well. If you tend to be perfectionistic yourself, be aware that you are liable to fall into a parent-child dynamic that makes you want to please your boss as if she were your parent. If you fall into this temptation, there is a good chance that your boss will fully exploit the situation.

*Pursue your own work style when it is safe to do so.* A perfectionistic, compulsive boss may ask for unnecessary attention to detail in completing a job. Some employees find that the best strategy for dealing with this is to say yes to everything and then go about the job their own way, making sure to complete the task but leaving out steps that add nothing to the result. This is simply a matter of work style, which is different for everyone. Do not adopt your boss's style if it is not right for you, but be careful—an extremely obsessive boss may check up on the details, in which case this strategy is inadvisable.

*Get frequent feedback from your boss about your work performance.* Ask for regular meetings and encourage direct feedback focusing on your areas of strength and weakness. Don't sit back and wait for an annual or semiannual job evaluation. The more you know about how your boss is feeling, the less you will imagine catastrophic outcomes based on your performance fears.

*Develop a support system of other employees.* Co-workers can help you reality-test your perceptions of the ill effects of your boss's perfectionism. They may share with you their own frustration in dealing with his unrealistic demands. This support can give you strength to cope and help you gauge your perceptions as to what is reasonable.

*If necessary, consider altering the working arrangement.* If your boss refuses to listen to feedback, will not alter unrealistic expectations, or cannot allow you to do the work your own way even if you complete tasks satisfactorily, you may need to seek a change. You might request to work under a different boss, to move to a different work site, or even consider quitting your job. Although quitting may create insecurity and upheaval in your personal life, you do not have to stay with a job in which your perfectionistic boss proves utterly impossible to work with.

## THE PERFECTIONISTIC COMPANY

If you work for a company that is perfectionistic as a whole, you need to be sure you are up to the task of working in an environment in which never-enough thinking predominates. If you are a perfectionist, this type of company may initially feel like just the right place for you, as you will feel comfortable with others who expect just as much from themselves as you do from yourself. You will enjoy the ego boost of being associated with a company that prides itself on striving for perfection. The high-paced, driven mentality can initially be very stimulating.

The trick here is to recognize whether what the company management labels "striving for excellence" is in fact clear-cut perfectionism. Many of the differences between perfectionism and excellence on the individual level already enumerated throughout this book ought to be helpful in making this distinction. Signs of perfectionistic company management include the following:

1. discourages time off for vacations, personal needs, or illness
2. demands uniformity and strict compliance to procedures
3. does not honor individual differences in work styles; stifles creativity in meeting job demands

4. refuses or is reluctant to award employees recognition for excellence in performance but tends to quickly pounce on mistakes

5. emphasizes volume of sales more than providing good service to customers

6. does not demonstrate to employees by word and deed that they are its most important resource; instead treats them as replaceable and interchangeable

If you work for a perfectionistic company, be prepared to receive little support unless your work exceeds that of all others you are competing against. As with perfectionistic bosses, in perfectionistic companies motivation is often by way of fear and criticism rather than support and praise. A spirit of cutthroat competition with other companies as well as with one's own colleagues is typically encouraged.

Assuming you work for a perfectionistic company but have yourself seen through the fallacy of viewing perfectionism as a virtue, here are some strategies to help you survive in this environment.

*Begin to educate those with whom you work.* Do not be afraid to subtly suggest to your colleagues, at least those whom you know well, that the perfection they are aiming for is unachievable. Point out how each of them is paying a stressful price in chasing a goal that is unreachable and unhealthy for them as individuals and for the company as a whole. Express your feelings carefully and tactfully and be alert to the reaction. Don't push your view on others if they show resistance.

*Resist the temptation to get caught up in the whirlwind of setting higher and higher goals.* No matter how competitive you may feel with your colleagues or how much company management glorifies competition, compare your own more reasonable goals with what is expected by the company.

*Do not become a slave to your work environment.* Be sure to engage in personal activities that act as a buffer from the perfectionistic work setting. A stable, loving relationship, sports activities or hobbies, an exercise routine to release the daily work stress—all of these will help ameliorate the temptation to let work become your entire focus.

*As much as possible, set your own pace for your work.* Shield yourself from contests, rivalries, challenges from colleagues, or grandiose ego needs that push you to measure up to someone else's idea of perfect performance. Determine what level you need to attain to meet minimal company performance standards, and then refuse to allow unrealistic company goals to influence what you aim for.

*Spend as little time as possible socializing with colleagues who share the company perfectionistic line.* They will only try to push you to conform to the company ethic and will be of no support to your more realistic standard. Instead, spend time with those who will support your moderate stance.

*As a last resort, consider quitting.* If all your efforts to fit within the perfectionistic company structure fail, remember that you have the option to quit and find a company that will not make you crazy with never-enough thinking. Do not expect management to understand or take seriously the difference between striving for excellence and falling into the perfection trap. If this distinction was clear to them, you would not be faced with these problems! Consider finding a company that appreciates the toll that perfectionistic thinking takes on everyone.

# TEN

# THE AGONY
# OF DEFEAT:
## *The Perfectionist at Play*

*Every victory contains the germ of future defeat.*

C. G. JUNG

As PERFECTIONISTS, WE TEND to apply our demanding standards to all major areas of our lives. The needs that motivate us toward perfectionism do not get turned off simply because we move from one sphere of activity to another. While some of us may be able to contain our perfectionism within the world of work, many of us bring our desire for perfection into our recreational lives as well. We may become compulsive exercisers and take sports and games very seriously. Our competitiveness and need for victory often push us beyond healthy and reasonable limits.

## COMPULSIVE EXERCISE

As in the other pursuits we have discussed, in the area of exercise there is a fine but critical line between those who strive for excellence through hard, consistent workouts, and perfectionists who are addicted to pushing their limits, in some cases to the point of physical endangerment. Adhering to the myth that more is better, they may exercise when they are sick or injured and aggravate their physical problems. They tend to fear they will lose the benefits of their fitness program if they skip a workout, even for good reason.

Exercise addicts sometimes become so obsessed with exercise that they have few other interests. They may isolate themselves from their families as relationships become secondary to the exercise program and the need to look perfect. They may avoid social outings and events that interfere with their exercise routine or make them too tired to work out.

Some exercise addicts, like obsessive-compulsive personalities and perfectionists in general, have a conscious or unconscious fear of being out of control of their lives. Following a rigid exercise and diet routine provides them with the illusion of outer control while they are unable to master the inner world of their own thoughts and emotions.

Maintaining a diet program or a workout schedule does require some degree of inner control, but this surface control often masks a more subtle and unconscious fear of loss of control of thoughts and emotions. *It is this unconscious fear breaking through to conscious awareness that is ultimately most threatening to perfectionists.* They may be unhappy with or overwhelmed by other aspects of their lives, such as work or home, and may compensate by throwing themselves into exercise as a way to cope with stress, anxiety, and feelings of emptiness. Rather than face these inner threats directly, they prefer to work toward establishing outer control of their bodies.

Some exercise addicts have distorted body images and may suffer from unrealistic fears of gaining weight and aging. No matter how good they look, they tend to view their appearance as never good enough, so they push themselves in exercise, hoping to stay "forever young." They identify with their bodies as the primary source of their sense of self-worth. They fear they will be less desirable to others if they fail to maintain their image of the ideal physique. They believe they can exercise their way to perfection.

Donna, 33 and single, was a graduate student and compulsive runner who would not forgive herself if she did not run at least 8 miles every day. She enjoyed the high that came from her morning run, but then she felt tired the rest of the day. Donna felt inadequate in her graduate studies despite doing reasonably well. She struggled to maintain a positive image of herself as a perfectionist while, at the same time, feeling that she fell short in her own eyes and in the eyes of her friends. She believed her women friends were more attractive than she.

Even though Donna's strict dieting and excessive running caused her menstrual periods to stop, she would not consider cutting down. Nor would she obey her doctor's orders to stop running when she suffered a knee injury.

She cited fatigue as the reason she did not date. What socializing she did was limited to fellow runners, with whom she prepared for frequent 10-kilometer races. Donna claimed to prefer being thin but complained when a man she liked told her she was "all skin and bones." She said to me, "When I see myself naked in the mirror, I look like I just came out of a concentration camp." Nevertheless, she resisted the suggestion that she gain weight, believing that added weight would "only slow me down."

In therapy, Donna slowly realized how her perfectionism was doing more harm than good. She began to face what had been her unconscious desire to remain young and physically undeveloped (symbolized by her amenorrhea), so as to avoid strong conflicts regarding her sexuality, especially Oedipal feelings toward her father. In facing this central conflict, she gradually became less rigid and compulsive. She cut back her running, changed her diet, and gave more attention to other areas of her life. Her romantic life also began to blossom.

Like Donna, most exercise addicts were raised by perfectionistic parents who emphasized the importance of looking good.[1,2] They earned conditional approval only when they measured up to their parents' image of how they should look. Internal qualities and intellectual talents were not valued as much as the physical.

## MORE THAN JUST A GAME

Sports represent another arena in which perfectionists may attempt to prove themselves the best. Sports perfectionists, like exercise addicts, become compulsively involved in their chosen activity, sometimes losing all sense that they are playing a game. For the sports perfectionist, personal worth and self-respect are on the line every time he competes. To lose a game or a competition is to lose part of his tenuous sense of self. Proficiency at the chosen sport becomes a personal challenge that determines the athlete's sense of personal value.

Sports perfectionists often prefer individual sports such as running, golf, tennis, surfing, and swimming as opposed to team activities. In these sports, there are no outside influences, no other team members or game schedules, to moderate their compulsive dedication. Individual sports also are more compatible with the perfectionists' desire to continually strive to improve their "personal best." The outcome is not dependent on anyone else; winning or losing is determined by their efforts alone. Thus, they can enjoy the glory that comes with victory without having to share it with teammates.

Of course, sports perfectionists can be found in team sports as well. Whether as part of a team or in an individual sport, perfectionists often take the agony of defeat as a personal humiliation, a statement that they are inadequate and have not lived up to their perfect image. They can't separate losing a game from feeling like a loser as a person. Because of this, sports perfectionists tend not to be good team players. They may blame teammates for their own loss of self-esteem. They may have difficulty realizing that, even when the team loses, teammates may be playing their best.

Ron, 29, couldn't stand to lose in league basketball games with his company team. Ron loved basketball as a kid but concluded he was too short to play in high school or college. He wishes now he had tried out. In analyzing Ron's decision not to try out, it became apparent that it was not so much his height but his *fear of failure* that stopped him. In addition, his father never encouraged him in high school sports. To the contrary, his father discouraged Ron from playing football, in which he was also interested, claiming the risk of injury was too great.

Ron prided himself on his athletic ability and now, many years later, jumped at the chance to play on his company's basketball team. But he was very critical of the mediocre playing skills of his teammates and opponents. He couldn't understand how anyone could want to play unless he was very good. "How could they stand the embarrassment of being lousy players?" he wondered. "Don't they care how the others will judge them?"

For Ron, it was inconceivable that the other players felt no need to prove themselves on the court. They were there for other reasons that were difficult for Ron to understand: enjoying the game, getting exercise, establishing friendships, building company solidarity, and networking with other companies.

On the court, Ron couldn't restrain himself from laughing uncontrollably when he witnessed the poor shooting and guarding of other players. When we analyzed this reaction, Ron recalled that this same kind of inappropriate laughter was how his father had responded when Ron was learning to play as a child. His father, out of his own sense of inadequacy, needed to humiliate Ron in order to feel superior. His father needed to come out on top when he played head-to-head, even with his own son. Instead of strengthening Ron's confidence by teaching him as friendly ally and supporter, his father demeaned and humiliated him. Thus, despite his skill, Ron never had the confidence to go out for team sports.

When he felt unjustly fouled by an opponent and the foul was not called, Ron would fly into a rage. He would scream at his opponent and promise to pay him back with a foul of his own, or criticize the referee for not responding. When his team lost and Ron believed his own performance to be less than he demanded of himself, he would be depressed for days. His teammates began to comment on his poor sportsmanship.

It was Ron's all-or-nothing thinking about winning and his need to prove self-worth by way of his skill that ensnared him in the perfection trap. Obsessed with winning, he often derived no real enjoyment from a game he claimed to love. His inability to remember it's *only a game* distinguishes him from those who strive to play their best but are able to enjoy the game even when they lose.

## Peak Performance—Not Perfection

It is common knowledge in sports psychology that athletes who compete in national and world-class competition are striving to achieve peak performance, not perfection. Peak performance means the highest level possible for the athlete under the given internal and external conditions on a given day. In studying the attitudes of accomplished athletes, psychologist Charles Garfield discovered that "the peak performer is not a perfectionist. Perfection is an illusion and the top performer knows this. He or she tends to see the perfectionist as paralyzed by unrealistically high standards. The people we talked to were not so much interested in perfection as doing the best job they could."[3]

The peak performer is the athlete who is striving for excellence. He or she has already learned the lesson that I had trouble learning when I was young and that many other competitors never learn. Because perfectionists are so focused on perfection, they are quickly disarmed and lose their concentration when they make mistakes. Unable to recover easily, they further reinforce the blunder by punishingly critical self-talk. This creates a downward spiral that often leads to further mistakes and a negative attitude.

Especially in sports like golf, in which the player has a lot of time between executions to think about what he or she is doing, critical self-talk and negative thinking can become powerful enough to destroy any chance of excellence. This is one reason so many serious athletes now utilize self-hypnosis, visualization exercises, relaxation tapes, and positive thinking programs as techniques for modifying self-talk.

## DISENGAGING PERFECTIONISM FROM PLAY

Here are some strategies for allowing yourself more time to play and disengaging perfectionism from your recreation.

*Do not make play time dependent on completing all work projects.* Play is not something you should have to earn but an activity that should be a regular part of your lifestyle. You need not feel guilty for indulging yourself even if there is work left undone.

*Schedule specific play time.* Do not just hope for a free hour to open up in your schedule. Achieving good mental and physical health and balance in your life means making recreational time as important as other activities.

*Use your desire to excel as a reinforcer to give yourself more play time.* The satisfaction that accompanies your efforts toward proficiency can be a motivator to spend more time with your chosen hobby, activity, or sport. Remember that proficiency does not mean perfection!

*Engage in play activities with those you care about.* Besides acting as further motivation to make more time for play, this is a good way to connect to those who matter to you by sharing enjoyable time together.

*Adopt the Zen attitude of beginner's mind.* Use play as a safe time to experiment creatively with new interests, allowing yourself to be a beginner and to make mistakes. *Beginner's mind* means a fresh, open approach to play that carries no performance expectations. It means suspending all judgments and evaluations during play activities.

*Discover what brings you back to your childlike curiosity and wonder.*
Beginner's mind also means recapturing your innocent, childlike
wonder of the world. Go to a natural setting, like the woods, ocean,
mountains, or desert, and be especially attuned to the various forms
of nature unfolding. Pay attention to all sights, sounds, smells, and
tactile sensations. Allow your attention to be totally focused on your
senses, which will bring you into the present and increase your sense
of aliveness and wonder.

## Goalless Play Activities

During play, allow yourself to temporarily sever any connection between your feelings of self-worth and your end goal. Focus on the
process of play rather than the end goal. Below are some play activities that have no goal attached to them. You might come up with
some of your own, too.

*Active goalless play.* Play at the beach in the sand and water. Wander in
the desert, mountains, or forest. Take a leisurely drive to "nowhere"
on a Sunday afternoon. Play your favorite musical instrument. Play a
game of volleyball with family or friends without keeping score. Play
card games and board games without keeping score. Walk through a
shopping mall just to enjoy window shopping. Go to an amusement
park.

*Passive goalless play.* Listen to music. Watch a movie or TV show. Read
for enjoyment. Attend a concert. Immerse yourself in a hot tub or
Jacuzzi. Take a bubble bath. Look at a picture album. Watch fire-
works. Watch the waves break at the beach. Listen in on an engross-
ing conversation between strangers.

Perfectionists have trouble finding goalless activities meaningful.
We must shift our attention from the goal to the process and realize
that the process is enough all by itself. This realization is also central
to creativity.

## Perfectionism and Creativity

Perfectionism stifles creativity in the same way it inhibits play. The desire of the perfectionist to pursue a goal does not allow for the free-form experimentation that is the life-blood of true creativity. To perform a task creatively requires doing it a new or different way, thereby risking the possibility of failure that the perfectionist struggles to avoid. Perfectionism inhibits the creative process in a number of other ways. The perfectionist:

1. is constrained by preconceptions of what is creative and how something should be done; these preconceptions leave little room for working with unfamiliar ideas, systems, methods, and outcomes

2. is unable to stay in the present and become immersed in the process of creating something out of nothing; focus on the end goal pushes the perfectionist's attention into the future

3. is quick to pounce on and edit out all perceived mistakes

4. is quick to compare and critically judge the product

5. expects a perfect creative result without exerting much effort

6. is unable to trust the spontaneity of the creative process; tries to engineer a creative product in a preplanned manner

7. is embarrassed to show off the creation; fears critical judgments by others

### Overcoming Inhibitions to Creativity

The following suggestions can help overcome the inhibitions that stifle creativity for the perfectionist.

*Give up all preconceptions about what it means to be creative.* To be creative is to do something new and unusual. There is no one right way to experiment creatively. When you suspend the need to do it right, you can allow yourself to express your unique personality in new and unusual ways. All of your self-expression is meaningful and need not be compared to anyone else's standards or to your own internal standards as to what is creative.

*Stay present-centered; focus only on the process of creation.* Give up any concern for the end goal and allow yourself to get lost in what you are doing. If you can stay present-centered, you will enjoy the process of self-expression and likely will end up with a product that positively reflects your total immersion in the creative process.

*Do not interrupt yourself by stopping to edit out mistakes.* The critical mind is often too quick to judge as a mistake what may be a creative but unfamiliar solution. Resist this temptation and refuse to interrupt your creative flow until you have finished a project. Allow your product to sit for a couple of days before you attempt to edit or correct it. Remember that mistakes are part of the creative process.

*Make no judgments or comparisons regarding your finished product.* Refuse to compare your product to your image of the perfect product. Allow your product to be acceptable just as it is. Use your "appreciative mind" to find qualities in your creation that you like. Focus on the idea that what you have created is unique to you and need never be compared to anyone else's creations.

*Remember that learning any skill requires the discipline of repeated practice.* Give up the idea that anything, including creative projects, should be easy the first time you try. The ability to skillfully improvise likewise becomes easier with practice.

*Resist the perfectionistic temptation to control or engineer your creative product.* Give yourself over to the process and let go of the need to know what is going to happen. Mechanical plotting of an outcome is the antithesis of creativity. Trust that you have something unique waiting to be expressed and that it *will* be expressed—if you can only get beyond your need to control the process of expressing it.

*Make sure you show your finished creation to others.* Don't hide your work. Get feedback from others to neutralize your own critical judgments. Try to avoid, however, the perfectionistic need to seek approval.

## WORKING WITH THE CONCEPTS

If you are unsure whether you are a compulsive exerciser, consider your answers to these questions: How do you react if you must break your exercise schedule? What effect does skipping exercise have on your mood? If you become depressed or hostile to others when you have not had your exercise "fix," watch out! This is a strong indicator of being addicted to exercise.

Has anyone who knows you well told you that you don't make enough time for them because of your exercise schedule? Do you continually increase the amount of time you exercise? Do you feel you could give up your exercise routine for a week without any ill effects?

In the same vein, if you are dedicated to a particular sport, how often do you use playing your sport as an excuse not to do other things with family or friends? How often do you find yourself talking only about your sport? How much money do you spend on equipment related to your sport? Do you ever go into debt because you can't say no to a new tennis racket, ski outfit, sailboat, racing bike, or golf clubs? Are your vacations ever planned solely around your sport? How much time do you spend watching your sport on TV or reading magazines or books related to it?

What is your attitude toward winning a game, contest, or match? How do you react when you lose? What do you tell yourself about your loss? How long does a loss affect you? If others who matter to you watched you lose an important game or contest, how would their witnessing it affect you?

# ELEVEN

# A Match Made
# in Heaven:
## *The Perfect Relationship*

*If you think you will find a better person then there is no limit to "better." You will go on searching and you will not find any 100% perfect partner.*

BABA HARI DASS

RICHARD, SINGLE AND NEVER MARRIED , was 41 when he came to see me because of what he described as a relationship problem. He couldn't find a woman worthy of him, no matter how hard he tried. Each time he thought he had found the perfect partner, something would happen to reveal her imperfections. Either she turned out to be not quite as smart as she initially appeared, or her attractiveness began to wane, or both. Maybe she wasn't a meticulous enough housekeeper or an experienced enough lover. Or perhaps his friends didn't approve of her because she wasn't sophisticated enough.

Over a period of three years, I watched Richard run through dozens of women, none of whom he dated for more than a few months. Since he was always looking for the perfect woman, he never passed up an opportunity to ask out a woman who caught his eye, even if he was dating someone else at the time. So, instead of having meaningful relationships, Richard found himself settling for rela-

tively brief sexual encounters. Yet he never gave up what clearly became the central theme of his life: the search for the perfect partner.
Periodically, he would come in and tell me the same story: how his
initial excitement about a new possibility was now blemished beyond
repair, spoiled by the reality of imperfection. He struggled to lower
his standards to the point where a woman might make it over his
various hurdles and, as he put it, "qualify for the semifinals." But no
one ever did.

Richard would scrutinize the woman he was dating, viewing her
critically from various angles. He would watch her closely in different kinds of light to determine the effect of the sun on her face and
whether she showed any sign of wrinkles. He would disqualify a
woman from the "semifinals" if her teeth weren't perfectly straight or
her hair was the wrong length or texture. The wrong voice could
spell immediate failure, despite any other assets the woman might
possess.

He liked his women full-figured, but they had to have just the
right proportions. While breasts could never be too big for him, hips
and thighs certainly could. If she wasn't a world traveler or didn't have
the right cultural background, she didn't fit the bill. In his narcissistic
perfectionism, Richard wanted a woman who was "as perfect in
every respect as I am."

You might wonder why anyone would want such a picky guy
who only seems to be interested in the surface. But because Richard
was tall, well-proportioned, blond, and tanned, he found no shortage
of attractive women who wanted to go out with him. Because he was
a plastic surgeon, many women saw him as a good catch financially.
They might also have thought, "Here's a guy who can take care of my
cosmetic surgery needs without charge—can't beat that!" In the
"beautiful body" culture of Southern California, this was no small
bonus in terms of his social marketability.

Despite his good looks, professional status, and smooth manner,
Richard's perfectionism made him a difficult person for others to be
around. He was critical of those who didn't seem to care enough

about their appearance; he believed this was an important reflection of one's feelings of self-worth. He had to bite his tongue not to correct other people's incorrect grammar. In conversations, he wanted not only to have the final word but to be the final arbiter of accuracy in all matters of fact. Richard thought he knew the answers to almost everything.

But he couldn't find the answer to maintaining a solid relationship with a woman. His unrealistic standard of perfection masked a deep fear of intimacy and attachment to a woman. As long as he didn't let himself get too involved, he did not have to face his fear of becoming emotionally dependent on a woman, which would entail being out of control of his feelings. And, if no woman was good enough, he wouldn't have to get too involved.

Over the course of therapy, Richard realized that his need to impress others by flaunting his knowledge was based on a longing to impress his father and thus earn love and admiration. As well, he became aware that his mother had unconsciously programmed him to believe that, compared to her, no woman would ever be good enough for him. When the powerful unconscious influence of his childhood program was brought to his awareness, Richard was able to loosen his standards. He was finally able to initiate and sustain a satisfying long-term relationship with a woman.

## WHEN THE HALO WEARS OFF

The beginning of a love relationship carries the joy and magic of entrancement, of feeling enveloped in the other. If you have been in love, you know what this stage is like. Your partner seems almost perfect in every way. Your infatuation colors your perception to fit this perfect picture. You tend to overlook what may be significant differences and to downplay flaws. You imagine this joyful state will last forever, and you look forward to a wonderful future. Psychologists call this tendency to see everything our partner does in an unre-

alistically positive light the *halo effect.* The warm glow of our love be-
stows the halo of a saint upon our beloved. When we are smitten by
love, it is as if our partner can do no wrong.

In love relationships that we expect to lead toward marriage or
other long-term commitment, we are usually influenced by a conscious or unconscious desire to have our partner fill some of the gaps
in our own psychological development. *We look for a partner who will
complement what we already have and who will supplement what we believe is missing.* Thus we attempt to make ourselves (as Jung put it)
complete through the other—to create what we think will be a perfect couple. As Richard's case shows, some of us never get beyond the
stage of finding fault with potential partners. For the perfectionist, it
is not easy to give up enough control to fall into anything, let alone
love. Perfectionists prefer to step gingerly into love. And so we find it
harder than nonperfectionists to allow ourselves to melt into the early
ecstasy of entrancement.

As we spend more time with our lover, the halo effect begins to
wear off. The reality of differences in temperament, attitudes, values,
and habits begins to exert its sobering influence. For some, this occurs
a matter of months into the relationship. For others, it may take a few
years. But sooner or later, the entrancement of perfect love gives way
to the reality of two imperfect people who begin to feel something has
changed. We may wonder, "What happened to the person I fell in
love with?"

What happens is that we begin to see the personality quirks and
idiosyncratic habits of our partner. We see parts of him or her that
reflect unresolved psychological problems, issues tracing back to
early family life. Earlier, we didn't notice these things, or we conven-
iently overlooked them. And our partner sees similar unfinished issues in our behavior.

Instead of becoming the perfect couple, we slowly discover we
are two imperfect adults projecting our own unresolved issues onto
the other. Instead of feeling easy and playful, the relationship begins
to feel like work. With the weakening of the "good enough" partner

created by the halo effect, we are forced to come to grips with our unrealistic expectations of what the perfect romance and perfect marriage should be.

In all healthy relationships, it is necessary to strip away the unrealistic expectations that promote an idealized perception of the partner in order to move to the next, deeper phase of the relationship. It is necessary, in other words, to let the halo fall away in order to see our partner as he or she really is.

We do not necessarily lose the sparkle we see when we look in our lover's eyes, nor do we stop seeing him or her as "special." But the unreality of the halo effect prevents us from clearly seeing and accepting exactly who our lover is. And this unreality is highlighted in the thinking of the marital perfectionist.

## THE MARITAL PERFECTIONIST

Psychiatrist David Burns identifies five types of perfectionists: the career perfectionist, the marital or interpersonal relationship perfectionist, the emotional perfectionist, the moral perfectionist, and the sexual perfectionist.[1] These categories are somewhat arbitrary; as we have said, a perfectionist in one area of life is often a perfectionist in other areas as well. In this chapter we focus on marital and sexual perfectionism.

Marital perfectionists want to live up to an image of what they believe the perfect marriage should be. They apply this same image to other couples as well. They view their loved ones as extensions of their own egos, and find it threatening when others are not perfect. They think they and all other couples should always be loving to each other and never fight or show any anger toward each other. When family members or friends fall short of these expectations (as they are bound to do), marital perfectionists become frustrated and depressed.

In his own partnership, the marital perfectionist is unwilling to let the halo drop away. He can't stand to be assaulted by reality; he prefers his image of perfection, an image that straightjackets him and his partner in rigid values, beliefs, and forms of self-expression.

On the surface, the halo effect may seem worth clinging to. But it is not the original entrancement of blissful love that the marital perfectionist desperately wants to preserve. Rather, it is the fear of seeing the imperfections in himself and in others that freezes the marital perfectionist into rigidity.

This pattern is compounded when both partners are perfectionistic, when both feel the need to project an image to the outside world of being the perfect couple. Frequently, such a couple seem to relate to each other in inauthentic ways. They tend to be overly careful in the way they talk to each other in front of others. They may go out of their way to be agreeable and placating with each other, no matter what the issue or how they are really feeling.

Below the surface there is a lot of tension and resentment. Some perfectionistic couples periodically "let down the mask" and express anger in the privacy of their own home. Others who are even less secure never feel safe enough to express angry feelings to each other. To do so would make them face the threatening reality that their relationship is less than perfect.

## UNREALISTIC EXPECTATIONS

Marital and sexual perfectionists tend to be burdened with unrealistic, often unconscious, expectations and distorted thinking. These expectations need to be challenged and given up if the relationship is to survive with anything more than a caricature of true intimacy. Following are some examples of such expectations.

*"Sex ought to be perfect to begin with and stay perfect forever. My partner ought to be telepathically tuned in to exactly what I need and know how to please me."* As a nonperfectionistic couple spends more time together,

the initial sexual excitement usually begins to wane. While each partner becomes more familiar with the other's sexual preferences and more willing to trust and open up physically to the other, they also begin to feel that the excitement they experienced during the halo phase is cooling down. This does not mean there is anything wrong with the couple's sexual life, only that they have moved into a different phase together.

Sexual perfectionists, however, get trapped in the unrealistic expectation that they should *always* be interested in sex, *never* have their partner deny them sex for any reason, *never* have to tell their partner what they want, and *always* be able to function absolutely perfectly. They are confined in the celluloid prison of the Hollywood movie image of perfect romance. This image ignores the normal changes in frequency of lovemaking that occur with age and years together, and the cooling down that results from seeing one's partner as less than perfect.

For example, women who are sexual perfectionists fear they are unresponsive and inadequate if they don't achieve orgasm every time they make love. They further complicate this belief by thinking they should be able to reach orgasm through intercourse and only through intercourse. If they require manual or oral stimulation by their partner to achieve orgasm, they think something is wrong with them, or they may blame their partners for being insufficiently experienced.

Such beliefs are partly the result of incorrect or inadequate information about general sexual response and normal sexual functioning in long-term relationships. But in a deeper sense the sexual perfectionists' all-or-nothing thinking is the result of linking security and self-worth solely with sexual performance, so that they are especially sensitive to any deviation from their image of the perfect sexual response pattern.

Men who are sexual perfectionists are very concerned about performance. They get depressed and feel sexually inadequate if they fail to achieve an erection "upon command." Because erection is an involuntary response, men are especially vulnerable in this way, as they can't will themselves to achieve one. They leave no room for being physically, mentally, or emotionally exhausted. Nor do they leave room for being preoccupied with finances, work, or other matters that impede concentration on lovemaking. They think, "If my wife is ready and wants it, I should be ready to perform."

In part this belief in "instant erection" is a result of patterns of thinking developed in youth. It comes from a "scarcity" model that dictates to young men that sexual intercourse (and pretty much anything leading up to it) is not going to come your way every day; it is a very desirable commodity that one cannot afford to pass up when an opportunity presents itself. One result of this thinking is the willingness to engage in casual sex with any obliging partner, whether he is attracted to her or not. This scarcity thinking is carried into adulthood and the marital relationship.

Male sexual perfectionists feel terrible when they are unable to maintain an erection as long as they would like or are unable to bring their partner to orgasm every time they make love. Premature ejaculation is enough to make them feel like the world is coming to an end. They may feel they haven't measured up if they do not achieve Perfect Mutual Orgasm with their partners. Some middle-aged and older sexual perfectionists feel less virile when they cannot ejaculate as powerfully and plentifully as they could when younger.

While sexual performance is an emotionally loaded area for all couples, it is especially trying for the sexual perfectionist. He or she can't stand the feeling of not being perfect in an area in which our culture places so much emphasis on performance. Sexual perfectionists are continually judging their own performance and that of their partners. They may become so interested in the technical aspects of pleasing the partner that they act as a detached spectator rather than getting lost in the spontaneity, emotion, and sensual pleasure that accompany healthy lovemaking.

*"We should never disagree about anything, nor should we ever get upset or argue with each other. We should never show others that we are not the*

*perfect couple by arguing in public."* In a healthy relationship, the appreciation of differences is essential to the growth of each person's individuality. Not only is it necessary for each person's growth, it is essential nourishment as well for the blossoming relationship. This is what finding completeness through the other is all about. Without difference, there will be nothing new brought to the relationship, nothing to nourish it so that each partner can learn and grow from the other.

It is common knowledge that all marriages are heavily influenced by what each partner has learned in his or her family of origin. If you watched your parents avoid arguments or disagreements of any kind, this is likely to become your model for interaction with your partner. However, some people react in the opposite way to what they have grown up with, realizing how destructive to true intimacy some family patterns can be. For example, if your father expressed anger through uncontrollable outrage and even violence, you may react to the terror that you experienced and decide never to lose control, never to experience or express anger. If you have never been exposed to the healthy, controlled expression of anger, you may not even know that healthy anger is possible.

Periodic (but not chronic or violent) arguments are healthy in a thriving relationship. They foster an acceptance of the expression of strongly felt individual differences in opinion and belief. In addition, they help establish a solid ground of trust between partners. If I don't have to worry that you will walk out on me if I get mad at you, I am free to tell you how I really feel. And you are free to do the same. In this way, I make room for you, rather than try to manipulate you to adopt my beliefs, opinions, and preferences.

This need for ongoing expression of difference by each partner reminds me of something Woody Allen said in his classic movie *Annie Hall:* "A relationship is like a shark—it needs to keep moving forward or it dies." He then looks at his girlfriend, played by Diane Keaton, and says, "What we have here is a dead shark." Without the free expression of individual difference, as well as the trust and security that make room for the expression of anger, relationship perfectionists end up with a dead shark.

*"Our friends and acquaintances ought to be just as perfect as we are. If they don't hold the same political, social, and religious beliefs that we do, they are falling short of the mark."* Relationship perfectionists are often self-righteous, seeing the world through the narrow lens of their own beliefs, habits, and values. Feeling threatened by others who think and act differently, they may be intolerant of those who express different cultural values and ways of making sense of the world. Perfectionistic thinking may act as a cover for simple prejudice.

*"My partner ought to have the same interests I have but not be better than I am at any activity I take seriously. There is only room for one of us to be the best in this relationship, and it's got to be me."* While our culture has predominantly taught men to take on this superior posture, it is sometimes assumed by women as well. We want our partner to have enough interests in common with us so that we can enjoy activities together. At least, our partner should be open to joining in and learning about our interests. But, for the perfectionist, "joining in" does not mean being as good as he is, especially if the activity is one in which he feels he has some expertise.

In one form or another, the hardcore perfectionist competes with *everyone* in his life, including his wife and children. He may push his mate ruthlessly to learn to cycle, swim, or run—but just up to the point where she can offer him good-enough competition. Should she actually excel him, all hell breaks loose! The unwritten law a male perfectionist lays down for his partner is: "Don't *ever* humiliate me by beating me or upstaging me in any activity I take seriously!"

*"My partner and I should look young forever, no matter what it takes. I refuse to accept the normal process of aging."* We have already looked at

the consequences of this expectation as it relates to cosmetic surgery for women (and growing numbers of men) in an effort to resist the normal effects of time. Because of their emphasis on physical appearance and sexual performance, marital perfectionists are committed to staying young psychologically and physically.

Because of his need to prove that he has not lost his virility with age, the male relationship perfectionist may become dissatisfied with his partner as she begins to show age. To feel like a "real man," he needs a young, fresh woman on his arm. He may have affairs with other women or seek a divorce. Many women married to such men react by doing whatever is necessary to keep looking young.

The perfectionist is not committed to his partner "forever," since his only real commitment is to perfection. So he simply changes partners, trading in his aging wife for a younger model. This form of narcissism is based on a panic response to middle age based on the fear that old age, infirmity, and death are just around the bend. According to Christopher Lasch:

> The irrational terror of old age and death is closely associated with the emergence of the narcissistic personality as the dominant personality structure in contemporary society. Because the narcissist has so few inner resources, he looks to others to validate his sense of self. He needs to be admired for his beauty, charm, celebrity, or power—attributes that usually fade with time.[2]

A recent news story told of a couple in their mid-40s who methodically planned joint suicide. Devoted to each other, they had been married 22 years and had no children. Both were successful in real estate sales. They quit their jobs, withdrew their savings, and settled into their home for a few months before carrying out their suicide plan. They paid all their bills and got everything in order in preparation for ending their lives.

They made a short video for their relatives to explain their actions. They wanted to choose their own time of death, they said. Life had been good but they were terrified of having to grow old. They wanted to get out when they were at the prime of life. So they blew their brains out with a shotgun (and even took their two poodles along with them). This story is the epitome of the raw, irrational terror of growing old.

## Toward Relationship Excellence

In this book, we have used the term *excellence* to mean striving to accomplish at the highest individual levels possible but without the all-or-nothing, anxiety-driven characteristics of perfectionism. Within the context of relationships, however, we need to alter the meaning of this term. Relationship excellence means striving to build the most secure, trusting, nourishing, loving, and mutually satisfying intimate relationship that is possible.

Just as we defined self-actualization as both a process and an end goal, relationship actualization is both the process of creating moment-to-moment satisfaction and a long-term goal of mutual security and happiness. The emphasis, as with self-actualization and the healthy pursuit of excellence, is placed more on the process of getting there, than on the long-term outcome.

For example, a couple can look back on their marriage after a number of years and agree that they have a more trusting, secure, loving, and satisfying relationship than they had many years earlier. In recognizing how far they have come, the couple is moving toward excellence as a goal. The essence of the couple's day-to-day work together remains in allowing mutual opportunities for the relationship to continue to grow. This is relationship excellence as process. The relationship perfectionist, who freeze-frames the relationship according to some perfect image, is unable to recognize or appreciate this process.

## The I That Is We

John, 42, and Susan, 40, are an example of a couple working toward relationship excellence. They have been married 12 years and have one daughter, Tina, age 6. Both work as professionals and are satisfied with their careers. Susan does not worry about John's commitment to her. She feels they are "securely bonded" to each other and therefore does not experience jealousy if John comments about an attractive woman who walks by. In fact, Susan may agree with him. She does not feel threatened by John's passing remarks about women he works with or sees in the movies or on TV.

John and Susan have a deep trust built over the course of their marriage. Each has remained faithful to their wedding vows of sexual fidelity. They openly share the good feelings this faithfulness brings to them. Through years of open discussion and experimentation, they have learned to please each other sexually so that neither worries about sexual performance. They frequently make loving remarks to each other and are comfortable showing affection to each other both privately and in public. Susan says, "We have a shared identity of 'we' that is more than just me alone or John alone. We do our best to respect and build this 'we' part of us."

Each month, John and Susan mark their anniversary date in some small way. On their yearly wedding anniversary, they share a loving ritual to mark the importance of their commitment to each other. In their home, Susan puts on her wedding dress and they repeat their vows, which John wrote. Then they dance to the same music they danced to at their wedding, and they discuss anything they want to add to or subtract from the original vows.

Susan and John both are strong willed and have definite preferences in the ways they like things to be done, but each tries not to push the other to agree. Instead, each offers the other an option through modeling his or her own creative way of thinking. For example, Susan is more tuned in to fashion than John. She cares more about color schemes and the impression that clothes make on others than

does John, who tends to like to dress casually and without much regard to style. Susan tolerates his lack of interest in clothes and does
not demand that John dress to please her.

At the same time, John realizes clothes shopping brings Susan
pleasure, and he appreciates her taste and her creative style of putting
outfits together. The agreement he made when they got married was:
"I will accept your interest in clothes and not ask you to dress like me,
and you will accept my lack of interest in fashion and not make me
into a clothes horse." For the most part, they have been able to live up
to their agreement. John has gradually changed his thinking about
clothes over the years under Susan's influence, without feeling he was
being forced to change his own style. And John has had some influence in Susan's gradual movement toward less flashy accessories.

They both share in the responsibilities related to bringing up
their daughter. Each spends time with her individually, and much of
their free time is spent together as a family. But they also take time to
nourish their marriage, leaving Tina with a sitter occasionally so they
can get away for a few hours or a romantic weekend.

When they disagree with each other, they sometimes raise their
voices and argue. Both are comfortable with the open expression of
anger and value the need for free expression of differences. They
have an understanding that no matter how far apart they may be on
an issue or how angry they may get, they do not make threats about
separation, divorce, or feeling unloved. They frequently share fantasies of where they would like to travel together, and both feel a level
of commitment to the relationship that allows them to comfortably
imagine spending the rest of their lives together.

## Relationship Tools

The following suggestions can help couples avoid the pitfalls of mutual marital perfectionism.

## Five Freedoms

In contrast to marital perfectionists, who feel the need to rigidly control their own and their partner's behavior, those in healthy relationships honor what Virginia Satir, a pioneer in family therapy, has called the five freedoms:[3]

1. The freedom to see and hear what is here and now, rather that what was, will be, or should be—and to be able to share it with your partner.

2. The freedom to think what you think, rather than what you think you should think—and to be able to share it with your partner.

3. The freedom to feel what you feel, rather than what you think you should feel—and to be able to share it with your partner.

4. The freedom to want and to choose whatever you want, rather than what you think you should want—and to be able to share it with your partner.

5. The freedom to imagine your own self-actualization, rather than playing a rigid role or always playing it safe—and to be able to share it with your partner.

*Step 1.* Examine your expectations of your partner with regard to communication, sex, bringing up kids, shared interests, finances, values, and future direction together. Do you have any expectations that are likely never to be fulfilled? What expectations have you been holding onto because they are part of your image of how your perfect partner should be? A good place to start is any area in which either of you is critical of the other on a regular basis.

*Step 2.* Ask your partner how he or she experiences you as having unrealistic expectations, using those broad areas mentioned in Step 1.

Discuss how mutual unrealistic expectations about your relationship may hamper you from accepting each other more fully just as you are and honoring the five freedoms.

## Daily Communication

Make an agreement with your partner to schedule some time every day—at least half an hour—to talk openly about the day's events. Do not let anything get in the way of this daily habit. Give up all excuses about lack of time, conflicts with kids' bedtime, work, or fatigue. Settle for nothing less than this minimal amount of time to reconnect with each other.

*Step 1.* Begin to share with your partner on a daily basis at least one thing he or she has done that day for which you feel genuine appreciation. Look first at those habitual behaviors that you may appreciate but have learned to take for granted.

*Step 2.* Begin to express to your partner on a daily basis at least one characteristic about him or her than you genuinely appreciate. This appreciation is not for what the person has done but for *who* he or she is. Does it feel any different to express this appreciation than the type expressed in Step 1? Many people find they feel more vulnerable in sharing appreciation for *who their partner is* than for *what they do,* and this appreciation feels more meaningful to the partner. Do not force yourself to make something up. Choose only those qualities that you truly appreciate but for which you have not shared your appreciation with your partner.

## Nourishing the Relationship

At least once a month, schedule a mutually enjoyable activity with your partner as an opportunity for playful relationship nourishment. Do not include kids, friends, or anyone else. It does not matter what activity you do or how you do it. The only thing that is important is that you are doing something together to enhance the playful side of your relationship. Let your childlike side meet your partner's child-like side and forget about being mature adults for a while.

*Step 1.* Every month celebrate your anniversary. Remind each other that another month of marriage has passed and mark this occasion in some small way. This observance will help keep you both apprecia-tive of your commitment to each other.

*Step 2.* On your annual marriage anniversary, repeat your marriage vows. You might include the music that was featured at your wed-ding, or bring some object from your marriage ceremony into this remarriage ceremony. Consciously recommit yourself, discussing whether there is any part of your vows that no longer feels true for you or anything you might like to add to the original vows.

This can be a powerful way to realize that you are choosing your partner again and again, each day, week, month, and year, and that you can alter whatever is not right and celebrate everything that is. It can help reconnect you to the original feelings that led you to choose your partner to begin with. It can bring back (in a healthy way) some of the deliciously romantic halo effect.

## Acknowledge Good Intentions

Try to remember that no matter how it appears on the surface, your partner's intentions are not to hurt you but to end up feeling good about himself or herself. Although he or she may use ineffective or harmful means to further these aims, if you can identify these good intentions, you can see behind the means.

Good intention refers to the desired internal experience behind a surface goal; it is an image, thought, or feeling that is conducive to one's well-being. Good intentions may include the desire to feel more acknowledged, more complete, more capable, more sexy, more loved, more appreciated, or more secure.

By exploring your partner's possible positive intentions you are more likely to stay in touch with his or her basic goodness, and to keep the positive aspects of the halo effect alive in your relationship.[4]

# PART FOUR

# ESCAPING
## FROM THE
# TRAP

# TWELVE

# CREATING ROOM FOR YOURSELF:
## *Learning to Live with a Perfectionist*

*You cannot know your own perfection*
*until you have honored*
*all those who were created like you.*
A Course in Miracles

IF YOU ARE THE spouse, lover, friend, parent, or child of a perfection-ist (or wondering whether to get emotionally involved with a perfec-tionist), this chapter is addressed to you. If you are a perfectionist yourself, read this chapter from the point of view of someone who might be trying to live with or relate to you.

Perfectionism is a difficult character trait to abolish, even when we seriously desire to give it up. As we have shown, the lifelong condi-tioning of perfectionism contributes to an overall personality style that helps us get through the world. Even though we clearly suffer more than we need to from our perfectionistic thinking and be-havior, they help us cope. You can be sure we are not easily going to give up feelings of pseudosuperiority that have been a primary source of our self-esteem and self-support.

Since most perfectionists have little desire to give up striving for perfection, those who try to teach us new behaviors will have a strug-gle on their hands. We tend to be stubborn, self-righteous, and firm in our convictions. Our intellectual defenses are strong. It is not easy for us to give up the very thinking and behavior that bolster our identity.

In addition to the best of self-help efforts, it frequently requires professional psychotherapy to change the perfectionistic thinking and behavior that have been shaped over a lifetime. As we have shown, there are significant psychological, social, and religious influences that must be confronted if the perfectionist is to make any real behavioral change. Why should anyone give up a personality style that is largely applauded and positively reinforced by the society in which we live?

As perfectionists, we will consider giving up our striving for perfection only when we have suffered so much from its consequences that we can no longer tolerate the pain. Perhaps we have experienced unbearable guilt, shame, and self-loathing in our repeated failures to measure up. Maybe we have been profoundly unhappy and lonely for many years and realize something is wrong. Perhaps through our continued rejection of others, we have alienated so many people in our lives that we realize it is time to make a radical change. But until the pain is enough to crack through our strong intellectual defenses, we are unlikely to walk into a psychotherapist's office and ask for help.

Our reluctance to alter our style of thinking and behavior doesn't mean that we can't accomplish some positive change through self-help methods such as this book. By working with the concepts and tools offered in this book, we may question our need to hold perfection as our goal. We can realize that holding on to the image of ourselves as perfectionists simply causes more pain than it is worth. We can begin to transform the energy that has gone toward perfection into a more realistic, practical, and satisfying goal of excellence. We can learn to use the positive traits of our perfectionism in modified ways that satisfy our need for high performance.

I believe it is more worthwhile and effective to try to reorient perfectionism in the direction of striving for excellence than to try to give up perfection-seeking totally. For those perfectionists who need to drastically alter their thinking and behavior, the psychotherapist has his or her work cut out. But, as I have seen in my own practice, good psychotherapy with a motivated patient can be quite effective.

When they are not too extreme, perfectionistic thinking and behavior have some redeeming personal and social values. Before you take on the formidable project of trying to teach an old perfectionist new tricks, be aware of these positive values. You don't want to throw out the proverbial baby with the bath water.

## THE UPSIDE OF LIVING WITH A PERFECTIONIST

Assuming the typical degree of compulsivity, perfectionists tend to be neat, clean, and orderly in personal hygiene, dress, and housekeeping habits. Often we have methodical minds that are above average or superior in the ability to intellectually analyze and solve problems. Even though we fall far short of our desire to attain perfection, we often reach high levels of achievement as a result of our strong drive to perform well. We may be top performers in our chosen work and may have accumulated many of the material goods that confer status in our society. Because of this, we appear on the surface to be well-adjusted and successful winners and are typically viewed as good catches as marital partners. We are often thought of as good providers.

A mild to moderate degree of compulsivity can go a long way in keeping home, job, and body functioning smoothly. As perfectionists, we tend to be conscientious, reliable, punctual, and to take obligations seriously. In addition, we tend to be dedicated and concerned (sometimes overconcerned) parents, careful with money, and ethical and law-abiding citizens. These attributes make us relatively stable, trustworthy, and predictable partners for those living with us.

Because of our desire to be acknowledged and admired by others and our strong beliefs about how things ought to be done, we may offer our time and skills to community organizations. We may spearhead political groups or head committees working for charitable causes. We often work hard at these commitments, anxious for recognition and appreciation for our donation of time, energy, and skills. Those living with us may indirectly enjoy enhanced social status because of our accomplishments and the recognition and respect we are accorded. We are able to feel passionately about the things we become interested in. Our energy, intensity, and commitment to projects can be contagious and keep life exciting for those living with us.

Undeniably, life with a perfectionist has its more problematic aspects as well. The following deal with the downside.

## STRATEGIES FOR LIVING WITH A PERFECTIONIST

*Don't try to tell a perfectionist that he or she should be less perfectionistic.* This is definitely a losing proposition, as you will find out if you try it. The perfectionist will interpret the suggestion to mean that he has not measured up in his attempt to be a "good" perfectionist. The reaction will be one of hurt or anger.

In either type of reaction, the perfectionist feels unappreciated for his efforts to be the best he can be. The neurotic perfectionist thus has one more thing to feel inadequate and guilty about. Feeling unappreciated, the perfectionist may try even harder to measure up, still hoping to win the approval and admiration of the loved one. For perfectionists, more is always better. The perfectionist may stubbornly hold on ever tighter to aiming for perfection. The resulting self-righteousness only aggravates the discord between the perfectionist and the partner.

Since perfectionists tend to think of their affliction as a virtue, they don't understand how you could want them to be less virtuous. It's like telling a quarterback to throw fewer touchdown passes—it sounds contrary to what he knows is right. The alternative is to tell the perfectionist specifically what you want.

*Learn to communicate your feelings to the perfectionist.* If you are to live with a perfectionist and not lose your own sense of identity, it is paramount that you be verbally assertive. You must not be afraid to speak up and take care of yourself. Otherwise your partner will tend to dictate to you how to live. Before long, you will feel like you have lost your own sense of self and are living as a satellite to the needs of the perfectionist. You will begin to harbor anger and resentment that will gradually undermine the foundation of the relationship. Finally you may either withdraw or explode.

One helpful fill-in-the-blank formula for expressing to the perfectionist how you feel is the following: "When you _____, I feel _____. What I would like is for you to _____." For example, "When you harp on me to pick up the newspapers, I feel disregarded. What I would like is for you to wait until I have had a chance to read them." Or: "When you are critical of my hair not being just right, I feel like you are trying to shape me into being what you want me to look like. What I would like is for you to lay off and let me wear my hair the way I want." Or: "When you get anxious when I'm not ready to go on time, I feel rushed and forced to act at your pace. What I would like is for you to understand that I'm not always going to be ready to go just when you are and for you to be able to cope with that."

With narcissistic perfectionists (as contrasted to more neurotic perfectionists), you may find that often they don't really think or care about how others feel when they make a decision to do something. They simply do what they want. The perfectionist's partner and others often feel insulted or deliberately ignored.

The truth, unfortunately, is worse: the narcissistic perfectionist has not even considered anyone else. Far from trying to insult you, the narcissist is not giving you any thought whatsoever. This can either make you feel that the narcissist is hopeless, or help you see that it is not a personal slight—the narcissist is simply too wrapped up in himself to recognize what's going on with you. This is why you have to speak up.

You can slowly teach the narcissist to begin to pay attention to your presence. Many people resent having to be responsible for this kind of teaching of a spouse or friend. It is sometimes a lot easier simply not to get involved when you see strong signs of narcissistic self-preoccupation. But if, for whatever reason, you're "stuck" with a narcissist, then the only solution is to teach him or her to *be more aware of and make room for you.*

Here is an example. Let's say you're at lunch with your friend, who happens to be a narcissistic perfectionist. She is going on melo-dramatically at great length about her own life. You like your friend and care about how she is feeling, but you also begin to feel left out of the conversation. In fact, you notice it isn't a conversation at all, but a monologue. You begin to feel resentful that your friend doesn't seem to realize that she has left you out—she could just as well be talking to a chair. What do you do?

You can sit and listen indefinitely and later walk away feeling un-comfortable and discounted by your friend. Or, after 10 or 15 min-utes pass and you notice your friend has not stopped talking about herself or shown any interest in you, you could say something like "Excuse me, Linda, but are you aware that we have been sitting here for 15 minutes and you've been doing all the talking? I get the feeling you're not much interested in what's going on with me."

This could lead to a discussion of how your friend tends to dump her emotions out to you repeatedly without showing much interest in you. If you're not willing to help your friend become aware that she is wrapped up in her own world and that you want attention too, you are likely to end up feeling bitter and used.

You might be surprised how many people put up with such treat-ment from their friends and are unwilling to say anything about it. They think it's better to preserve whatever it is they are getting from the friendship than risk speaking up and losing a friend. But when it comes to someone with whom you are living, failure to speak up will only result in your feeling like you've been used.

The narcissist forgets that others are the center of their own sub-jective worlds. He acts as if others exist and are valuable only so far as they can help satisfy his needs and wants. It takes someone with good ego strength, who is not afraid of confrontation and compromise, to be able to live with a narcissistic perfectionist without becoming a small satellite orbiting around the partner's sun.

*It is important that a couple be able to share the different meanings a particular behavior may have for each of them.* For example, one man complained that his perfectionistic wife became enraged whenever she found an empty milk carton in the kitchen sink. She believed that he purposely left it there for her to dispose of and to annoy her. This happened repeatedly, and each time, they would fight about it.

In a couples therapy session it emerged that the man's mother had always told him to put an emptied milk carton in the sink, wash it out, and let it sit until it dried out. He had never told his wife *why* he did this, despite their frequent arguments over it. When she finally understood the meaning of his action and saw that it wasn't meant to annoy her or to make her pick up after him, she was able to tolerate this behavior without becoming enraged.

*Understand that perfectionists are not out to hurt you or purposely make your life miserable.* Making your life miserable is simply a by-product of making their *own* lives miserable. They usually have little control over their perfectionism. This means that, within limits, you will have to learn to tolerate some of the thinking and behavior that the perfectionist is unwilling to alter. If you can't or won't learn to tolerate what the perfectionist is unwilling to change, it is best not to make a commitment to live with a perfectionist.

We said "within limits." This means you must set some boundaries.

## Setting Boundaries

You need to set appropriate boundaries (as to what you are willing to take) and limits (as to how much of it you will take) with the perfectionist. This is necessary to ensure that your personal differences in thinking and behavior are respected. Unless you set personal boundaries, the perfectionist may eventually swallow your individuality. Let us examine some of the perfectionist's typical beliefs and ways of expressing these beliefs that commonly become issues of contention in relationships. You will see that the limits and boundaries you set can be quite narrow and firm. In this way, you can effectively help alter the perfectionist's behavior if he or she is willing to engage your confrontations and truly wants to make the relationship work.

*Issue #1: Confronting blame.* The neurotic perfectionist tends to blame himself and others when things don't go right. You can cope with the perfectionist's self-blame by calmly and gently trying to help him see that little is gained by blame. If the perfectionist doesn't blame himself, he is likely to blame you. Your coping strategy is this: *Don't accept the assignment of blame.*

Accept responsibility—not blame. Blame is condemning of oneself or another through unhealthy guilt. Responsibility means acknowledging, that "This is my doing. I won't blame myself and unnecessarily feel guilty, nor do I need to blame you and make you feel guilty." When we have done something that transgresses our ethical or moral guidelines, it is appropriate for us to feel healthy guilt. This leads to making amends and letting go of the guilt. Blame just tends to make us feel guilty in an unhealthy way. It breeds resentment and reinforces old shame. So don't allow the perfectionist to blame you for what is none of your business. Here is an illustration of how you can accept responsibility while rejecting the blame being assigned by the perfectionist:

> *John:* There you go again—leaving your papers scattered all over my desk. How can you be so sloppy? It's your fault that I can't get my report finished—you know I can't begin work with a cluttered desk!

> *Mary:* John, stop blaming me because you're having trouble completing that project. Yes, I did leave my papers on your desk

and sometimes I *am* sloppy, but you know very well that my sloppiness has nothing to do with your procrastination.

*Issue #2: Confronting "shoulds."* The perfectionist will often tell you what you should feel, think, and do. Keeping in mind Albert Ellis's dictum that "shouldhood equals shithood," you must not allow these "shoulds" to be foisted upon you. Assert yourself calmly but firmly each time the perfectionist tells you how you should be doing something. Let him know that this approach is not the way to get you to do what he wants. Tell the perfectionist that it would be more effective for him to simply offer his own best judgment for your consideration—not to tell you what you should do.

For example, most people are more accepting of a comment like "I'd take the chance and go for the new job if it were me, honey," rather than "You should take the new job." We all want to be given advice (whether or not we ask for it) in a diplomatic way that *preserves our sense of adult autonomy*—not in a way that makes us feel like children being told what to do.

Of course, you need not be a perfectionist to offer "shoulds." Most parents get caught in the trap of "shoulds," and most of us have some experience in confronting our parents' attempts to control our lives with "shoulds." Draw on this experience when you confront the perfectionist. Before long, you will be able to teach the perfectionist to find more acceptable ways to offer an opinion. If he must, let him continue to speak of "shoulds" when it comes to his own behavior.

There may be occasional exceptions to the rule of never accepting "shoulds." At times, you may ask for advice from your perfectionistic partner and it may come in the form of a "should." If it does, accept it without comment. There is no need to make an issue out of the use of this word. It is *the need to set limits* as to how much the perfectionist will dominate your decision-making and behavior that is important here, not hang-ups on language.

*Issue #3: Questioning demand statements.* Statements of demand imply absolute necessity, but they are usually based on irrational beliefs.

Almost always the "necessity" is no more than a preference. Demand statements by a perfectionist can be difficult to cope with. The perfectionist usually puts demands in absolute, all-or-nothing terms and desires their immmediate fulfillment. The irrationality of these statements will be easy for you to spot. Examples:

- "I've *got* to be the one who sells the most this month or I can't live with myself."

- "We *must* win this game or we'll never get another chance to make it into the league finals."

- "You *must* keep the bathroom spotless or I'll never be comfortable using it."

- "I *need* that new dress or I can't go to the dance."

The all-or-nothing nature of the demands as well as the immediacy with which they should be fulfilled can be trying for the one living with the perfectionist. You get the feeling that for the demanding perfectionist (as Meryl Streep put it), "instant gratification isn't fast enough."

The best way to handle demand statements is to counter the perfectionist's irrational demands with a rational statement. Since perfectionists tend to respect and listen to logical, rational thinking, this approach is often effective. You can say something like, "You've *got* to have that new car? Or you mean you'd *like* that new car but it isn't really necessary, just desirable?" Or, "Yes, it would be nice if you had a new dress for the dance, but we need that money for the house payment, and you know you'll look great in one of the dresses you already have."

To defuse the all-or-nothing urgency of the demand, put the issue into perspective by comparing it to the larger picture. For example, "Yes, I can see that winning the game seems very important to you, but compared to Jim's losing his job last week, you know it really isn't the end of the world if you don't win."

*Issue #4: Neutralizing catastrophic beliefs.* As with demand statements, it is helpful to challenge the validity of the perfectionist's irrational catastrophic beliefs. Remember, you are confronting the perfectionist not just because you care about how she tortures herself. As well, you are trying to avoid letting the perfectionist's irrationality affect your own thinking and behavior. You are protecting yourself by creating room for yourself and by establishing a clear self-boundary.

Catastrophic beliefs assume that the worst possible result will follow if the perfectionist doesn't get what she wants. Examples:

- "If I don't close that sale tomorrow, I'll never get another chance and the boss will think I'm dog meat."

- "If we don't go away for a vacation sometime this year, I'll go out of my mind. I wonder if we'll ever take a vacation again."

- "If I go in for the mammography, I know they'll find something terrible."

- "If we don't follow the directions exactly, we'll get lost and never find our way back to the main road."

- "If I don't get an A in chemistry, I'll never get into medical school."

- "If we don't get our bid accepted for that house, we'll never find another one as nice."

It is necessary to challenge the if-then logic of the catastrophic belief. For example: "Honey, even if you don't close that sale tomorrow, it doesn't mean your boss will be angry or judge you harshly. It's just another account." Or: "Even if we do get lost, we could enjoy the side roads. We're not in a hurry and I'm sure we'll eventually get back to the main road."

*Issue #5: Coping with intolerance statements.* Intolerance statements are exaggerations that overdramatize the perfectionist's position. For example: "I *can't stand* the way Jane keeps leaving her clothes on the floor!" Or: "I *just can't cope* with the way your brother always interrupts me when I'm speaking!" Or: "*I'll just stop eating and die* if Jim doesn't call me for a date."

Sometimes humor is an effective strategy for dealing with intolerance statements. Playfully repeating back to the perfectionist her own statement can make the point: "Yes, I know you'll just *fall over and die* if my brother interrupts you one more time!" Or: "Yes, I know *the world will just come to an end* if you don't get that new dress!"

At other times, a slap of reality will do the job: "Come on now, you know very well that it doesn't matter whether he interrupts you—you *can* stand it and you *will* stand it, unless you're willing to tell him how you feel." Or: "Yes, I know it's frustrating and stressful to drive in heavy traffic on these narrow streets, but you *can* cope with it until we get out of the city. Just try to relax and listen to the music."

Intolerance statements, like whining and complaining, can be irritating to listen to, but remember they are not really aimed at you. If you simply make the perfectionist aware of how often he uses these exaggerations of intolerance, he may stop using them so automatically.

*Issue #6: Confronting rating statements.* This issue is one of the most challenging to relationships. While the perfectionist's intolerance statements and catastrophic beliefs are irritating but self-directed, rating statements (along with blaming and "shoulds") will be aimed at you and others. To the perfectionist, virtually everything and everyone is open to being judged and rated. If you accept this perpetual comparing game, you can be sure the ratings you receive will be no better than what the perfectionist gives himself—and usually worse! Examples of the comparing game include:

- "I'm smarter than you."
- "My car is more expensive than yours."
- "I have a better sense of fashion than you."

- "I can dance better than you."
- "My house is fancier than yours."
- "She doesn't have as nice a body as I do."
- "Mary, why can't you get high grades like your brother?"
- "I wish you were as sociable as my old boyfriend."

A variation of this comparing game is to imply superiority by continually putting down everyone else. "John has a good forehand, but I can get him every time on his backhand." "So what if she does have big breasts—look at her horse mouth!" "He has a lot of publications, but look what journals they come out in—they're not very prestigious, if you ask me."

Behind much of the comparing game is the perfectionist's need to inflate his ego at the expense of others. Comparing also serves to establish dominance and control over others. If the perfectionist can convince himself that he is better than the next guy, he thinks this makes him more worthwhile as a human being.

Behind much of the need to put others down is unconscious envy. As we defined it in chapter 8, envy is the painful or resentful awareness of an advantage enjoyed by another and the desire to possess the same advantage. We want what the other has and we can't stand seeing him have it when we don't. Because perfectionists are so acutely tuned in to their relative position on the status totem pole, any perceived advantage on the part of another is experienced as a diminishing of oneself. No wonder domination and control become so important.

How can you deal with the unconscious envy and need to be superior that fuel the perfectionist's rating game? Again, heightening awareness is a helpful tool. If you point out to the perfectionist how often he puts down others, this behavior may become less automatic. When the rating is aimed at you, make it clear you are not interested in being compared to others and would like to be appreciated for your own uniqueness.

Be aware that perfectionists have a difficult time truly understanding this idea of individual uniqueness. To threaten to take away
their comparing game is to throw them into confusion. They don't
see how they can really matter if they can't compare favorably to
others.

Don't be afraid to simply point out, "Jim, you're comparing me to
your ex-wife (mother, sister, etc.). I love and value you for who you
are—I would like for you to do the same with me." Or: "Jennifer,
when you keep telling me I can't cook as well as you do, I feel like you
need to put me down and see me as less than you. Is there anything
I'm doing to threaten you in any way?"

This question—"Is there anything I'm doing to threaten you?"
may make the perfectionist think twice about why he is playing the
comparing game. The best you can hope for with a perfectionist is to
diminish the frequency and intensity of the comparing. It is unrealistic to expect the perfectionist to relinquish the habit entirely. This
is where your willingness to be compassionate and to compromise
comes into the picture.

In confronting the various irrational beliefs and statements of
the perfectionist, you will slowly begin to feel you are creating a safe
boundary so that you can be confident your sense of separateness will
not be engulfed. Working with these boundary issues in a conscious
and thorough manner will help you learn to live with a perfectionist.

## Additional Strategies

*Don't let yourself get trapped in rational argument alone.* Even if logic
seems to persuade the perfectionist to your thinking, focus on feelings too. Perfectionists are much more confortable with cool rationality than they are with strong emotions. While your rationality
will be an invaluable tool to get through to the perfectionist, it is natural for you to want to experience your partner as able to be vulnerable, gentle, and willing to feel. A hard-driving, overly logical,

competitive, and unemotional partner may make you feel like you're living with a robot. It's like trying to live with the Tin Woodsman in *The Wizard of Oz* before he gets a heart!

Perfectionists' comfort with logic and rationality is ironic, given the numerous irrational thought patterns they utilize. But our point here is that if you want to help make the perfectionist in your life more tolerable to live with, it is helpful to bring him or her back to a focus on feelings.

One useful strategy is to periodically inquire of the perfectionist, "What are you feeling now?" Or, "How do you feel when John doesn't give you what you want?" It is much easier for many perfectionists to feel anger, resentment, and hostility than it is for them to acknowledge softer, more vulnerable feelings. When the perfectionist does express tenderness, gentleness, sensitivity, or affection in loving ways, let him know how good it makes you feel to see this kind of emotional vulnerability.

*Without giving up your sense of self, allow the perfectionist to make many decisions that affect both of you but that you don't really care about.* The perfectionist usually prefers to be in control and dominate the decision-making. As long as the decisions aren't too important, it doesn't hurt to reinforce this sense of control. But make your feelings heard when it comes to big decisions. In this way, you can let your perfectionistic partner have a sense of control without damaging the relationship. The important thing here is to realize that all issues and decisions are not equally important and to know what matters to you.

Do you really care what color the bathroom tile is if your partner is affectionate and sexually responsive? Does it matter that your partner keeps stacks of papers and magazines at her bedside for months if she is tender, loving, and treats you with respect? As long as she consults with you on issues that both of you consider important, the small stuff is really not worth fighting about. In this way, following a tenet of Eastern philosophy, you can be more in control by being strong enough to give up some of your control.

*Last but not least, give your perfectionistic partner some ego-strengthening compliments.* "Feed the hungry bee," as author Ken Kesey put it. In other words, let the perfectionist hear often how special he is to you. Tell him often how attractive he is and how much you appreciate his positive qualities. Let him know how good it feels, for example, to know you can trust and rely on him.

On the surface, it may sound like I am suggesting that you feed the perfectionist a dose of exactly what it seems he has too much of: inflated grandiosity, a sense of being superior and special. But remember, beneath the surface the perfectionist longs to feel genuinely loved and admired by parents, family, and peers to make up for feeling *never enough.* So be generous with authentic compliments, with the hope of filling some of the insecurity that lies below the surface bravado. Eventually you might find that the perfectionist has become someone you want to live with rather than without.

# THIRTEEN

# TRANSFORMING PERFECTIONISM:
## Tools Toward Excellence

*When the mind is no longer resisting, no longer avoiding or blaming*
*what is but is simply passively aware, then in that passivity of the*
*mind you will find there comes a transformation.*

J. KRISHNAMURTI

IN THIS CHAPTER WE focus on ways to transform perfectionistic
thinking and behavior into striving for excellence. It is possible to utilize the best that perfectionistic thinking has to offer without having
to embrace its unrealistic and self-defeating aspects. Our aim is to be
able to experience the personal satisfaction that goes with knowing
when good enough is really enough even though it falls short of perfection. One aspect of perfection-seeking that we have not yet examined closely is the assumed connection between striving for perfect
performance and the desire to feel satisfaction. As others have
pointed out,[1] breaking this long-held and unconsciously assumed
connection is an important step in transforming perfectionism. We
must realize that it is possible to feel deep satisfaction with ourselves
and our projects even when we don't perform perfectly. Because finding alternative routes to satisfaction is a key to letting go of perfectionistic standards, we will concentrate on tools to help us find these
alternatives. The tools include rational inquiry; a record form for re-
defining the terms of personal satisfaction; exercises for confronting

fear and anxiety and becoming grounded in the present; challenging false beliefs; and applying elements of excellence to help transform perfectionism.

We may experience satisfaction as a feeling of wholeness, completeness, pleasure, or integrity. It may come from many sources other than perfect performance: doing a job well, filling our inner emptiness, finding our true inner goodness and self-worth, winning the respect and admiration of others, or connecting with our own original perfect nature. Despite self-critical judgments of our performance, we continue to desire satisfaction. Think about your answers to the following questions:

How much satisfaction do you get from the process of striving for perfection? How much satisfaction do you derive from your actual accomplishments? When was the last time you experienced satisfaction because you actually measured up to your own perfectionistic expectation? For the sake of argument, let's say that you can remember when you last measured up to your standard and experienced a sense of satisfaction. Compared to the far greater number of times when you felt frustration, self-torture, regret, and inadequacy, does it really seem worthwhile to subject yourself to all this turmoil? Aren't the odds of achieving satisfaction heavily stacked against you when you link satisfaction to perfection?

Can you imagine finding satisfaction in your projects and activities even when you do not perform perfectly? Try this simple visualization: Imagine a common situation in which you perform well but less than perfectly. See the actual outcome in your mind's eye and compare it to your image of the perfect performance. How different are the two? Are they so different that good-enough performance should bring you any less satisfaction than some idealistic goal of perfection?

Now, using this same outcome, imagine feeling *very* satisfied with your performance, more than you would ordinarily allow yourself to feel. Notice that you have a choice as to how much satisfaction you feel. It is simply a conditioned response to feel less pleasure with a less-than-perfect performance.

## Redefining the Terms of Satisfaction

The connection between satisfaction (or pleasure) and perfection was made for us long ago, in childhood. For the most part we don't even think about it anymore, but the way we experience it is quite obvious: we feel little satisfaction and too much self-critical pessimism. The self-acceptance and satisfaction we could be enjoying are replaced by a self-critical sense of inadequacy. Instead of stroking ourselves gently with soothing gratification, we bat ourselves over the head for not being good enough.

For example, let's say your expectation of perfection involves playing tennis. You have an image in mind as to what it would be like to play the game perfectly. You always end up feeling you have fallen short, since your image of perfect tennis means committing no unforced errors. While you may occasionally play a match in which you have few unforced errors, you may have never played a match with none. Consequently, you feel less satisfaction with your performance than you could have felt had you lowered your expectation from perfection to excellence. More satisfaction would be possible if you allowed yourself a healthy dose of good-enough feeling for simply playing the best you could.

Your degree of satisfaction, then, is a matter of consciously giving yourself permission to feel more enjoyment with a less-than-perfect performance. How much satisfaction you allow yourself to feel about anything is up to you. You can reinforce this concept by saying, "I will allow myself to feel a high degree of satisfaction with 10 or fewer unforced errors in any given match." Thus, you redefine the terms of satisfaction. The goal of 10 or fewer unforced errors becomes your standard of excellent performance. If you reach that goal, you will allow yourself to feel just as much satisfaction as if you had played with no errors.

Your ability to feel greater satisfaction may be constrained by unconscious psychological programs that continue to exert powerful influence. This is where the help of a good psychotherapist can enable you to accomplish more than you can on your own.

## ASSIGNING GOOD-ENOUGH PERFORMANCE

In learning to break the connection between satisfaction and perfect performance, it is helpful to keep a record of the degrees of satisfaction you derive from various activities. You can do this by using the Performance-Satisfaction Record Form, in which you specify in objective, measurable terms what constitutes good-enough performance for various activities.[2]

This exercise is helpful for two reasons. First, it encourages you to define and refine your expectations in realistic, attainable terms. Second, it helps you set up the conditions that will enable you to give yourself approval and feel satisfaction upon achieving your goal. If you have set your terms too high, you will see this clearly as you continue to keep your record. You can then lower the objectives accordingly.

This exercise forces you to realize the difference between perfect performance and good-enough performance. It also helps you allow yourself to feel satisfaction even when you fall short of your goals and even when you don't think you will derive much satisfaction from an activity.

First, identify an activity. Then decide what you want your good-enough performance to be. Put it in objective, measurable terms, if possible. After you have tackled the tasks, enter (as a percentage) how close you feel you came to achieving your good-enough performance. In the last column, estimate the degree of satisfaction (again as a percentage) you derived from your performance of the task. A sample form shows a record for several different activities.

Working with this record form for a few weeks will help you think in terms of measurable performance until doing so becomes second nature. In this way, you are less likely to judge yourself as falling short simply because you feel you have not performed perfectly. It will require your subjective judgment in assigning a percentage score for how you measured up to your objective goals. And, of course, your assessment of how satisfying the activity was is also purely subjective.

## PERFORMANCE—SATISFACTION RECORD FORM

| Activity | "Good Enough" Performance | % Attained | % Satisfied |
|---|---|---|---|
| Work report | Reads easily, covers all aspects of topic, turned in on time, gets boss's approval | 75% (it didn't read as smoothly as I wanted it to; wasn't thorough) | 90% (enjoyed writing it and boss loved it!) |
| Sunday golf | Make at least 9 pars, 2 birdies; beat all other players, shoot 78 or better | 80% (shot 77, had 9 pars, 1 birdie but lost to Ron, who shot 76) | 100%! (exciting, came down to last hole) |
| Put stain on new shingles | Complete the job; don't spill paint; do it within 1 hour | 100% (So what?) | 20% (back hurts from bending over; hate painting) |
| Tennis with Ricky | 10 or less unforced errors in 2 sets; practice serve and volley game; practice putting spin on serve | 50% (had more than 20 errors; not enough volleys) | 85% (beautiful day, enjoyed exercise; controlled temper; nice lunch) |
| Chapter 13 of book | Complete at least 8 pages; clearly explain connection between satisfaction and good enough performance. Illustrate by way of sample record form. | 70% (only completed 6 pages; record form graphics could be jazzier) | 90% (like way it looks; creative adaptation of Burns' form) |

*Figure* 13-1

In working with this record form, you may discover the following:

- Performance is *not* always positively related to satisfaction.

- Performance in objective, measurable terms gives you something realistic to shoot for rather than an unreachable standard.

- You can equate good-enough performance to excellence and need not depend upon the standards of others to determine whether you have achieved excellence.

- Much more than you might think, it is possible to enjoy activities in which you don't measure up to perfection or even to good-enough performance.

- Most importantly, you can begin to see how much control you actually possess in the regulation of your own internal states of satisfaction and pleasure, regardless of the activity itself or the actual outcome of your performance.

## A Self-Acceptance Philosophy

As you work with the Performance-Satisfaction Record Form, an underlying philosophy of self-acceptance will facilitate your greater satisfaction with a less-than-perfect performance. Here, then, is a short statement of the philosophy of pursuing satisfaction and self-acceptance that is appropriate in working to transform perfectionism to excellence:

> I am a unique human who will live for a limited period of time, so I'd better try to discover what I really like and dislike, and engage, within reason, in as much of the liking and as little of the disliking behavior of which I am capable.
>
> I shall try not to rate or measure my 'self,' my 'totality,' my 'personality,' my 'essence,' or my 'being' at all, for these entities are too vague and global to be given single, over-generalized

ratings. I shall neither esteem nor devalue my 'self' but shall try to accept my aliveness and my potentiality for continued aliveness and enjoyment *whether or not* I perform well and *whether or not* I am approved by others. But at the same time, I shall strive to do well, to be approved, and to help my society because these goals will probably bring me and it a longer and better existence.[3]

## GOOD-ENOUGH AFFIRMATIONS

The following statements of affirmation should be repeated frequently during the day (either internally or out loud) as an aid in transforming perfectionistic thinking to excellence thinking. Affirmation statements put into positive words those beliefs that lend direction and support to a chosen goal. Obsessive-oriented perfectionists often do well with affirmations, because they tend to repeat various statements to themselves anyway in an effort to maintain self-control.

After reading the following list, choose one affirmation that feels right for you. Repeat it whenever you find yourself standing in line, driving, waiting for something, and at other moments when your mind is not occupied. Sometimes, if you repeat an affirmation many times, you may find that it begins to repeat itself without any conscious effort on your part. Repeat the affirmation for at least two or three days, then choose another one to focus on. The value of these affirmations is that they may slowly begin to counter your unconscious negatively programmed beliefs and help instill new, positive ones. Use these affirmations only in a constructive manner—do not become obsessed with any of them, and keep in mind they are only mental tools.

- Perfection is impossible; I will be satisfied with excellence.
- I am entitled to feel satisfaction without having to perform perfectly.

- I will allow myself to feel deeper levels of satisfaction and pleasure.
- I will open to and accept the feeling of being good enough.
- I will not judge others harshly for failing to live up to my standards.
- I will not make my self-worth depend on my performance.
- I will note and neutralize as quickly as possible all critical self-talk.
- I will counter all critical self-talk with positive statements.
- I am a unique human being of value; my value can never be taken away.
- Since there is nobody in the world just like me, I need not compare myself to others to feel special.
- I am special simply because of my uniqueness.
- I am good enough just as I am.
- No matter how much I enjoy material possessions, I will not make my self-worth dependent upon having them.
- Enjoying material comforts and possessions has nothing to do with my value as a human being.
- I am not less just because I *have* less; I am not more just because I might *have* more.
- Momentary perfection comes as I settle into the present and accept myself as the best person I can be.
- I will continue to grow toward wholeness in every way possible.
- The pursuit of excellence will help me feel a sense of self-respect.
- I vow to give my best and most conscious effort to everything I do.

- When I fall short of good-enough performance, I will remember that I have still made my best effort.
- I will not feel guilty unless I know that I haven't made my best effort.

## BEYOND ANXIETY AND FEAR

We have emphasized that the perfectionist is fueled by anxiety and fear rather than by the anticipatory excitement that leads to the satisfaction of good-enough performance. *Anxiety is the uneasiness caused by an inability to allow yourself to settle gracefully into the present. It is always related to something in the future* that you imagine may happen, even if that future is only the next few seconds, minutes, or hours.

In order to give up a driven, perfectionistic mentality, you must be willing to examine closely the feelings of anxiety and fear that support it. This inquiry requires that you be able to tolerate a certain degree of discomfort that comes from *staying with* unpleasantness rather than avoiding it. This tolerance will be easier to achieve if you know that you won't get caught in unpleasantness beyond your control. The next exercise will help you learn to stay with an experience, and the following one will help you feel more in control as you learn how to pull yourself out of anxious thoughts if they become too uncomfortable.

### Exercise: Grounding into the Present

Grounding into the present means coming back to the immediacy of your senses. Anxiety cannot survive without your thoughts going into the imagined dreadful future. Coming back to your senses will usually bring you out of any anxious thought. You can use the points of contact between your body and other objects as grounding points to bring yourself back to the present at any time, whenever you begin to fade away into the fantasyland of fearful or anxiety-tinged thought.

Begin to focus on exactly what you are now experiencing through your senses. Become aware of what information is coming through each sense. Notice any sounds in your environment. Notice any physical sensations in your body. Notice the feeling of touch—your hands on the book, your bottom on the chair, your feet on the floor, and any other parts of your body that are touching anything.

What do you actually experience through this contact? Do you experience the pressure of gravity of your foot against the ground? Do you feel a hardness or softness of your fingers touching the book cover? Do you notice any sense of vibration between your body and the object it is touching?

### Exercise: Shuttling

Knowing that you have the anchor of your senses to bring you back to the present, consciously and willfully experiment with one thought that you know will make you a little bit anxious. Choose a thought or image around some area related to your perfectionism—maybe a fear that a certain work project won't be good enough . . . or thoughts about how an upcoming challenge or performance may not go perfectly . . . or whether a certain person will approve of you. Whatever it might be, let yourself purposely go to this mildly anxious thought related to future outcome. (You may find it easier to focus your thoughts with eyes closed.)

Once you have made contact with the thought or situation, stay with it and feel your mild apprehension. Don't go away from it! Stay for at least a minute, getting a clear image of exactly what negative outcome you imagine. Now, gently come back to the touch of your body against the chair and the touch of your hands on this book. Get completely present-centered by looking around your environment.

Once again, shuttle back to your mildly anxiety-provoking thought. This time stay a little longer, maybe two minutes, noticing exactly what makes it so uncomfortable for you. Now, again, shuttle back to the present, to the anchor points of the touch of your body.

Now, this time, shuttle back again to your situation, but change the image to one of getting your desired outcome. Notice the difference in how you feel. What happens to your apprehension when you change the outcome favorably? Now, come back to your present here-and-now experience.

Whenever you imagine a dreadful outcome, you have two quick tools to help pull you out of it: (1) coming into the present through your physical contact points; and (2) neutralizing the negative outcome by substituting a positive one.

## Confronting Fear

In addition to anxious thoughts, you must be willing to confront the fearful thoughts that support your perfectionism. Fear and anxiety may seem like the same thing. However, your fear may be deeper than any specific anxiety-arousing image or event. *While anxiety is usually conscious and on the surface, fear may be unconscious, denied, or suppressed.* Simply by being alert to your all-or-nothing thinking and your catastrophic expectations, you can begin to notice the part fear plays in maintaining this mentality.

If you weren't so afraid that something terrible would happen if you failed to measure up, there would be no reason to hold on to such an aggravating, self-torturing, and self-defeating program. But you have convinced yourself that you're actually helping yourself by upholding such a high standard.

Allow yourself to feel your fear *to the bone.* Until you see how fear helps motivate your driven, anxious feelings of needing to perform perfectly, you won't seriously consider giving up what you have stubbornly believed to be a virtue. The following are some of the common fears behind perfectionism:

- I'm afraid I'll lose my standard for guiding my behavior. If I don't have perfection as my goal, what will I use to guide me?

- I'm afraid I'll simply give up, that without perfection as my goal, I'll fall apart and lose all motivation to do anything.

- I'm afraid of dying without having made a significant mark in the world. I can't stand the thought of being average, of not standing above the crowd.

- I'm afraid people won't like or respect me if I don't strive to reach perfection. They'll just pass me by; I'll be left in the dust.

- I'm afraid I can't survive financially unless I get ahead of the crowd by striving for perfection. After all, everyone knows it's a dog-eat-dog world.

- Life's too short for good enough to ever be enough for me. I'm afraid of dying, so I like to go for the gusto, and that means nothing short of perfection.

- I'm afraid of giving up the feeling of specialness that I enjoy in identifying myself as a perfectionist.

- I'm afraid I'll lose respect for myself unless I strive for perfection.

- I'm afraid I'll never feel whole and complete unless I strive for perfection.

- Without my fantasies of attaining perfection, I'll feel like a nobody.

Do some or all of these fit you? If so, which ones? Can you think of any other fears behind your perfectionism? Now, consider this: for any of the above fears that relate to giving up something that you believe is worth keeping, you can substitute good-enough striving for excellence in place of perfectionism. Think about it and see if this is not true for you. For example, if you are afraid of losing the feeling of specialness that you enjoy in identifying yourself as a perfectionist, you can just as easily feel special in identifying yourself as a striver for excellence. Or, if you are afraid of losing respect for yourself unless you strive for perfection, you can just as easily make striving for excellence your standard. This is not just a matter of substituting one word for another. The difference between striving for excellence and perfectionism is crucial in allowing yourself to lower your standards to a more realistic and attainable level.

## CHALLENGING FALSE BELIEFS

One or more of the false beliefs presented below are commonly part of the self-talk that maintains perfectionistic thinking. Often the beliefs are unconscious and unchallenged by the perfectionist and therefore exert considerable influence. Once you recognize them as false beliefs, you can replace them with true counter beliefs. In this way, you can begin to dismantle the assumptions that support perfectionism. In addition, you may want to pick an affirmation from those listed earlier in this chapter that supports a specific true counter belief.

*False Belief 1:* Perfectionism means following the rules to the letter, never deviating from what you're told.

*Counter Belief:* It's OK not to take things literally; it's OK to think for yourself and find creative solutions without relying strictly on rules and regulations.

*False Belief 2:* I will be punished if I don't always try to be perfect.

*Counter Belief:* I will be punishing *myself* if I keep trying to be perfect.

*False Belief 3:* I ought to feel guilty if I don't perform perfectly.

*Counter Belief:* I need not feel guilty as long as I try my best.

*False Belief 4:* Thinking like a perfectionist makes me more perfect.

*Counter Belief:* Thinking like a perfectionist makes me more miserable.

*False Belief 5:* Being critical of others helps me feel superior to them.

*Counter Belief:* Being critical of others only reveals my own need to feel superior to them and my underlying insecurity.

*False Belief 6:* People can be as perfect as smoothly running machines.

*Counter Belief:* People are more like machines that continually need to be adjusted, tuned, and periodically given complete overhauls.

*False Belief 7:* Trying to keep things frozen in a state of stability will make for a more perfect life.

*Counter Belief:* Without change, there would be no room for growth and new possibility.

As we all sooner or later become painfully aware, the very nature of life is constant change. According to Eastern philosophy, it is the ability to skillfully surf the waves of this ongoing change that puts us in the perfect flow of life. Do you let yourself become part of this perfect flow or do you struggle to swim upstream? Healthy striving for excellence means using all of your skills and talents to make creative adaptations to this ongoing flow—not to struggle to fight the changing nature of life.

While stability and security are legitimate and powerful needs, they are only one side of the coin. We must confront our fear of the other side—the side that represents the need for new stimulation, surprise, change, and even disruption, chaos, and transformation.

One way this acceptance of change is experienced by those striving for excellence is the ability to enjoy the process of getting to the goal, rather than focusing on the goal itself. The perfectionist tends to forget that it is the process of getting there that is what creative adaptations to life are all about—not just reaching some artificial goal, which is then quickly replaced by another goal, and then another.

## "Anything Worth Doing Is Worth Doing Poorly"

As a tool to confront your compulsive tendency to do things perfectly, choose a small task and intentionally do a poor job. Choose an activity that is not very important or a project that can easily be redone later. Consciously allow yourself to experience what it is like to do a poor job (however you define it). Observe that your world does not have to come down around your ears, and that it is even possible to enjoy doing something poorly.

For example, you can experiment with washing the dishes poorly. If you know they will later end up in the dishwasher anyway, see how it feels to do a poor job of washing them by hand. At first, you may have some trouble leaving food stains on plates. But if you keep at it, you can get to the point where you are able to let some food smudges remain. Little by little, you can get pretty good at doing a poor job— but watch out for the trap of needing to be perfect at doing a poor job!

Another example: If you like things neat and orderly, purposely leave things lying around sometimes. Fight the compulsive urge to put them away. Face the slight anxiety of having your room or office less than squeaky-clean. Delay reading the mail immediately. Stay sweaty for a while after working out instead of jumping right into the shower. Change your morning wake-up routine in some way. Experiment with expanding your limits of comfort.

In altering your routine, choose those areas that you know will generate only mild discomfort. Your focus doesn't have to be on a project or activity that involves the compulsive aspect of your perfectionism. Any alteration in your everyday habits can become a small but significant challenge. For example, after 20 years of wearing my watch on my right wrist, I decided to experiment with wearing it on my left wrist. While this was a rather nonthreatening change, I noticed that I was initially resistant to making the switch. Even small changes can be significant in showing us that we can cope with change without getting too anxious. This awareness can then lead to a decreased fear of larger risks, helping us to break compulsive patterns of safety and stability.

## FACING RISK AND TAKING CHANCES

Taking risks requires confronting what the perfectionist dreads the most—fear of the unknown and of failure. So it is important to "put your head into the lion's mouth," to dare to take some risks that you know will challenge your image as a perfectionist. This means doing some things that you know you are not very good at, and letting yourself feel OK as a beginner. Allow yourself to be a vulnerable novice with the attitude of "beginner's mind" discussed in chapter 10.

For example, try jogging if you're not a jogger, preparing a simple meal if you never cook, drawing or painting a picture, learning a new dance step, traveling to a distant city or foreign country that seems too far away and scary for you, or sitting down and writing a passionate letter or short story if you've never liked writing. It doesn't matter what you choose—the idea is to take a risk.

Along with trying new things, try some activities that you know you like but have avoided because you don't think you do them well enough. Let yourself recapture the interest and excitement you felt with these activities before you cut off your excitement and decided you were not good enough.

Think about activities and projects that you started but never completed because of a fear of never being good enough. Go back to those dance lessons, learn to play that instrument, or take that language class. Give yourself a new chance, with an attitude of allowing for mistakes but enjoying yourself anyway. Approaching an activity with a new attitude, you may experience much more pleasure than you previously allowed yourself.

You must be willing to face your embarrassment of not measuring up and your need to be in control at all times. The more you see that you can cope with being out of control and manage your embarrassment at knowing little about what you are doing, the more you will be ready to accept that good-enough performance is, indeed, something worthy of feeling real satisfaction from. This understanding puts you squarely on the path toward transforming your perfectionism into the healthy pursuit of excellence.

The emotion of embarrassment is important in another way. In embarrassment, the recognition of your uniqueness is turned against yourself instead of being a reason to love yourself. To find "perfection in imperfection," you have got to be at peace with your own uniqueness. This means overcoming your embarrassment of your individual differences.

As perfectionists, we have a deep fear and mistrust of our individual differences. While we want to stand above others and be recognized as superior to them, at the same time we fear feeling *different*. For example, you might be embarrassed about a body part that is not perfectly proportioned, or about your voice, manner of speaking, or style of walking. Each of these examples may be experienced as making you different and therefore out of step with others—or it may be experienced as an expression of who you are that need not be altered for the sake of pleasing others. *One sign of healthy adult maturity is coming to accept, appreciate, and honor your individual differences rather than being embarrassed by them.* This means taking the risk of allowing yourself to truly be yourself. To do so you must view your individual differences through the lens of an attitude called *appreciative mind.*

### Appreciative Mind Versus Judging Mind

It is possible to give up the need to constantly judge your behavior, others' behavior, and the world in general, and to cultivate a nonjudging appreciation of things as they are. While the judging mind focuses on differences that lead to evaluating and comparing everything and everybody, the appreciative mind allow things to be as they are without comparison. One way to work with the concept of appreciative mind is to walk around for a day with one simple idea in mind: that everything you do and everything you see others doing is to be appreciated just as it is. To appreciate something means to take pleasure in it, to receive satisfaction from it, and to honor and respect it. The way to appreciate your own behavior and that of others is to view it as perfect in its imperfection.

For one day, see everything that you do as just right in its imperfection. Begin to notice how you can switch your perception from judging and comparing to appreciating all behavior just as it is.

## THE ELEMENTS OF EXCELLENCE

So far in this chapter we have presented ways of confronting the self-defeating aspects of the perfectionistic mind. We have offered some tools for beginning to transform these negative aspects into the more healthy characteristics of striving for excellence. We will now look at some elements of excellence that the perfectionist probably already possesses. The perfectionistic view of these qualities can be shaped into a more moderate form in realizing the good-enough mentality. This is not an exhaustive list but only an indication of those elements that I believe are most important in the pursuit of excellence.

*Knowledge.* Are you willing to acquire, through reading, study, and experience, the basic and advanced knowledge of your discipline that is necessary to thoroughly perform your skill at a high level? Have you chosen an area in which you are capable of obtaining this knowledge? Is this knowledge interesting and meaningful to you?

*Compatibility.* Does the area in which you wish to excel follow naturally from those skills and talents that you already possess? If not, is it an area in which you have a realistic possibility of learning at a high level, given your natural limitations? Are your temperament and personality compatible with the skills and talents necessary to perform at a high level? If others are involved in your chosen area, can you work with them well enough to do the job you desire?

*Dedication.* How much does it matter to you whether you excel? Are you willing to practice your skills in your chosen area as much as is required to reach a high level of proficiency? Are you, within reason, willing to sacrifice certain pleasures and diversions if necessary? Are you willing to hang in there without quitting even after repeatedly falling short of your goals?

*Motivation.* Are you sufficiently motivated to not allow yourself to be distracted by other interests? Are you, without being driven, strongly pulled toward reaching the top? What makes it so important for you to excel in this particular area? What are your true motivations for caring about it? Do you have any ulterior motives that you don't like to admit?

*Commitment.* Is reaching excellence in this area a short-term goal for you? Or are you willing to be committed over the long term, refining your skills even after you reach your desired level of competence? What will you do when your attention is captured by another, equally interesting area? How much are you willing to dedicate your life to truly becoming an expert over time?

*Satisfaction.* Do you derive satisfaction from incremental steps toward your goal of excellence? Do you know how to break your goal into various subgoals that bring you enjoyment, pleasure, self-respect, and sense of well-being? Is there anything else you'd rather be doing than this particular area of striving? Are you able to make your efforts a dance toward excellence rather than an all-consuming struggle?

## Moving from Perfectionism to Excellence

In transforming perfection to excellence, the perfectionist's attitude toward these six elements can evolve in the following ways.

*Knowledge and excellence.* We can move from knowledge that confirms an air of superiority to knowledge that ensures adequate grounding in a chosen discipline. We can learn to use knowledge to gain confidence and to acquire skills rather than to feel superior to others or to boast about our intelligence and learning. We can learn to give up the narcissistic attitude that our superior knowledge entitles us to special attention and treatment.

*Compatibility and excellence.* We can learn to choose pursuits that are right for us, not just those that carry high status or reflect what our parents and friends think we should do. We can find the work and projects that fit our personal style. We can move from a viewpoint of "me against the world" to "we're in it together." We can learn how to cooperate with others for the mutual benefit of others and ourselves. We can move beyond jealousy, envy, and vindictiveness to take an interest in and feel joy for the triumphs of others. Instead of thinking there's only room at the top for one, we can believe there's room enough for everyone.

*Dedication and excellence.* Instead of conditional dedication based on easy reward and low frustration, we can cultivate dedication based on personal integrity. We can move beyond blaming others when something isn't easy. We can persist even after failures. We can learn to tolerate second-best, if necessary. We can make use of constructive criticism.

*Motivation and excellence.* We can move from motivation by fear of failure to motivation derived from personal satisfaction and achievement. Instead of desperate performance to avoid shame, we can practice spirited, interested engagement and find reward in both the process and the goal. Instead of compulsively moving on without taking time to savor our achievements, we can make room for the celebration of success as a way to gain nourishment for further challenges. We can use our obsessive tendencies positively to sustain motivation despite distractions.

*Commitment and excellence.* Instead of commitment based on short-term ego gratification, we can seek commitment based on strong investment in the skill or work itself. From surface-level narcissistic gratification we can move to a deeper sense of right livelihood, or doing work that we enjoy that is consistent with our ethics, temperament, and personal beliefs and that fulfills our personal needs. We can transcend short-term interest based on fad and fashion.

*Satisfaction and excellence.* In place of momentary relief based on temporarily fending off anxiety and the fear of failure, we can achieve deeper satisfaction and contentment based on a sense of pride of accomplishment and enjoyment of the process of reaching it. We can shift our focus from the end goal to enjoyment of the incremental steps toward the goal; from frustration and fragmentation to a sense of wholeness and completeness.

Are you willing to make these changes and to address the elements of excellence you may be lacking? If you are, you will be in a strong position to break out of the good-enough-is-never-enough mentality. As Lao Tze put it, "He who knows when enough is enough will always have enough."

## More Tools Toward Excellence

Additional tools and ideas which may be helpful in striving for excellence include the following:

*Restrict the amount of time you engage in perfectionistically driven activities.* Purposefully cut back in those areas that you devote large amounts of time to but where your performance does not seem to improve. There is a delicate balance between the commitment of time and energy needed to excel versus compulsive overcommitment. At a certain point, striving becomes self-defeating; it is possible to try too hard. You may spend too much time doing and redoing things in an effort to get them perfect. Research on leadership suggests that a moderate amount of motivation (leading to moderate time investment) tends to be related to best performance.[4]

*Always break large goals into smaller subgoals.* As with end goals, try to put subgoals into objective, measurable terms. In this way, you can give yourself nourishment along the way toward your end goal and reinforce enjoyment of the process of reaching it. For example, in writing this book each chapter was a subgoal toward the end goal of completing the manuscript. With the completion of each cha~ became further motivated to continue to the next. In d/

subgoals, be careful not to set them too high or you will defeat the purpose. If you set the subgoals too low, on the other hand, you will not feel worthy of any satisfaction when you meet them.

*Break the habit of being critical.* Refrain from criticizing others' performance, no matter how strong an urge you feel to comment on their shortcomings. If you can break the habit of being critical of others, you will also tend to be less critical of yourself. You will begin to see that it is not necessary to continually compare yourself to others. This is not easy to do, since our culture gives continual reinforcement to the comparing game.

*Try journal writing to help you along the path of accomplishment.* Write about those projects and activities that matter to you, and compliment yourself when you reach subgoals and end goals. Let your journal be a record of your successes, and return to it for support whenever you tackle a new challenge. Reading about your successes will help give you the confidence to tackle larger and riskier projects. Use your well-practiced compulsivity in a positive way to ensure that you make entries in your journal regularly.

*Keep company with people who support your projects.* It will be much easier for you to reach your goal of excellence if you are in the company of others who value excellence in their own lives and are willing and able to support your efforts. Refrain from spending too much time around heavily critical people who are unable to appreciate your desire for excellence or who put you down out of their own feelings of envy, inadequacy, and perfectionism.

*Keep in mind that the final determination of excellence is up to you.* The goal of excellence is not a matter of the outside world giving you approval or applause. While it is gratifying to receive approval and recognition from others, the real gratification comes only when you have accepted yourself at a deep enough level so that you can view your own projects and your very existence in this world as good enough. *The ultimate judge, jury, and trial reside within.*

There is no substitute for learning to love and accept yourself. All of the glitter and recognition in the world cannot make you feel good enough if you are unwilling or unable to give yourself what only you have the power to give. Without this self-acceptance you will always feel like more is never enough.

# FOURTEEN

# Natural Wonder, Natural Self:

## *Finding Perfection in an Imperfect World*

*The perfect man employs his mind as a mirror. It grasps nothing; it refuses nothing; it receives but does not keep.*

CHUNG TZU

IN THE TOWN WHERE I live there is a pixieish fellow with a long, gray Santa Claus beard. Known as Number 1, he is the unofficial town greeter. Almost every day he can be found standing on the main street corner in the center of town, waving to everyone passing by on foot and in cars. Number 1 calls out to passersby, "You're perfect!" Sometimes he shortens it to "Perfect!" This is his greeting to one and all.

While tourists and residents alike find Number 1 to be a colorful and friendly addition to the flavor of our beach town, few really understand the intent of his words. Some nod appreciatively, wanting to believe his words, if only for a moment. But they soon lapse back into critical self-judgments that leave no room for feeling perfect just as they are.

In this final chapter we will briefly examine the question of human perfection. Are we really prefect just the way we are because of our individual uniqueness? In what ways is this true and in what ways not true?

In addition, we will suggest how to find perfection in an imperfect world. While human perfection in terms of projects will always be a dancing chimera that we may approach but never attain, there is still much that may be experienced as perfect when we look to the natural world in which we are embedded.

## DOES UNIQUENESS MEAN PERFECTION?

We may think of our own individual uniqueness as making us perfect in the sense that we are the only (and therefore the best) example of ourselves. Genetic inheritance makes us similar to—but never the same as—other family members. It can be enlightening to contemplate the overwhelming sense of personal power and worthiness that may accompany this realization: never in the history of humankind has there been a human being exactly like you, nor will there ever be again. In this sense, you are "pure, absolute, and undiluted"—one of the definitions of perfect.

Each of us is also perfect in the sense that each human being is a reflection of our original nature, thus whole and complete. We are, in essence, "lacking nothing that properly belongs," which is another definition of perfect. It is this original nature that Eastern philosophies have suggested we strive to regain.

But, as we have emphasized in this book, when we start to think of our desire to perform perfectly, we use a very different meaning of perfection. We are not perfect in the sense of being absolutely correct, beyond criticism, or incapable of error. Nor are we perfect in the sense of being able to perform any task or activity in a way that could never be improved upon. Nor are we perfect in the sense of being at the highest possible point of our growth. We are not ripe or finished, always having more work to do in our quest to fully realize our perfect nature.

This, then, is the paradox we confront: while our highest and most pure nature as human beings is indeed perfect, we are always a step away from truly realizing it. We separate ourselves from our own perfection and end up striving to find it through our projects. We are in search of something that is part of our basic nature and yet is something most of us never fully realize. *We are both perfect in our deepest nature and yet imperfect in our realization of this nature.*

If we can keep in mind the ways in which our uniqueness qualifies us as being perfect for *who we are,* perhaps we may feel less compelled to prove ourselves in the competitive world of *what we do.* With greater inner security, perfectionism can slowly be transformed into the pursuit of excellence. We pursue this excellence because we must do the very best that we can in order to establish and fortify our self-respect and integrity.

This pursuit of excellence is what the psychologist Abraham Maslow meant when he said that no person will feel good about himself if he knows he has not made his best effort to realize his potential. Although we might be able to fool others, we cannot fool ourselves. If we know we are not giving our projects our best efforts and actualizing the latent abilities within us, we are not going to feel much pride, self-respect, or dignity. This drive toward self-actualization is part of what pushes us in search of excellence.

Our early dependence upon our parents was necessary to sustain life in infancy and childhood. But, as we have indicated, psychological and emotional maturity means moving beyond looking for the nod of parental approval. As the outcome of good psychotherapy has repeatedly shown, it is possible to overcome the past despite emotional wounds and shortcomings. With awareness and insight, the right tools, and sufficient motivation, we can transform the negative aspects of perfectionism into the positive striving for excellence.

But we need to remember that the achievement of excellence itself is just another goal from which we hope to derive joy, satisfaction, self-acceptance, self-worth, and contentment in our lives. If excellence, as well as fame, fortune, and power do not lead to these feelings, what is the value of pursuing them? In and of themselves, these achievements will leave us feeling hollow and empty, longing for something that has not been satisfied.

Who you *are* is perfect but what you *do* isn't, *and it never will be.* Perfection in the realm of doing is impossible.


## PERFECTION NATURALLY

We can't find perfection in the world of doing, nor can we find perfection in the behavior of human beings toward each other. We certainly can't find perfection in human suffering. Is there anything in this imperfect world in which we *can* find perfection?

Yes. We can find perfection in the beauty of the natural world that surrounds us. We can find perfection in the ocean, the mountains, the deserts. We can find perfection in the shape of clouds, in the color of the sky as the sun rises and sets. We can find perfection in the basic elements of earth, wind, fire, and water and our relationship to each of them.

There is, as well, perfection in the natural rhythms of nature: the rhythms of day and night, of sun and moon, and the seasons of the year. We can find perfection in the cycles of change and repetition that make up our lives. There is perfection in the rhythm of creation and destruction of the natural world, the various checks and balances that nature provides to keep things in order. There is perfection in the natural circadian rhythms of our bodies and their adaptation to changing conditions. There is perfection in the physical life cycle: birth, development, full maturation, decay, and finally death. And there is perfection in the predictable passages we go through as we make transitions from one stage of life to another.

There is perfection in the universe, the solar system, the stars and galaxies upon which we gaze with mystery and wonder. This gazing may give us perspective, helping us realize our relative place in this much larger universe.

We may find perfection in the animal world, in the way that various creatures possess the anatomy and genetic inheritance that are required for survival in a particular habitat. And there is perfection in the evolutionary food chain, with more complex and sophisticated animals at the top and less evolved species on the bottom.

We can find a certain perfection in material things—in their beauty and usefulness, or the security, comfort and esteem they may bring to us. Beautiful art objects, tools of our trade, technological gadgets that make our lives easier, antique relics of the past that bring meaning and perspective to the present—we can find perfection in all of these when we look for it.

There is perfection in the sounds and rhythms of music, the vibrations that impact our ears in just the right manner to create an inner sense of harmony with the outer world. This includes the natural pulses of movement that are never far from us, from the rhythms of the baby's heart pounding in its mother's womb to the continual dance of rhythm that pervades our daily life.

And there is perfection in the timing of the natural pulse of life. It can be the perfect timing of a good joke wittily conceived from an occurrence in the moment; the timely arrival of a letter or a visit by a friend or loved one when we most need it; the learning of certain lessons in life just when they are most important for us to grasp.

There is the perfection that may come when everything in our world seems peaceful and orderly, when we feel "God's in His heaven and all's right with the world."

## Every Moment At Just the Right Time

When we learn to live with our attention centered in the present, more and more of the world can feel perfect to us. To present something means to bring it forth for consideration. What life presents to us can feel just right for our needs, even if it is unpleasant or painful. We begin to sense the meaning of the Zen phrase that "every moment occurs at just the right time." To be in this perfect flow of life requires a surrendering to the present.

For the perfectionist, to surrender to the moment is to risk not being prepared for whatever may come in the next moment to threaten his security. As we have shown, the perfectionist views the present as the gateway to a future filled with apprehension, doubt, and possible failure.

To face this apprehension directly is the first step to settling more gracefully into the present. The present then becomes pregnant with possibilities that may lead to projects of excellence. When we learn to live in the present, we do not give up striving for excellence. We do not give up having goals. But we *do* give up the perfectionist's paralyzing anxiety and fear. We learn that the present is the fulcrum or balance point that empowers us to tackle projects without fear or procrastination. Our immediate involvement in living brings us an excitement and willingness to engage the world that allows us to direct our energy into meaningful projects.

As we become more adept at accepting what life "brings forth for our consideration," we find the strength, courage, and resources to manage and transcend our everyday survival needs. We may find the motivation to meet those psychological needs, like feeling good enough about our right to be in this world and to pursue excellence, that lend depth, challenge, and meaning to a satisfying existence. And we can do all this without becoming ensnared in the perfection trap.

# NOTES

## Chapter 1 Perfection or Excellence?

1. See, for example, D. D. Burns (1980). *Feeling Good: The New Mood Therapy.* New York: William Morrow.

2. A. Ellis (1973). *Humanistic Psychotherapy: The Rational-Emotive Approach.* New York: McGraw-Hill.

## Chapter 2 When Good Enough Is Never Enough

1. Reuven P. Bulka (1987). Guilt from, guilt towards, *Journal of Psychology and Judaism* 11(2):81.

2. H. B. English and A. C. English (1958). *A Comprehensive Dictionary of Psychological and Psychoanalytic Terms.* New York: David McKay.

3. This impostor complex has also been observed by David Stoop in his clinical work with perfectionistic patients. D. Stoop (1987). *Living with a Perfectionist.* Nashville: Oliver Nelson, p. 70.

## Chapter 3 The Perils of Perfection

1. D. A. Thompson, K. A. Berg and L. A. Shatford (1987). The heterogeneity of bulimic symptomatology: Cognitive and behavioral dimensions. *International Journal of Eating Disorders* 6(2):

215–234. See also R. G. Druss and J. A. Silverman (1979). Body image and perfectionism of ballerinas. *General Hospital Psychiatry* 2:115–121.

2. C. Gordon, E. V. Beresin and D. B. Herzog (1989). The parents' relationship and the child's illness in anorexia nervosa. *Journal of the American Academy of Psychoanalysis* 17(1):29–42.

3. R. G. Owens and P. D. Slade (1987). Running and anorexia nervosa: an empirical study. *International Journal of Eating Disorders* 6(6):771–775.

4. D. R. Inbody and J. J. Ellis (1985). Group therapy with anorexic and bulimic patients: implications for therapeutic intervention. *American Journal of Psychotherapy* 39(3):411–420.

5. See, for example, J. S. Tamerin and C. P. Neuman (1974). The alcoholic stereotype: Clinical reappraisal and implications for treatment. *American Journal of Psychoanalysis* 34(4):17.

6. Brian L. (1985). *Perfectionism.* Center City, MN: Hazelden, p. 2.

7. For a more thorough discussion of these points and other problematic issues related to self-help groups and 12-step programs in particular, see S. J. Katz and A. E. Liu (1991). *The Codependency Conspiracy: How to Break the Recovery Habit and Take Charge of Your Own Life.* New York: Warner Books. See also W. Kaminer (1992). *I'm Dysfunctional, You're Dysfunctional.* Reading, MA: Addison-Wesley.

8. See, for example, John Bradshaw's (1988) best-seller *Healing the Shame That Binds You.* Deerfield Beach, FL: Health Communications. While I believe that Bradshaw has overemphasized the importance of the concept of shame, the idea that we all judge ourselves as "less than enough" is closely associated with the desire for parental approval, one motivator for perfectionism. As I point out in chapters 4–6, reducing addiction, perfectionism, or any other problem to a single psychological dynamic is overly simplistic and does not do justice to the complexity of the human

mind, emotions, or behavior. Moreover, various cultural factors simply cannot be reduced to single events or feelings, even those as powerful as childhood trauma and shame.

9. This statement was made by Anne Wilson Schaef, quoted by Matthew Fox in an interview with Mark Matousek (1990). Toward a spiritual renaissance. *Common Boundary* 8(4):18.

10. M. Miles (1984). Type A personality: Bad business? *Computer Decisions* (April). See also T. W. Smith and S. S. Brehm (1981). Cognitive correlates of Type A coronary-prone personality pattern. *Motivation and Emotion* 3:215–223.

11. C. Brod (1984). *Technostress: The Human Cost of the Computer Revolution.* Reading, MA: Addison-Wesley, p. xii.

12. Technostress (1990). *Los Angeles Times* (May 11):E1.

13. M. Green (1986). *Zen and the Art of the Macintosh: Discoveries on the Path to Computer Enlightenment.* Philadelphia: Running Press, p. 80. Although it is long out of date, those who work with computer graphics will appreciate this book both for its instruction and its humor. It is also of interest as a "historical" document regarding the early possibilities of computer graphics.

14. Ibid., p. 83.

15. Ibid., p. 142.

16. Brod (1984). *Technostress,* p. 98.

17. P. L. Hewitt and G. L. Flett (1991). Perfectionism in the self and social contexts: Conceptualization, assessment, and association with psychopathology. *Journal of Personality and Social Psychology* 60(3):456–470.

18. D. D. Burns (1980). The perfectionist's script for self-defeat. *Psychology Today* (November): 34–52.

19. D. E. Hamachek (1978). Psychodynamics of normal and neurotic perfectionism. *Psychology* 15:27–33.

20. H. A. Meyersburg, S. L. Ablon, and J. Kotin (1974). A rever-berating psychic mechanism in the depressive processes. *Psychiatry* 37:372–386.

21. P. L. Hewitt and D. G. Dyck (1986). Perfectionism, stress, and vulnerability to depression. *Cognitive Therapy and Research* 10(1): 411–420. See also P. L. Hewitt and G. L. Flett (1991). Dimensions of perfectionism in unipolar depression. *Journal of Abnormal Psychology* 100(1):98–101.

CHAPTER 4 A SOCIETY DEVOTED TO PERFECTION

1. J. Faust (1987). Correlates of the drive for thinness in young female adolescents. *Journal of Clinical Child Psychology* 16(4): 313–319.

2. D. A. Thompson, K. A. Berg and L. A. Shatford (1987). The heterogeneity of bulimic symptomatology: Cognitive and behavioral dimensions. *International Journal of Eating Disorders* 6(2):215–234.

3. E. D. Luby and M. Weiss (1984). Case study: Anorexia nervosa: A girl and her father. *Women and Therapy* 3(3–4):87–90.

4. W. C. Roedell (1984). Vulnerabilities of highly gifted children. *Roeper Review* 6(3):127–130.

5. See, for example, *Iron John* by men's movement leader Robert Bly (1991). Reading, MA: Addison-Wesley. Also Sam Keen (1991). *Fire in the Belly.* New York: Bantam.

6. R. K. Gilbert (1992). Revisiting the psychology of men: Robert Bly and the mytho-poetic movement. *Journal of Humanistic Psychology* 32(2):41–67.

7. Pop! goes the Donald (1990). *People* (July 9):29.

8. Ibid., 32.

9. Pulling a slick one (1990). *Los Angeles Times* (May 31): Sports section, pp. 1, 18.

10. Ibid.

11. An epidemic of college cheating (1990). *Los Angeles Times* (May 2): View section, p. E14.


Chapter 5 The Perfectionistic Mind

1. S. Freud (1961). New introductory lectures. In J. Strachey (ed. and trans.). *The Standard Edition of the Complete Psychological Works of Sigmund Freud* (vol. 22). London: Hogarth. (Originally published 1933.)

2. C. G. Jung (1959, 1969). The archetypes of the collective unconscious. In *The Collected Works of C. G. Jung* (vol. 9). Princeton, N.J.: Princeton University Press. (Originally published 1936.)

3. For an extended discussion on working with inner voices and accessing contents from the unconscious mind, see S. J. Hendlin. (1989). *The Discriminating Mind: A Guide to Deepening Insight and Clarifying Outlook.* San Francisco: HarperCollins.

4. O. Fenichel (1945). *The Psychoanalytic Theory of Neurosis.* New York: W. W. Norton.

5. For a solid discussion of the role of the conscience in perfectionism from both psychological and religious perspectives, see R. L. Timpe (1989). Perfection: Positive possibility or personal pathology? *Journal of Psychology and Christianity* 8(1):25–34.

6. S. Freud (1938). *An Outline of Psycho-analysis.* London: Hogarth.

7. F. Perls (1969). *Gestalt Therapy Verbatim.* Moab, UT: Real People Press, p. 33.

8. M. Woodman (1982). *Addiction to Perfection. The Still Unravished Bride.* Toronto: Inner City Books, p. 25.

9. Ibid., p. 52.

10. Ibid., p. 173. See also M. Woodman (1980). *The Owl Was a Baker's Daughter: Obesity, Anorexia Nervosa and the Repressed Feminine.* Toronto: Inner City Books. For an extended account of the concept of the Great Mother, see E. Neumann (1972). *The Great Mother* (Bollingen Series XLVII). Trans. R. Manheim. Princeton, NJ. Princeton University Press. For an account in popular-psychology form of the role of the literal mother-daughter relationship in perfectionism (especially in relation to eating disorders) from Kohut's self psychology perspective, see C. Dowling (1988). *Perfect Women: Daughters Who Love Their Mothers But Don't Love Themselves.* New York: Pocket Books.

11. Woodman (1982). *Addiction to Perfection,* p. 188.

12. C. F. Monte (1980). *Beneath the Mask* (2d ed.). New York: Holt, Rinehart and Winston.

13. A. Adler (1971). *The Science of Living.* New York: Doubleday. (Originally published 1929.)

14. A. Adler (1973). Compulsion neurosis. In H. Ansbacher & R. Ansbacher (eds.), *Superiority and Social Interest* (3d ed.). New York: Viking Press, p. 117. (Originally published 1931.)

15. A. Adler, Religion and individual psychology. In Ansbacher & Ansbacher (1973), *Superiority and Social Interest,* p. 125.

16. Ibid. See also Timpe (1989). Perfection: Positive possibility.

17. A. H. Maslow (1971). *The Farther Reaches of Human Nature.* New York: Viking Press. See also A. H. Maslow (1968). *Toward a Psychology of Being* (2d ed.). New York: Viking Press.

18. Maslow (1971). *The Farther Reaches,* p. 45.

19. Maslow (1971). *The Farther Reaches,* p. 36.

20. Maslow (1971). *The Farther Reaches,* p. xvi.

21. See, for example, Timpe (1989). Perfection: Positive possibility, p. 29.

22. Maslow (1971). *The Farther Reaches,* p. 217

23. Ibid.

24. See, for example, M. J. Mahoney and D. B. Arnkoff (1979). Self-management. In O. F. Pomerleau and J. P. Brady (eds.). *Behavioral Medicine: Theory and Practice.* Baltimore: Williams & Wilkins, pp. 75–96. See also A. R. Beck (1976). *Cognitive Therapy and the Emotional Disorders.* New York: International Universities Press.

25. K. Horney (1950). *Neurosis and Human Growth: The Struggle Toward Self-realization.* New York: W. W. Norton.

26. K. Horney (1937). *The Neurotic Personalty of Our Time.* New York: Norton. See also Timpe (1989). Perfection: Positive possibility, p. 26.

27. K. Horney (1942). *Self-analysis.* New York: Norton.

28. A. Ellis and R. J. Yeager (1989). *Why Some Therapies Don't Work.* New York: Prometheus, pp. 18, 92. See also: A. Ellis (1962). *Reason and Emotion in Psychotherapy.* Secaucus, NJ: Lyle Stuart and Citadel Press. A. Ellis (1973). *Humanistic Psychotherapy: The Rational-Emotive Approach.* New York: McGraw-Hill. A. Ellis and W. Dryden (1987). *The Practice of Rational-Emotive Therapy.* New York: Springer.

29. Ellis and Yeager (1989). *Why Some Therapies Don't Work,* p. 20.

30. For a good book in popular-psychology form on the various ways women tend to purposefully intensify the dramatic aspects of their lives, see J. Davidson (1988). *The Agony of It All. The Drive for Drama and Excitement in Women's Lives.* Los Angeles: J. P. Tarcher.

31. Ellis and Yeager (1989). *Why Some Therapies Don't Work,* p. 20.

32. Ibid. pp. 20–21.

33. For a popular explanation of psychological pessimism, see S. Bodian (1990). Love is the healer: an interview with Joan Borysenko. *Yoga Journal* (May–June):44–49, 94–98. For recent

applications of the concept of psychological pessimism, see G. Oettingen and M. E. P. Seligman (1990). Pessimism and behavioral signs of depression in East versus West Berlin. *European Journal of Social Psychology* 20(3):207–220. Also, P. Schulman, C. Castellon, and M. E. P. Seligman (1989). Assessing explanatory style—The content analysis of verbatim explanations and the attributional style questionnaire. *Behavior Research and Therapy* 27(5):505–512. For his research on the contrasting optimistic orientation and its relation to success, see M. E. P. Seligman (1991). *Learned Optimism.* New York: Knopf.

34. See, for example, D. Levin (1987). Clinical stories: A modern self in the fury of being. In D. Levin (ed.). *Pathologies of the Modern Self: Post-modern Studies of Narcissism, Schizophrenia, and Depression.* New York: New York University Press, pp. 479–537. Also, E. Zaretsky (1976). *Capitalism, the Family, and Personal Life.* New York: Harper and Row.

35. P. Cushman (1990). Why the self is empty: Toward a historically situated psychology. *American Psychologist* 45(5):599–611.

36. Ibid., p. 604.

37. See, for example, C. Lasch (1978). *The Culture of Narcissism: American Life in an Age of Diminishing Expectations.* New York: Norton. Also, D. Levin (1987). Psychopathology in the epoch of nihilism. In Levin (ed.), *Pathologies.*

38. T. I. Rubin (1981). Goodbye to death and celebration of life. *Event* 2(1):64.

39. O. Kernberg (1975). *Borderline Conditions and Pathological Narcissism.* New York: Jason Aronson, p. 264. See also A. Lowen (1983). *Narcissism: Denial of the True Self.* New York: Macmillan, p. 6.

40. J. Masterson (1981). *The Narcissistic and Borderline Disorders.* New York: Brunner/Mazel, p. 30.

41. H. Kohut (1971). *The Analysis of the Self.* New York: International Universities Press.

42. H. Kohut (1977). *The Restoration of the Self.* New York: International Universities Press.

43. H. Kohut (1984). *How Does Analysis Cure?* Chicago: University of Chicago Press.

44. H. Kohut (1971). *Analysis of the Self.* See also B. Sorotzkin (1985). The quest for perfection: Avoiding guilt or avoiding shame? *Psychotherapy* 22(3):566.

45. Sorotzkin (1985) The quest for perfection, p. 567.

## CHAPTER 6 LOOKING GOD IN THE EYE

1. J. E. Hamilton (1983). Perfectionism. In R. Taylor (ed.) *Beacon Dictionary of Theology.* Kansas City, MO: Beacon Hill Press.

2. V. A. Harvey (1964). *A Handbook of Theological Terms.* New York: Macmillan.

3. J. A. Wood, ed. (1885). *Christian Perfection as Taught by John Wesley.* Chicago: Christian Witness Co.

4. Ibid.

5. Psalms 19:7; James 1:25.

6. 2 Corinthians 12:9.

7. W. Barclay (1956). *The Gospel of Matthew* (vol. 1). Philadelphia: Westminster Press.

8. See, for example, D. A. Seamonds (1981). Perfectionism: Fraught with fruits of self-destruction. *Christianity Today* (April 10):24. See also D. Stoop (1987). *Living with a Perfectionist.* Nashville: Oliver Nelson, p. 84.

9. I. Epstein, ed. (1961). *The Talmud* (18 vols.). London: Soncino Press. Avot, 2:21.

10. R. P. Bulka (1987). Guilt from, guilt towards. *Journal of Psychology and Judaism* 11(2):81.

11. For example, it has been argued that the identification of one's innermost essence with Christ-consciousness or Buddha-mind may be seen as the core teaching of all the world's religions, i.e., "They call him many who is really one." For a comparison of the various religious and spiritual traditions, see K. Wilber (1978). *The Spectrum of Consciousness*. Wheaton, IL: Theosophical Publishing House.

12. See, for example, K. Wilber (1983). *A Sociable God*. New York: McGraw Hill. Also, D. Anthony, B. Ecker, and K. Wilber, eds. (1987). *Spiritual Choices: The Problem of Recognizing Authentic Paths to Inner Transformation*. New York: Paragon House; see especially pp. 35–105.

13. See S. J. Hendlin (1989). *The Discriminating Mind: A Guide to Deepening Insight and Clarifying Outlook*. San Francisco: Harper-Collins, pp. 226–229. See also Wilber (1983). *A Sociable God*, pp. 65–72.

14. K. Wilber (1980). *The Atman Project: A Transpersonal View of Human Development*. Wheaton, IL: Theosophical Publishing House. See also K. Wilber (1978). *Spectrum of Consciousness*, p. 75.

15. For example, see H. Coward (1985). *Jung and Eastern Thought*. New York: State University of New York, pp. 52–53. See also K. Wilber (1978). *Spectrum of Consciousness*.

16. Wilber (1980). *Atman Project*, pp. 100–110. See also K. Wilber (1981). *Up from Eden: A Transpersonal View of Human Evolution*. Garden City, NY: Anchor/Doubleday.

17. Wilber (1980) p. 167.

18. For more on the dynamic interplay between the relative and absolute nature of self, see Hendlin (1989). *Discriminating Mind*.

19. Wilber (1980) p. 107.

20. See, for example, James Stewart's (1991) best-seller *Den of Thieves*. New York: Simon and Schuster. Also, M. Lewis (1991). *The Money Culture*. New York: Norton.

21. See A. J. Deikman (1991). *The Wrong Way Home: Uncovering the Patterns of Cult Behavior in American Society.* Boston: Beacon. This book examines how people's need to be taken care of, feel secure, and to feel their life is meaningful make them susceptible to various forms of cultish behavior in everyday institutions.

22. J. A. Gordon (1990). Why spiritual groups go awry. *Common Boundary* 8(3):25. See also, J. A. Gordon (1987). *The Golden Guru: The Strange Journey of Bhagwan Shree Rajneesh.* New York: Viking-Penguin.

23. Gordon (1990). Why spiritual groups go awry, p. 26.

24. For an account of how men in positions of authority may take advantage of their power by sexualizing professional relationships, see P. Rutter (1989). *Sex in the Forbidden Zone: When Men in Power—Therapists, Doctors, Clergy, Teachers and Others—Betray Women's Trust.* Los Angeles: J. P. Tarcher. See also A. J. Deikman (1991). *The Wrong Way Home.*

25. Hendlin (1989). *Discriminating Mind.* For some of the difficulties in thinking and practice that arise for those pursuing New Age spiritual groups, see also S. Hendlin (1983). Pernicious oneness. *Journal of Humanistic Psychology* 23(3):61–81. Also, S. Hendlin (1984). Pernicious oneness: Taking a hard look at the spiritual marketplace. *Yoga Journal* (May–June):32–36.

## CHAPTER 7 THE PROMISE OF SPECIALNESS

1. Can Yuppie offspring keep pace? (1990). *Los Angeles Times,* View section (September 2):E1, E11.

2. A. A. Brooks (1989). *Children of Fast-Track Parents. Raising Self-Sufficient and Confident Children in an Achievement-Oriented World.* New York: Penguin.

3. Can Yuppie offspring keep pace?, E11.

4. See, for example, chapter 4, and especially pp. 105–107, in S. Grof (1976). *Realms of the Human Unconscious.* New York: Dutton. Grof argues that even the bliss of the womb itself may be disturbed by physical assaults that may result in various unconscious psychological issues surfacing later in life. He especially focuses on the trauma of birth and its relation to psychological development.

5. See D. N. Stern (1985). *The Interpersonal World of the Infant.* New York: Basic Books. Also M. S. Mahler, F. Pine, and A. Bergman (1975). *The Psychological Birth of the Infant.* New York: Basic Books.

6. See, for example, D. E. Hamachek (1978). Psychodynamics of normal and neurotic perfectionism. *Psychology* 15:27–33.

7. A. Miller (1981). *Prisoners of Childhood.* New York: Basic Books.

8. C. Dowling (1988). *Perfect Women: Daughters Who Love Their Mothers But Don't Love Themselves.* New York: Pocket Books.

9. R. J. Ackerman (1989). *Perfect Daughters: Adult Daughters of Alcoholics.* Deerfield Beach, FL: Health Communications.

10. See, for example, J. Bradshaw (1988). *Healing the Shame That Binds You.* Deerfield Beach, FL: Health Communications. Also, C. L. Whitfield (1987). *Healing the Child Within.* Deerfield Beach, FL: Health Communications.

11. A. Lowen (1983). *Narcissism: Denial of the True Self.* New York: Macmillan, pp. 105–106.

12. Ibid., p. 107.

13. Major network news program, May 14, 1990.

14. "Designer Kids" segment on TV news magazine show "20/20," June 15, 1990. Updated in October 1991.

15. C. Brod (1984). *Technostress: The Human Cost of the Computer Revolution.* Reading, MA: Addison-Wesley, pp. 125–139.

## Chapter 10 The Agony of Defeat

1. Exercise addiction (1990). *Orange Coast Magazine* (April).

2. A. Yates. (1991) *Compulsive Exercise and the Eating Disorders: Toward an Integrated Theory of Activity.* New York: Brunner/Mazel.

3. C. Garfield (1982). Better than good. *Mgr.* 2:8.


## Chapter 11 A Match Made in Heaven

1. D. D. Burns (1983). The spouse who is a perfectionist. *Medical Aspects of Human Sexuality* 17(3):219–230.

2. C. Lasch (1978). *The Culture of Narcissism: American Life in an Age of Diminishing Expectations.* New York: Norton, p. 356.

3. V. Satir (1976). *Making Contact.* Milbrae, CA: Celestial Arts, p. 11.

4. For a simple-to-read book on improving intimate relationships, see K. Keyes, Jr. (1990). *The Power of Unconditional Love: 21 Guidelines for Beginning, Improving and Changing Your Most Meaningful Relationships.* Coos Bay, OR: Love Line Books.


## Chapter 13 Transforming Perfectionism

1. For example, see D. D. Burns (1980). *Feeling Good: The New Mood Therapy.* New York: William Morrow, pp. 309–337.

2. A similarly conceived but differently focused form was created by David Burns. He calls it the pleasure-perfection balance sheet. See D. Burns (1980). The perfectionist's script for self-defeat. *Psychology Today* (November): 50. Burns asks the reader to estimate the degree of satisfaction he thinks he will derive and later compare it to his actual satisfaction. My focus is more on having the reader identify in measurable terms what constitutes a good-enough

performance and then compare this standard to his performance. However, the idea that satisfaction is not necessarily related to performance is common to both approaches.

3. A. Ellis (1990). Let's not ignore individuality. *American Psychologist* (45)6:781 (comment).

4. W. D. Criddle (1975). Don't try too hard! *Rational Living* (10)2:19.

# BIBLIOGRAPHY

Ackerman, R. J. (1989). *Perfect Daughters: Adult Daughters of Alcoholics.* Deerfield Beach, FL: Health Communications.

Adler, A. (1971). *The Science of Living.* New York: Doubleday. (Originally published 1929.)

Adler, A. (1973). Compulsion neurosis. In H. Ansbacher and R. Ansbacher (eds.). *Superiority and Social Interest* (3d ed.). New York: Viking Press. (Originally published 1931.)

Adler, A. (1973). Religion and individual psychology. In H. Ansbacher and R. Ansbacher (eds.). *Superiority and Social Interest* (3d ed.). New York: Viking Press. (Originally published 1933.)

Anthony, D., B. Ecker, and K. Wilber, eds. (1987). *Spiritual Choices: The Problem of Recognizing Authentic Spiritual Paths to Inner Transformation.* New York: Paragon House.

Barclay, W. (1956). *The Gospel of Matthew* (vol. 1). Philadelphia: Westminster Press.

Bassett, P. M., and W. M. Greathouse (1985). *Exploring Christian Holiness* (vol. 2). Kansas City, MO: Beacon Hill Press.

Beck, A. R. (1976). *Cognitive Therapy and the Emotional Disorders.* New York: International Universities Press.

Bly, R. (1991). *Iron John.* Reading, MA: Addison-Wesley.

Bodian, S. (1990). Love is the healer: An interview with Joan Borysenko. *Yoga Journal* (May–June): 45–49, 94–95.

Bradshaw, J. (1988). *Healing the Shame That Binds You.* Deerfield Beach, FL.: Health Communications.

Brian, L. (1985). *Perfectionism.* Center City, MN: Hazelden.

Brod, C. (1984). *Technostress: The Human Cost of the Computer Revolution.* Reading, MA: Addison-Wesley.

Brooks, A. A. (1989). *Children of Fast-Track Parents. Raising Self-Sufficient and Confident Children in an Achievement-Oriented World.* New York: Penguin.

Bulka, R. P. (1987). Guilt from, guilt towards. *Journal of Psychology and Judaism* 11(2): 73–90.

Burns, D. D. (1980). *Feeling Good: The New Mood Therapy.* New York: William Morrow.

Burns, D. D. (1980). The perfectionist's script for self-defeat. *Psychology Today* (November): 34–52.

Burns, D. D. (1983). The spouse who is a perfectionist. *Medical Aspects of Human Sexuality* 17(3): 219–230.

Coward, H. (1985). *Jung and Eastern Thought.* New York: State University of New York.

Criddle, W. D. (1975). Don't try too hard! *Rational Living* 10(2): 19.

Cushman, P. (1990). Why the self is empty: Toward a historically situated psychology. *American Psychologist* 45(5): 599–611.

Davidson, J. (1988). *The Agony of It All. The Drive for Drama and Excitement in Women's Lives.* Los Angeles: Jeremy P. Tarcher.

Deikman, A. J. (1991). *The Wrong Way Home: Uncovering the Patterns of Cult Behavior in American Society.* Boston: Beacon.

Dowling, C. (1988). *Perfect Women: Daughters Who Love Their Mothers But Don't Love Themselves.* New York: Pocket Books.

Druss, R. G., and J. A. Silverman (1979). Body image and perfectionism of ballerinas. *General Hospital Psychiatry* 2:115–121.

Elliot, M., and S. Meltsner. (1991). *The Perfectionist Predicament: How to Stop Driving Yourself and Others Crazy.* New York: Morrow.

Ellis, A. (1962). *Reason and Emotion in Psychotherapy.* Secaucus, NJ: Lyle Stuart and Citadel Press.

Ellis, A. (1973). *Humanistic Psychotherapy: The Rational-Emotive Approach.* New York: McGraw-Hill.

Ellis, A., and W. Dryden (1987). *The Practice of Rational-Emotive Therapy.* New York: Springer.

Ellis, A., and R. J. Yeager (1989). *Why Some Therapies Don't Work.* New York: Prometheus.

English, H. B., and A. C. English (1958). *A Comprehensive Dictionary of Psychological and Psychoanalytic Terms.* New York: David McKay.

Epstein, I., ed. (1961). *The Talmud* (18 vols.) Avot, 2:21. London: Soncino Press.

Faust, J. (1987). Correlates of the drive for thinness in young female adolescents. *Journal of Clinical Child Psychology* 16(4): 313–319.

Fenichel, O. (1945). *The Psychoanalytic Theory of Neurosis.* New York: Norton

Freud, S. (1926, 1959). Inhibitions, symptoms, and anxieties. In J. Strachey (ed. and trans.). *The Standard Edition of the Complete Psychological Works of Sigmund Freud* (vol. 20). London: Hogarth.

Freud, S. (1933, 1961). New introductory lectures. In J. Strachey (ed. and trans.). *The Standard Edition of the Complete Psychological Works of Sigmund Freud* (vol. 22). London: Hogarth.

Freud, S. (1938). *An Outline of Psycho-analysis.* London: Hogarth.

Friedman, M., and R. H. Rosenman. (1974). *Type A Behavior and Your Heart.* New York: Knopf.

Garfield, C. (1982). Better than good. *Mgr.* 2:8.

Gilbert, R. K. (1992). Revisiting the psychology of men: Robert Bly and the mytho-poetic movement. *Journal of Humanistic Psychology,* 32(2): 41–67.

Gordon, C., E. V. Beresin, and D. B. Herzog (1989). The parents' relationship and the child's illness in anorexia nervosa. *Journal of the American Academy of Psychoanalysis* 17(1): 29–42.

Gordon, J. A. (1987). *The Golden Guru: The Strange Journey of Bhagwan Shree Rajneesh.* New York: Viking-Penguin.

Gordon, J. A. (1990). Why spiritual groups go awry. *Common Boundary* 8(3): 24–29.

Green, M. (1986). *Zen and the Art of the Macintosh: Discoveries on the Path to Computer Enlightenment.* Philadelphia: Running Press.

Grof, S. (1976). *Realms of the Human Unconscious.* New York: Dutton.

Hamachek, D. E. (1978). Psychodynamics of normal and neurotic perfectionism. *Psychology* 15:27–33.

Hamilton, J. E. (1983). Perfectionism. In R. Taylor (ed.). *Beacon Dictionary of Theology.* Kansas City, MO: Beacon Hill Press.

Harvey, V. A. (1964). *A Handbook of Theological Terms.* New York: Macmillan.

Hendlin, S. J. (1981). Every second at just the right time: A tale of intensive Zen practice. *Pilgrimage,* 9(1): 39–47.

Hendlin, S. J. (1983). Pernicious oneness. *Journal of Humanistic Psychology* 23(3): 61–81.

Hendlin, S. J. (1984). Room enough for everyone. In R. Resnick and G. Yontef (eds.), *James Solomon Simkin, Ph.D. Memorial Festschrift.* pp. 36–41. Los Angeles: Gestalt Therapy Institute of Los Angeles.

Hendlin, S. J. (1984). Pernicious oneness: Taking a hard look at the spiritual marketplace. *Yoga Journal* (May–June): 32–36.

Hendlin, S. J. (1985). The spiritual emergency patient: Concept and example. *The Psychotherapy Patient* 1(3): 79–88.

Hendlin, S. J. (1987). Gestalt therapy: Aspects of evolving theory and practice. *The Humanistic Psychologist* 5(3): 184–196.

Hendlin, S. J. (1989). Evolving spiritual consciousness: Is "religious maturity" all there is? *The Counseling Psychologist* 7(4): 617–620.

Hendlin, S. J. (1989). *The Discriminating Mind: A Guide to Deepening Insight and Clarifying Outlook.* San Francisco: HarperCollins.

Hendlin, S. J. (1991). (Chair). *Humanistic trends in contemporary psychoanalysis.* Invited symposium with R. D. Stolorow, M. J. Horowitz, M. C. Nelson, J. S. Grotstein and S. A. Tobin. Presented at American Psychological Association Convention, San Francisco, August 16. APA audiotape #91-076

Hendlin, S. J. (1991). (Chair and participant). *The spirit and practice of transpersonal psychotherapy.* Symposium with S. Boorstein, K. R. Speeth, and R.W. Jue. Presented at American Psychological Association Convention, San Francisco, August 18. APA audiotape #91-079.

Hendlin, S. J. (1992). (Chair and participant). *Gestalt Therapy: Does the Here and Now Have a Future?* Symposium with E. W. L. Smith, R. L. Harman, and J. Latner. Presented at the American Psychological Association Centennial Convention, Washington, D.C., August 15.

Hewitt, P. L., and D. G. Dyck (1986). Perfectionism, stress, and vulnerability to depression. *Cognitive Therapy and Research* 10(1): 411–420.

Hewitt, P. L., and G. L. Flett. (1991). Dimensions of perfectionism in unipolar depression. *Journal of Abnormal Psychology* 100(1): 98–101.

Hewitt, P. L., and G. L. Flett (1991). Perfectionism in the self and social contexts: Conceptualization, assessment, and association with psychopathology. *Journal of Personality and Social Psychology* 60(3): 456–470.

Hinsie, L. E., and R. J. Campbell (1970). *Psychiatric Dictionary.* New York: Oxford University Press.

Horney, K. (1937). *The Neurotic Personality of Our Time.* New York: Norton.

Horney, K. (1942). *Self-analysis.* New York: Norton.

Horney, K. (1950). *Neurosis and Human Growth: The Struggle Toward Self-realization.* New York: Norton.

Inbody, D. R., and J. J. Ellis (1985). Group therapy with anorexic and bulimic patients: Implications for therapeutic intervention. *American Journal of Psychotherapy* 39(3): 411–420.

Jacobson, E. (1964). *The Self and Object World.* New York: International Universities Press.

Jung, C. G. (1954). *Answer to Job.* Princeton, NJ: Princeton University Press.

Jung, C. G. (1959, 1969). Aion. In *The Collected Works of C. G. Jung* (vol 9 ii). Princeton, NJ: Princeton University Press. (Originally published 1951.)

Jung, C. G. (1959, 1969). The archetypes of the collective unconscious. In *The Collected Works of C. G. Jung* (vol. 9). Princeton, NJ: Princeton University Press. (Originally published 1936.)

Jung, C. G. (1963). *Memories, Dreams, Reflections.* Recorded and edited by A. Jaffe. New York: Vintage Books.

Kaminer, W. (1992). *I'm Dysfunctional, You're Dysfunctional.* Reading, MA: Addison-Wesley.

Katz, S. J., and, A. E. Liu (1991). *The Codependency Conspiracy: How to Break the Recovery Habit and Take Charge of Your Life.* New York: Warner.

Keen, S. (1991). *Fire in the Belly.* New York: Bantam.

Kernberg, O. (1975). *Borderline Conditions and Pathological Narcissism.* New York: Jason Aronson.

Keyes, K., Jr. (1990). *The Power of Unconditional Love: 21 Guidelines for Beginning, Improving and Changing Your Most Meaningful Relationships.* Coos Bay, OR: Living Love Books.

Kohut, H. (1971). *The Analysis of the Self.* New York: International Universities Press.

Kohut, H. (1977). *The Restoration of the Self.* New York: International Universities Press.

Kohut, H. (1984). *How Does Analysis Cure?* Chicago: University of Chicago Press.

Lasch, C. (1978). *The Culture of Narcissism: American Life in an Age of Diminishing Expectations.* New York: Norton.

Levin, D. (1987). Clinical stories: A modern self in the fury of being. In D. Levin (ed.). *Pathologies of the Modern Self: Post-modern Studies of Narcissism, Schizophrenia, and Depression.* New York: New York University Press, pp. 479–537.

Levin, D. (1987). Psychopathology in the epoch of nihilism. In D. Levin (ed.). *Pathologies of the Modern Self: Post-modern Studies of Narcissism, Schizophrenia, and Depression.* New York: New York University Press.

Lewis, H. (1971). *Shame and Guilt in the Neurosis.* New York: International Universities Press.

Lowen, A. (1983). *Narcissism: Denial of the True Self.* New York: Macmillan.

Luby, E. D., and M. Weiss (1984). Case study: Anorexia nervosa: A girl and her father. *Women and Therapy* 3(3–4): 87–90.

Mahler, M. S., F. Pine, and A. Bergman (1975). *The Psychological Birth of the Infant*. New York: Basic Books.

Mahoney, M. J., and D. B. Arnkoff (1979). Self-management. In O. F. Pomerleau and J. P. Brady (eds.). *Behavioral Medicine: Theory and Practice*. Baltimore: Williams & Wilkins.

Mallinger, A. E., and J. DeWyze (1992). *Too Perfect: When Being Out of Control Gets Out of Control*. New York: Clarkson Potter.

Maslow, A. H. (1968). *Toward a Psychology of Being* (2d ed.). New York: Viking Press.

Maslow, A. H. (1971). *The Farther Reaches of Human Nature*. New York: Viking Press.

Masterson, J. (1981). *The Narcissistic and Borderline Disorders*. New York: Brunner/Mazel.

Matousek, M. (1990). Toward a spiritual renaissance. *Common Boundary* 8(4): 18.

Meyersburg, H. A., S. L. Ablon and J. Kotin (1974). A reverberating psychic mechanism in the depressive processes. *Psychiatry* 37: 372–386.

Miles, M. (1984). Type A personality: Bad business? *Computer Decisions*. (April).

Miller, A. (1981). *Prisoners of Childhood*. New York: Basic Books.

Monte, C. F. (1980). *Beneath the Mask* (2d ed.). New York: Holt, Rinehart and Winston.

Neumann, E. (1972). *The Great Mother* (Bollingen Series XLVII). Trans. R. Manheim. Princeton, NJ: Princeton University Press.

Oettingen, G., and M. E. P. Seligman (1990). Pessimism and behavioral signs of depression in East versus West Berlin. *European Journal of Social Psychology* 20(3): 207–220.

Owens, R. G., and P. D. Slade (1987). Running and anorexia nervosa: An empirical study. *International Journal of Eating Disorders* 6(6): 771–775.

Peters, J. L. (1985). *Christian Perfectionism and American Methodism*. Grand Rapids, MI: Eerdmans Publishing Co.

Pier, G., and M. Singer (1953). *Shame and Guilt: A Psychoanalytic and a Cultural Study.* Springfield, IL: Charles C. Thomas. (Reprinted 1971, New York: Norton.)

Roedell, W. C. (1984). Vulnerabilities of highly gifted children. *Roeper Review* 6(3): 127–130.

Rubin, T. I. (1981). Goodbye to death and celebration of life. *Event* 2(1): 64.

Rutter, P. (1989). *Sex in the Forbidden Zone: When Men in Power—Therapists, Doctors, Clergy, Teachers and Others—Betray Women's Trust.* Los Angeles: Jeremy P. Tarcher.

Satir, V. (1976). *Making Contact.* Milbrae, CA: Celestial Arts

Schulman, P., C. Castellon, and M. E. P. Seligman (1989). Assessing exploratory style—The content analysis of verbatim explanations and the attributional style questionnaire. *Behavior Research and Therapy* 27(5): 505–512.

Seamonds, D. A. (1981). Perfectionism: Fraught with fruits of self-destruction. *Christianity Today* (April 10): 24.

Seligman, M. E. P. (1991). *Learned Optimism.* New York: Knopf.

Smith, T. W., and S. S. Brehm (1981). Cognitive correlates of Type A coronary-prone personality pattern. *Motivation and Emotion* 3: 215–223.

Sorotzkin, B. (1985). The quest for perfection: Avoiding guilt or avoiding shame? *Psychotherapy* 22(3): 564–571.

Stern, D. N. (1985). *The Interpersonal World of the Infant.* New York: Basic Books.

Stoop, D. (1987). *Living with a Perfectionist.* Nashville, TN: Oliver Nelson.

Tamerin, J. S., and C. P. Neuman (1974). The alcoholic stereotype: Clinical reappraisal and implications for treatment. *American Journal of Psychoanalysis* 34(4).

Timpe, R. L. (1989). Perfectionism: Positive possibility or personal pathology? *Journal of Psychology and Christianity* 8(1): 23–34.

Thompson, D. A., K. A. Berg, and L. A. Shatford (1987). The heterogeneity of bulimic symptomatology: Cognitive and behavioral dimensions. *International Journal of Eating Disorders* 6(2): 215–234.

White, R. W., and N. F. White (1981). *The Abnormal Personality* (5th ed.). New York: John Wiley.

Whitfield, C. L. (1987). *Healing the Child Within.* Deerfield Beach, FL: Health Communications.

Wilber, K. (1978). *The Spectrum of Consciousness.* Wheaton, IL: Theosophical Publishing House.

Wilber, K. (1980). *The Atman Project: A Transpersonal View of Human Development.* Wheaton, IL: Theosophical Publishing House.

Wilber, K. (1983). *A Sociable God.* New York: McGraw-Hill.

Wood, J. A., ed. (1885). *Christian Perfection as Taught by John Wesley.* Chicago: Christian Witness Co.

Woodman, M. (1980). *The Owl Was a Baker's Daughter: Obesity, Anorexia Nervosa and the Repressed Feminine.* Toronto: Inner City Books.

Woodman, M. (1982). *Addiction to Perfection. The Still Unravished Bride.* Toronto: Inner City Books.

Yates, A. (1991). *Compulsive Exercise and the Eating Disorders: Toward an Integrated Theory of Activity.* New York: Brunner/Mazel.

Zaretsky, E. (1976). *Capitalism, the Family and Personal Life.* New York: Harper and Row.

# INDEX

# About the Author

Steven J. Hendlin, Ph.D., is a clinical psychologist in private practice in Irvine, California. The author of *The Discriminating Mind* and 70 other publications and papers, he sits on the editorial boards of two journals and holds membership in a dozen professional associations. His work has received national and international recognition. He lives in Laguna Beach, California.